ROUTLEDGE LIBRARY EDITIONS: CHRISTIANITY

Volume 3

AN INTRODUCTION TO THE STUDY OF CHRISTIANITY

AN INTRODUCTION TO THE STUDY OF CHRISTIANITY

FRANK DODD

LONDON AND NEW YORK

This edition first published in 2021
by Routledge
2 Park Square, Milton Park, Abingdon, Oxon OX14 4RN

and by Routledge
52 Vanderbilt Avenue, New York, NY 10017

Routledge is an imprint of the Taylor & Francis Group, an informa business

First published 1938 Allen & Unwin. Copyright 1938 Frank Dodd

All rights reserved. No part of this book may be reprinted or reproduced or utilised in any form or by any electronic, mechanical, or other means, now known or hereafter invented, including photocopying and recording, or in any information storage or retrieval system, without permission in writing from the publishers.

Trademark notice: Product or corporate names may be trademarks or registered trademarks, and are used only for identification and explanation without intent to infringe.

British Library Cataloguing in Publication Data
A catalogue record for this book is available from the British Library

ISBN: 978-0-367-62307-4 (Set)
ISBN: 978-1-003-10879-5 (Set) (ebk)
ISBN: 978-0-367-62380-7 (Volume 3) (hbk)
ISBN: 978-0-367-63159-8 (Volume 3) (pbk)
ISBN: 978-1-003-10917-4 (Volume 3) (ebk)

Publisher's Note
The publisher has gone to great lengths to ensure the quality of this reprint but points out that some imperfections in the original copies may be apparent.

Disclaimer
The publisher has made every effort to trace copyright holders and would welcome correspondence from those they have been unable to trace.

AN INTRODUCTION TO
THE STUDY OF CHRISTIANITY

by

FRANK DODD

> "On ne saurait en quelques pages épuiser un sujet à jamais inépuisable. Le parcourir à grandes enjambées serait déjà beaucoup."—CHARLES NORDMANN "*L'au delà.*"

LONDON
GEORGE ALLEN & UNWIN LTD

FIRST PUBLISHED IN 1938

All rights reserved
PRINTED IN GREAT BRITAIN BY
UNWIN BROTHERS LTD., WOKING

PREFACE

It may reasonably be asked why, in view of the immense mass of literature already existing on the subject of the Christian faith and its history, an "Introduction" such as the present should be thought necessary. The reply is that the vast bulk of such literature falls into one of two categories:—(a) works which assume on the part of the reader a preconceived willingness to accept unquestioningly the authority of a divinely inspired book, or rather of a collection of divinely inspired books; and (b) works which are avowedly hostile to the claims of Christianity.

The present treatise, while falling into neither of the above classes, and while assuming no pre-existing sympathy on the part of the reader, aims at opening up a line of thought likely to lead him to the acceptance of what is really essential in the Christian faith.

The author's design has been to make a rapid survey of the most elementary facts connected with the origin and growth of Christianity, and in so doing to suggest the conclusion that the many blemishes which cannot fail to impress the genuine truth-seeker are due rather to human imperfections, and to misconception as to the real teaching of Jesus and of his immediate followers, than to any shortcomings in the teaching itself.

In Christian countries young children are customarily taught at a tender age the rudiments of the faith in dogmatic form, by means of simple catechisms or other elementary expositions of doctrine. When such children become older, if they desire to acquire further knowledge they are, if Roman Catholics, taught how the faith as already inculcated harmonises with certain selected passages of Holy Scripture, the writings of the Fathers and the decisions of successive Popes and Councils. If on the other hand they are brought up as Protestants, they are made familiar with the actual text of Holy Scripture, and are similarly taught how such text harmonises with Christian doctrine as understood by theologians of the reformed religion. And in both cases the result in this twentieth century is felt to be unsatisfactory by a large and probably increasing number of earnest truth-seekers, both Catholic and Protestant, who find it difficult to reconcile the conclusions to which they eventually arrive concerning primitive Christianity with what they were in their early years taught about current dogma. It is to such truth-seekers that the present work is primarily addressed. It is suggested that misunderstanding almost inevitably arises owing to the fact that the student at a very early age absorbs dogmatic teaching, and only subsequently commences seriously to study the sacred records. The author of the present work has aimed first at setting forward very briefly the basic facts anent the genesis of Christianity, and subsequently at calling attention to the interpretations which successive generations of Christians have placed on such facts. It is believed that this course is likely to render Christianity more intelligible and its basic doctrines more credible than is the method which, owing to obvious circumstances, teachers of elementary theology find themselves obliged to adopt when imparting instruction to the young.

The general plan of this treatise is as follows:—A rapid summary has been made of the more striking events in the history of the faith from the commencement of the public mission of Jesus till the period, early in the thirteenth century, when Pope Innocent III was successful in elevating to its climax the power of the Western Church as a visible, homogeneous organisation. After the death of this Pontiff, however, no attempt has been made to present a consecutive narrative. Later Popes have been represented as being called upon to combat difficulties arising out of (*a*) Mohammedanism; (*b*) Decentralisation, and the tendency to demand independence, total or partial, for local Churches; (*c*) Protestantism; (*d*) Liberal theology, sometimes leading to scepticism; and (*e*) Mysticism. A short section has in consequence been devoted to each of these five subjects, the suggestion being made that the difficulties caused by these various factors eventually brought about a decline of the power of the See of Rome, and indeed of institutional Christianity in general. A final chapter is devoted to Christianity of the present day, an attempt being made to regard the body of believers, within and without the Roman fold, in the light of the conclusions drawn in previous pages.

NOTE

WHEN quotations have been made from the Bible, the English Authorised Version has usually but by no means invariably been adhered to. Among the exceptions may be specially cited the fact that the excellent translation of Dr. James Moffatt has in several instances been followed; though only in a few of these instances has the divergence seemed sufficiently important to call for a specific acknowledgment of indebtedness.

Moreover, acknowledgments are due for the assistance rendered by the scholarly treatise of Bishop Gore, *Roman Catholic Claims*, frequent quotations from which are made in the body of the work by kind permission of the publishers, Messrs. Longmans, Green & Co., Ltd. In my quotations from Dr. Gore's book I have of course accepted his use of the authorities he quotes.

CONTENTS

CHAPTER		PAGE
	PREFACE	7
I	EARLY CHRISTIAN DOCUMENTS	13
II	THE PAULINE EPISTLES	23
III	THE SYNOPTIC GOSPELS, ETC.	33
IV	THE FOURTH GOSPEL	53
V	THE CHRISTIANS AS A JEWISH SECT	76
VI	CHRISTIAN PROPAGANDA, THE INFLUENCE OF PAGANISM, THE FORMATION OF TRADITIONAL CHRISTIANITY AND THE CRYSTALLISATION OF DOGMA	96
VII	CHRISTIANITY AS AN INSTITUTION	148
VIII	CHRISTIANITY OF TO-DAY	268
	APPENDICES	295

A. Extracts from Bhagavad Gita.—B. Suffering and shame as factors in spiritual development—C. The Religion of the Albigenses—D. Portuguese Expeditions—E. Toleration towards non-Catholic bodies

| | INDEX | 303 |

CHAPTER I

EARLY CHRISTIAN DOCUMENTS

THE most important of the documents available for the study of the origin of Christianity may be placed under three headings, and will be discussed in the three chapters following. These headings are:

>   The Pauline Epistles   Chapter II
>   The Synoptic Gospels, etc.   Chapter III
>   The Fourth Gospel   Chapter IV

Before going into any details it may be well to say a few words having general reference to the above.

Types of Criticism

One of the first difficulties which the student will find himself compelled to face is the following. For many centuries the documents above mentioned have been the subject of conscientious criticism on the part of scholars, and the conclusions drawn by such scholars have been the most divergent possible. The Church of Rome, the most numerous and historically the most important body of Christians, pronounces a formal anathema on anyone who shall deny sanctity and canonicity not merely to the documents themselves "with all their parts" (*cum omnibus suis partibus*) but also to the authorised Latin translation (*in Veteri Vulgata latina editione*. Decree of Council of Trent, Session 4). In contrast to the foregoing J. M. Robertson (*Christianity and Mythology*) contends that:

> When every salient item in the legend of the Gospel Jesus turns out to be more or less clearly mythical, the matter of doctrine equally so with the matter of action, there is simply nothing left which can entitle anyone to a belief in any tangible personality behind the name.

Now it would appear at first glance evident that the two propositions above set forth are wholly incompatible one with the other. But it has nevertheless happened that during the last few decades the controversy has been complicated by the rise of a school of thought which goes nearly as far as Mr. Robertson in affirming the unhistorical nature of the Gospels, but which on the other hand claims to be not only Christian but also

Catholic, and this notwithstanding the uncompromising censure passed on the entire school by Pope Pius X (Encyclical *Pascendi*, September 8, 1907). Thus M. Alfred Loisy, perhaps the most eminent exponent of the doctrines in question, thinks (*Les Origines du Nouveau Testament*) that all four Gospels are quite unreliable, and were compiled in the first half of the second century, while Paul, who actually wrote portions only of some of the Epistles attributed to him, looked forward to Jesus as the Messiah which was to come. The reader is of course inclined to enquire why and on what grounds those who hold such opinions continue to call themselves Christian and Catholic. Father Tyrrell tried to meet the difficulty by assuming the existence of a "will-world" which for him was the only real world. He seems to imply that the Gospel narratives may not be true in the same manner as it is true that George IV died in 1830, but nevertheless we can by an effort of will make them true to ourselves. He tells us:

> The will cannot make that true which in itself is not true. But it can make that a fact relatively to our mind and action which is not a fact relative to our understanding. . . . It rests with each of us by an act of will to create the sort of world to which we shall accommodate our thought and action. . . . It does not follow that harmony of faith with the truths of reason and facts of experience is the best or essential condition of its credibility (*Lex Orandi*).

It has already been remarked how widely different are the standpoints of the scholars to whom reference has been made above. The orthodox Catholic theologian, starting from the principle that the Vulgate with all its parts is both sacred and canonical, finds himself bound to regard, for example, the last twelve verses of Mark's Gospel as being as trustworthy as the remainder of the text. The so-called modernist Catholic priest feels himself able to instruct his flock to pray to the Blessed Virgin to assist them by her intercession, while at the same time he may believe the whole history of the Queen of Saints to be mythical. The uncompromising rationalist rejects the orthodox history of early Christianity as a clumsily woven tissue of legends. And the three schools of thought seem to have but one characteristic in common, that is that they have little need for a genuine critical study of the New Testament writings. If one student considers himself bound by the above-cited Decree of the Council of Trent, he is obliged to regard as sacred and canonical "fourteen Epistles of the Apostle Paul," including one "to the Hebrews"; so he obviously has neither necessity nor inclination to enter into an impartial enquiry as to when and by whom the Epistle to the Hebrews really was written. And if a student of another school accepts the conclusion that Jesus was an obscure fanatic, he is not likely to maintain much genuine interest in any question regarding either the development of Christian doctrine or the history of the early Church.

In fine, the conclusion to which the reader seems led is that conscientious critical study of Christianity is only likely to be undertaken by those who are disposed to avoid the two extremes. Those who unreservedly accept the Decrees of the Council of Trent may study, but are not likely to criticise. Those who are unable to believe that the genesis of Christianity was a supernormal event, brought about by divine intervention with a view to reuniting man with God, may criticise but have no very obvious reason for studying. The reader is indeed reminded of Francis Bacon's contention that avowed atheists are unlikely to waste their time in propagating their theories. "If they did truly think that there were no such thing as God, why should they trouble themselves?" (*Essays* XVI). Similarly, to those who regard Jesus as a being as mythical as King Arthur, a study of Matthew is really not likely to be more interesting than a perusal of Sir Thomas Malory.

The Manuscripts

The books constituting the groups referred to at the commencement of this chapter were of course written at various dates, and it is generally believed that such dates commence early in the sixth decade of our era, and end certainly not later than 170 and probably very considerably earlier. Now there are known to scholars about 1,800 ancient Greek manuscripts containing the New Testament, in whole or in part. The text of these different manuscripts presents an immense number of variations. The vast majority of such variations are due to the ignorance or carelessness of copyists, and with respect thereto we can confidently believe that the scholarship of subsequent ages has enabled most of the mistakes to be definitely corrected. But we also have to consider an entirely different class of variations arising out of what we can affirm, with a greater or less degree of confidence, to be deliberate interpolations. Thus there is a well-known passage (1 John v. 7) "For there are three that bear record in heaven, the Father, the Word and the

Holy Spirit, and these three are one." These words are undoubtedly a late interpolation by some author who desired to express a certain theological belief, and who did not scruple to insert in the sacred text words calculated to support his views.

Now the best known and most important of the early manuscripts with which we are concerned, the *Codex Vaticanus* and *Codex Sinaiticus*, are believed to date from the fourth century. And seeing that we can verify, from the comparison of early manuscripts with later, that the latter are very frequently corrupt, it is reasonable to infer that in all probability the early ones are to some extent corrupt also. In other words it is impossible on reading any particular passage of the New Testament to assert with entire certainty that such passage is genuine.

Verbal Accuracy

An account of a speech can obviously be made in one of two ways, sometimes called respectively "direct" and "indirect" narration. One can say: *He asked: "Are you waiting there all day?"* or, alternatively, one can say: *He asked if they were waiting there all day*. Now when we in the twentieth century use the former mode, we consider it incumbent on us to use the speaker's exact words. But ancient writers did not feel themselves so bound. For example, when Herodotus narrates a private council-meeting at the court of Darius, King of Persia, and quotes a speech made by the monarch himself, we have no reason for supposing that the historian had any special facilities for reporting exactly what took place; but on the other hand we do not discredit him because he gives us, as the words of Darius, merely what he believes that Darius is likely to have said.

Similarly when we come to examine the early Christian documents, we find that frequently the form of the narrative suggests to a modern reader a claim to complete verbal accuracy, but nevertheless the respective authors did not apparently attempt to attain such accuracy. Indeed, unless we are prepared to adopt the theory of the verbal inspiration of Scripture, it is evident that circumstances rendered complete accuracy impossible. We notice that all four evangelists tell us that the Founder of Christianity was crucified, and that an inscription, stated by two of them to be tri-lingual, was placed on his cross. Of the four evangelists, only one actually claims to have been an eye-witness, and of the remaining three, one frankly gives us to understand that he had no first-hand knowledge of events (Luke i. 2). All four give what purports to be the Greek form of this inscription, and this Greek form is different in each case. The differences are in themselves unimportant, but are sufficient to justify the inference above set forth.

Miraculous Events

An important feature of much religious literature is a tendency to assume a belief in miracles, and as this is specially the case as regards the early Christian documents, it is desirable that some consideration should be given to the subject.

What may be called the typical scientific attitude is taken by Maurice Maeterlinck (*La Grande Loi*):

> No law of nature ever has been, will or can be transgressed; and if this were not the case nature would no longer be what it is, or rather would no longer exist. The transgressions that we think we have discovered exist only in our own ignorance.

On the other hand Cardinal Newman takes a diametrically opposite view when he tells us (*Apologia pro Vita Sua*):

> Miracles are not only not unlikely, but they are positively likely; ...
>
> I think it impossible to withstand the evidence which is brought for the liquefaction of the blood of Saint Januarius at Naples, and for the motion of the eyes of the pictures of the Madonna in the Roman States.

Newman's standpoint is of course the one commonly taken by Roman Catholic writers, who put their case in a very attractive form when they say, e.g. "The miracles of the Church seem to rest not so much upon faces or voices or healing power coming suddenly near to us from afar off, but upon our perceptions being made finer, so that for a moment our eyes can see and our ears can hear what there is about us always." (The quotation is from Miss Willa Cather.) But this observation can hardly be applied to the most widely known of the miracles adduced in support of the claims of the Roman Church. No one can reasonably think that incidents involving an alteration, at once supernormal and permanent, in the location of material objects (such for example as the translation of the "Holy House" from Nazareth to Loreto, to be described in a subsequent chapter of this work) are "about us always," but that our eyes cannot generally see them nor our ears hear them. It is of course quite possible to believe that such transient miracles as "the motion of the eyes of the pictures of the Madonna in the Roman States" are "about us always," but that our lack of spiritual vision normally prevents us from appreciating them. But this is equivalent to saying that the eyes seem to some people to move, and to others to remain still; or in other words that the apparent motion is a mere subjective phenomenon dependent on the mental or spiritual attitude of the observer.

In consequence nine readers out of ten will probably be inclined to agree with Maeterlinck that the universe is governed by fixed laws. In one of Byron's poems there is a dialogue between two young ladies, the subject under discussion being the possibility of their father being disturbed by a light. One of the girls says:

> He would but deem it was the moon
> Rising unto some sorcerer's tune
> An hour too soon.

Now it is clear that such a world as is above indicated, a world in which there was no established order, and in which it was quite comprehensible that the sun and moon would rise at such hours as sorcerers might think fit, would be quite unimaginable. Our mental processes are inevitably based on the assumption of the continuity of natural law.

But notwithstanding this fact, every decade opens out to our view the operation of such law in forms which would have been considered miraculous only a short time previously. Thus for example, if seventy or eighty years ago anyone had been rash enough to predict the fact that in the middle of the twentieth century inhabitants of Rome and of Buenos Aires would be able to sit at home and to adjust their watches by the sound of the chimes of Big Ben, the reply might very reasonably have been given that a miracle would be necessary to perform such a feat. In other words, the miracle of yesterday may be the commonplace of to-day.

It is suggested therefore that we should not believe that the laws of nature can be transgressed, but we should nevertheless remember that we are frequently forced to believe in the operation of laws of nature of which we know little or nothing. So when we come to consider the evidence brought forward in support of the occurrence of miraculous events, in places ranging from Bethlehem to Lourdes, our minds should surely be kept free from prejudice. We ought not to fall into the error of thinking that we can obtain favour with the Deity by pretending to believe the incredible, but we should not affirm categorically that events could not have taken place merely because we do not understand by what means such events could have been brought about. It is undoubted that there has been, on the part of many theologians, undue temerity in affirming, for controversial purposes, the authenticity of alleged supernormal phenomena; but on the other hand it seems likely that there has on occasion been similar temerity in denying such authenticity. Thus Dean Inge (Essay on *Roman Catholic Modernism*) tells us that "The Catholic saints did not fly through the air . . . as the mendacious hagiology of their Church would have us believe." It seems probable that this statement is more definite than the facts warrant. The student who commences to investigate alleged phenomena of levitation will read of a vast number of incidents, differing widely from one another as regards time, place and circumstance, but nevertheless all tending to the conclusion that certain exceptional individuals, when in a condition of trance or ecstasy, act as if they had temporarily lost a portion of their weight; and that in rare cases the body actually leaves the ground and becomes suspended in the air. All investigators are agreed that much of this evidence is not merely unreliable but is definitely untrue; the problem is to determine what element of truth, if any, does really remain. Now while rigid scientific examination of individual phenomena of levitation is, by the nature of the case, nearly always impossible, nevertheless the instance of D. D. Home (1833–86) may be cited as that of a subject who submitted himself, both in England and on the Continent, to tests carefully devised by scientists. Sir William Crookes was one of the observers who examined his feats of levitation and emphatically pronounced them genuine. Home never received payment for exhibiting his powers, and, notwithstanding the lengthy period during which his name was prominently before the public, he was never convicted of fraud. It seems therefore that it would be wrong to affirm definitely that he was an impostor; the utmost that a sceptic could reasonably say is that the evidence is not conclusive.

Now it is hardly necessary to observe that if Home's phenomena were in fact genuine, it does not follow that the laws of nature were thereby violated, but rather that Home, consciously or otherwise, availed himself of a principle of nature of which we are almost ignorant. In somewhat the same way, if an intelligent but uneducated man were to visit a steel-foundry for the first time, and were to see heavy masses of iron being moved, by means of electromagnets, through the air without any visible means of support, he would not say that he was witnessing a violation of the laws of nature, but rather would he confess that he was ignorant of the particular force which was causing the iron to appear to act as if the laws of gravitation had ceased to apply to it.

The case of Home was not ostensibly connected with Roman Catholic propaganda, but nevertheless it has some indirect bearing on the question under discussion, because if we feel compelled to admit at least the possibility of Home's claims being genuine, we equally find ourselves compelled to admit at least a similar possibility in the case of some of the Roman Catholic saints: e.g. Joseph of Copertino (1603-63). Considerations of space render it impracticable to discuss fully the miracles of levitation alleged to have been performed by St. Joseph, but if the student cares to examine the records he can hardly fail to be struck by the difficulties in the way of concluding either that all the witnesses were deceived or that the records themselves are the result of deliberate invention.

Let us now approach the subject of miracles from quite a different angle. Among the prodigies recorded in the Gospels which we are about to consider, one is specially noteworthy on account of the exceptionally wonderful nature of the alleged phenomena. We have four accounts of the death, by crucifixion, of the Founder of the Christian religion. What is apparently the most carefully written and reliable of these accounts is the only one which professes to be written by an eye-witness. This account gives no hint of any external manifestation of supernatural power on the occasion. Now it is comprehensible enough that some of the followers of Jesus, when describing the effects of his death, should perhaps have said that by this great event salvation was offered to all men, that as it were the veil of the Jewish Temple was torn apart and entrance to the Holy Places of God was made free to people of all kingdoms, nations and languages. So we are not surprised to find that the three remaining evangelists—all of whom probably wrote considerably over thirty years after the event—state, not figuratively but as a fact, that the veil of the Temple was actually rent at the time of the death of Jesus. And one of the three (Matthew) goes much further, for he tells us:

And behold the veil of the temple was rent in twain from the top to the bottom, and the earth did quake, and the rocks rent, and the graves were opened, and many bodies of the saints which slept arose, and came out of the graves after his resurrection, and went into the holy city and appeared unto many.

It would appear that we have here an example of the formation and growth of a legend, and we may reasonably infer that the statements made by Matthew are almost certainly untrue.

In fine the propositions which are suggested from the above considerations, taken as a whole, are:

(*i*) Like causes produce like effects, and there can be no conflict between religion, properly so called, and science.

(*ii*) We should not overlook, however, the fact that some very exceptional cause may produce some very exceptional effect, and such effect may appear to us to be miraculous.

(*iii*) It is not reasonable to admit the existence of any very unusual (and apparently miraculous) phenomenon without due and careful consideration. If Cardinal Newman had adhered to this rule he might possibly have followed the example of Renan,[1] and asked himself why the miracle of the motion of the eyes in pictures was only observed in the Roman States and not in such parts of Italy as were less subject to clerical influence.

[1] Renan, writing about a year before the appearance of Newman's *Apologia*, says: The miracle explains itself before a sympathetic public: it is indeed the public which performs it. But before a hostile public the question is quite different. This is clearly seen in the recrudescence of miracles which took place five or six years ago in Italy. The miracles performed in the Roman States were successful; on the contrary those which had the courage to show themselves in the Italian Provinces, submitted as they were to an examination, promptly stopped. People said to have been cured confessed that they had never been ill. The miracle-workers themselves, when examined, declared that they understood nothing about the matter but that, a rumour of their miracles having been circulated, they had believed that in fact they had performed them (*Vie de Jésus*, augmented edition, p. 496).

CHAPTER II

THE PAULINE EPISTLES

WE now commence our examination of the earliest of the Christian documents.

By the expression "The Pauline Epistles" we generally understand a series of thirteen letters written by Saint Paul from about A.D. 51 onwards, and addressed respectively to communities of believers in Rome, Corinth, Galatia, Ephesus, Philippi, Saloniki, and Colossæ, and also to three co-workers named Timothy, Titus and Philemon. The authenticity of some of these works, especially those addressed to Timothy and Titus, has been called in question by even conservative critics.

Paul before his Conversion

Paul, or Saul, of Tarsus was a man whose life falls into two sharply divided portions, consisting respectively of the periods before and after the event which we customarily call his conversion. He was educated as a Pharisee, which term corresponds to some extent to what we should to-day call a "strict Jew." Concerning his intimate religious convictions during the former period of his life we can say but little with certainty, but it seems probable that the strong tendency to mysticism which he exhibited during his later years was also shown by him during his earlier career. The true mystic is born rather than made.

The term "mystic" is extremely difficult to define, and further is used in more than one sense, so it will be well if it be here stated as clearly as possible what meaning will be attached to it throughout this book. If we consult the earliest literature that has come down to us from antiquity we find that man has consistently tended to believe in the existence of a Deity or Deities, by which term we understand extremely powerful, invisible beings, whose assistance and favour may be secured by a certain course of conduct, and whose wrath may be aroused by a different course. Thus if we open the Egyptian *Book of the Dead* at random, we may get a passage such as the following:

> The Scribe Ani triumphant saith:—May the God Ptah open my mouth, and may the God of my city loose the swathings

THE PAULINE EPISTLES

even the swathings which are over my mouth. Moreover, may Thoth, being filled and furnished with charms, come and loose the bandages, even the bandages of Set which fetter my mouth, and may the God Tem hurl them back at those who would fetter me with them, and drive them back.

In the Hebrew sacred writings this idea of a beneficent Deity is frequently set forth in terms of extraordinary beauty. For example one of the early poems contains the following:

My tongue shall sing of thy righteousness: thou shalt open my lips O Lord, and my mouth shall show thy praise. For thou desirest no sacrifice, else would I give it thee, but thou delightest not in burnt offerings. The sacrifice of God is a troubled spirit: a broken and contrite heart O God shalt thou not despise.

Coming to a wholly different class of literature, we find that Matthew Arnold, writing many centuries later, when seeking words to define his idea of the Deity, suggests "the Eternal Power, not ourselves, that makes for righteousness."

The three quotations above given are purposely chosen as being widely different in style, but nevertheless as showing a like conception of the Deity or Deities as a being or beings essentially different from the worshipper. It will be observed that Matthew Arnold goes out of his way to emphasise the point that the Eternal Power is "not ourselves." This appreciation of the immeasurable gulf existing between the Creator and the creature is the key-note of what we may call "non-mystical religion."

But on the other hand a large number of thinkers have formed a radically different conception of the relationship between God and man: the thoughts of such persons are most difficult to express in words, but in general one may say that these thinkers have sought, and believe that they have found God not without, but within. For such devout souls the word "atonement" is no mere figure of speech but is an expression of an actual fact—i.e. the Creator and the creature becoming one. Such men are called "mystics."

Let us by way of illustration turn to the *Divine Pymander*, a treatise of uncertain date, but possibly written in Egypt about the third century of our era. We there find a dialogue from which we extract the following:

Trismegistus. Why or how doth he that understands himself go or pass into God?

24 INTRODUCTION TO THE STUDY OF CHRISTIANITY

> *Pymander*. That which the Word of God said say I: Because the Father of all things consists of Life and Light whereof Man is made.
> *Trismegistus*. Thou sayest very well.
> *Pymander*. God and the Father is Life and Light, of which man is made. If therefore thou learn and believe thyself to be of the Life and Light, thou shalt again pass into Life.

Let us now take another example of somewhat similar language, taken this time from an early Brahminical work, the Bhagavad Ghita. We find that Chrishna instructs Arjuna as follows:

> He who is thus devoted and free from sin obtaineth without hindrance the highest bliss—union with the Supreme Spirit. The man who is endued with this devotion and who seeth the unity of all things perceiveth the Supreme Soul in all things and all things in the Supreme Soul. He who seeth me in all things and all things in me looseneth not his hold on me and I forsake him not. And whosoever, believing in spiritual unity, worshippeth me who am above all things, dwelleth with me in whatsoever condition he may be.

In the above extracts the dominating note is seen to be not the gulf between God and man, but their union: this is the language of mysticism, and, as has already been observed, it would seem likely that Paul was a mystic even before his conversion. In one of his Epistles there is an illuminating passage which sheds a very clear light on his interpretation of the Hebrew sacred writings, and it would seem probable that this interpretation was the one accepted by him before he became a Christian. It must be observed that the writings in question contained a legend to the effect that the early Jews, before occupying Palestine, wandered about the desert for many years, during which period they were happily prevented, by various miraculous events, from suffering such extreme privations as would otherwise have been inevitable. Notably on one occasion when water was lacking, their leader Moses struck a rock with his rod, and a stream consequently spurted out.

Now this legend, as has been the case with similar ones, has been customarily accepted by the majority of both orthodox Jews and Christians as being literally true. On the other hand it has been suggested that the whole narrative may be an allegory of the human soul, wandering about in this sinful world and seeking the promised land of union with the Divine

Being. Such indeed would appear to be the view taken by Paul who says:

> Brethren, I would not that ye should be ignorant, how that all our fathers were under the cloud, and all passed through the sea; and all were baptised unto Moses in the cloud, and in the sea; and did all eat the same spiritual meat, and did all drink the same spiritual drink; for they drank of that spiritual rock that followed them, and that rock was the Messiah ($Χριστος$) (1 Cor. x. 1-4).

The above passage raises the question of the meaning of the word $Χριστος$ (generally anglicised into "Christ" and here translated "Messiah," which is the English form of the Hebrew word). The literal meaning is "Anointed One." The Jews used the word as a title of peculiar dignity. For example Isaiah (xlv. 1) wishing to pay special honour to the Persian king Cyrus, says "Thus saith the Lord to his Messiah, to Cyrus, whose right hand I have holden." But the word had in addition a very special signification. The Jews believed that a great ruler would arise to restore the fortunes of the Hebrew nation, and to give them once more that pre-eminence which, as their sacred writings told them, they had enjoyed many centuries previously. This ruler was emphatically referred to as "The Messiah." *To restore and to build Jerusalem unto the Messiah the Prince, shall be seven weeks and three score and two weeks* (Dan. ix. 25).

But Paul's conception of the office of the Messiah is clearly at variance with the above. He did not regard the Christ as a successful general who would expel the Romans from Judea, but rather as a Divine Being whose kingdom was in the hearts of his disciples, whose spiritual food he gave himself to be.

We can therefore imagine the indignation of Paul on hearing, apparently in the fourth decade of our era,[1] that a preacher of humble birth had some years previously been going about the country claiming to be the Messiah; and further, notwithstanding the fact that this preacher had been ignominiously put to death, a considerable and increasing number of disciples continued to believe in his Messianic mission. This preacher was named Joshua (meaning *Jehovah is Salvation*), or to be more strictly accurate he had the Hebrew name of which Joshua is

---

[1] There is a passage (2 Cor. v. 16) which may be interpreted to mean that Paul had himself known Jesus personally. This however does not seem probable: it is more likely that the word "we" is used vaguely to imply "people in general" or "any of us who happened to have heard him preaching."

26 INTRODUCTION TO THE STUDY OF CHRISTIANITY

the Anglicised form. The name has come down to us in its Greek form 'Ιησους, and we customarily latinise it and say "Jesus."

In his desire to suppress what he regarded as a pernicious blasphemy, Paul exerted himself to stir up his fellow-countrymen to persecute the followers of Jesus. He obtained from the chief priests certain authority, as a result of which he was enabled to arrest and to take part in the condemnation to death of several members of the new body (Acts xxvi).

The Conversion

Now on a certain occasion, as Paul approached Damascus on a journey made with a view to the further persecution of the followers of Jesus, there occurred what we customarily call his conversion, an event of capital importance in religious history. "The Acts of the Apostles" gives us a considerable amount of information about this incident, but it is perhaps to be regretted that we have no detailed account in Paul's own writings. It is however clear that as a result of this experience his spiritual outlook was entirely changed. First and foremost he acquired a deep and unshakable conviction that that same Jesus whose teaching he had so bitterly opposed really was the Christ. And it is most important to notice that this belief in no way clashed with Paul's exalted and mystical view as to the spiritual nature of the Christ. On the contrary he seems to have arrived at the conviction that, while it is possible for Christ to be formed in every one of us, nevertheless he was actually formed in Jesus in a quite unique sense. Consequently Paul regarded Jesus as completely inspired by, and indeed identified with the Messiah.

In attempting to translate Paul's tenets into our own words we are met by the difficulty, which he himself so obviously experienced, of enunciating in everyday language principles which tend to transcend our ordinary human experience. But on the other hand, by taking a few passages from his writings we can form a not wholly inadequate idea of his conception of the nature and office of Jesus. He tells us for example in 1 Tim. vi. 13–16:

> In the presence of God who is the life of all, and of Christ Jesus who testified to the good confession before Pontius Pilate, I charge you to keep your commission free from stain, free from reproach, till the appearance of our Lord Jesus Christ—which will be brought about in due time by that

blessed and only Sovereign, King of Kings and Lord of Lords, who alone has immortality, who dwells in light that none can approach, whom no man has ever seen or can see.

Dr. Moffatt's translation has been chosen for the above extract, as the Authorised Version is somewhat awkwardly worded, and has indeed led careless readers to think that Paul believed Jesus, and not God, to be King of Kings and Lord of Lords. But there is really no ambiguity, because Paul tells us that Christ Jesus testified before Pontius Pilate and that no man has ever seen the King of Kings and Lord of Lords.

A second example is chosen from Eph. iii. 14–17:

> I bow my knees unto the Father of our Lord Jesus Christ, of whom the whole family in heaven and earth is named, that he would grant you, according to the riches of his glory, to be strengthened with might by his Spirit in the inner man, that Christ may dwell in your hearts by faith.

Points which strike us are:

(i) Paul obviously gives his readers no ground for thinking that he abandons the monotheism of the orthodox Jews. Whether he speaks of God or of the Father of our Lord Jesus Christ, he makes it clear that he worships one Deity only, whom he calls *one God and Father of all, who is over us all, who pervades us all, who is within us all* (Eph. iv. 6). And it is noticeable how Paul, as do other mystics, consistently based his theology on the unity of God and man. *He who joins himself to the Lord is one with him in Spirit* (1 Cor. vi. 17).

(ii) Jesus unquestionably was regarded by Paul as a historical character, who had really lived and had been tried by Pontius Pilate some years previously. But on the other hand the disinclination of Paul to write about the teaching, miracles and parables of Jesus is in general so obvious that we are justified in concluding that the former attached relatively little importance to the details of the earthly career of the latter.

(iii) Although we cannot trace that any fixed rule was followed by Paul when referring to "Christ" or to "Jesus Christ," nevertheless the tendency is to speak of "Jesus Christ" when referring to the man Jesus as illuminated and permeated by, and identified with the Christ Spirit. And the term "Christ," when used alone, rather means the divine Spirit which is ready to illuminate and to permeate any worshipper who will but prepare his heart accordingly. Many critics have seen in Paul's successive Epistles—assuming always that they were all really written by the same author—a gradual change in his theological outlook. It is indeed undeniable that the fundamental doctrine of the indwelling of the Christ Spirit is taught with greater clearness and emphasis in the later works than in the earlier. But even in what is believed to be the earliest of the Epistles, the First to the Thessalonians, we find that the author uses such unmistakably mystical phrases as: "The dead in Christ shall rise first" (iv. 16); "the Word of God which effectually worketh also in you that believe" (ii. 13); "God who hath given unto us his Holy Spirit" (iv. 8). So it seems fair to say that although Paul's conviction as to the indwelling of the Spirit became deeper and fuller as he gained in years and experience, nevertheless there was, after the decisive event of his conversion, no further change of standpoint.

Several passages in the Pauline Epistles show us that as a result of his conversion the author acquired an intense and earnest conviction that Jesus had in fact risen from the dead, and Paul believed that the Christ, having once experienced death and resurrection in the person of Jesus, had thereby conquered death, and that all those who receive Christ into their hearts similarly acquire immortality. Thus we are told (1 Cor. xv. 20):

> Christ is risen from the dead: and become the first-fruits of them that slept. For since by man came death, by man came also the resurrection of the dead. For as in Adam all die, even so in Christ shall all be made alive.

And again (Rom. vi. 9–10):

> Christ being raised from the dead dieth no more, death hath no more dominion over him. For in that he died he died unto sin once, but in that he liveth he liveth unto God.

The Apostleship of Paul

Further, as a result of his conversion Paul acquired the firm conviction that he had become an apostle, or in other words that he had received a special mission from God himself to preach the Christ. As he himself says: "God called me by his grace to reveal his Son in me so that I might preach him among the heathen" (Gal. i. 15, 16). Here by the expression "his Son" clearly we should understand "the Christ." Paul's view evidently was that we are all Sons of God in the sense that we are created by the All-Father, and we are capable of becoming Sons of God in the sense of bearing the Christ in our hearts (cf. John i. 12 and 1 John iii. 2), but nevertheless the Christ Spirit is rightly regarded as being in the supreme sense the Son of God.

But to revert to the subject of Paul's apostleship, it is very interesting to observe how logically and consistently he held to the position that what he had to preach was the result of a direct revelation. It would appear to us natural that as soon as possible after his conversion he should make a journey to Jerusalem with the objects of visiting the leaders of the Christian body, of expressing to them his sorrow for his hostility in the past, and of asking for first-hand information as to the actions and teaching of Jesus when on earth. But in point of fact Paul never seems to have manifested interest in the miracles or in the oral teaching of Jesus. He believed that everything vital to the doctrine of the Christ had been revealed to him by supernatural means. Hence we find that whereas Paul expresses deep regret for having "persecuted the Church of Christ," he adopts no very apologetic attitude when at Jerusalem he actually meets the leaders of the sect against which his persecution had been directed. And he is emphatic in refusing to admit that the personal acquaintance with Jesus, enjoyed by the elder members of the body, conferred on them any privileges which he himself did not share.

We can hardly suppose that Paul's attitude towards the elder Apostles failed to arouse a certain hostility. Passages in Chapter II of the Book of Revelation refer to people who claim to be apostles and who are not, and who have been found liars and who eat things sacrificed unto idols. Such passages may very probably have been inspired by opposition to the Pauline claims. And Paul himself, especially in his second letter to the Church at Corinth, clearly refers to the difficulties which his opponents placed in his way.

General Nature of the Pauline Epistles

To appreciate at their full value the series of letters which we are here discussing, it is necessary to have a certain acquaintance with other theological literature of antiquity, so that some sort of a comparison may be made. Such comparison will be found to be greatly to Paul's advantage. It is true that Paul obviously found it by no means an easy task to make his meaning clear when he expounded his mystical tenets as regards the relationship between God and man. We are not therefore surprised that Peter, or at least someone who wrote in Peter's name, should have used a little mild sarcasm in remarking that Paul's Epistles contained some things hard to be understood, which the unlearned and unstable were accustomed to wrest unto their own destruction (2 Peter iii. 16).

One feature which specially distinguishes Paul from other early theological writers is his comparative readiness to give reasons for his assertions. While theologians habitually dogmatise, Paul takes an obvious pleasure in arguing his case. It is true that his reasoning is not always extraordinarily cogent, but the fact that he argues instead of merely preaching compels our respect. Examples of his method may be given. Addressing readers who already accept as a fact the statement that Jesus rose from the dead, Paul argues therefrom the resurrection of all mankind. The weak point is obviously that *ex hypothesi* Jesus was not an ordinary man, and consequently the natural laws which applied to him do not necessarily apply to the rest of humanity. Paul supports his case by the analogy between a dead body buried in the earth and a seed sown in a field, taking occasion to affirm, "That which thou sowest is not quickened except it die" (1 Cor. xv. 36). Surely if Paul had possessed even a very elementary knowledge of agriculture, this statement would never have been made.

Again, the subject of the relationship between the sexes is discussed in some detail, and here again we are compelled to note a certain weakness in the argument. No one who has conscientiously tried to free his mind of prejudice in this matter can fail to be impressed by the magnitude of the difficulties surrounding it. Paul, as indeed is inevitable, does but little to remove these difficulties. He tells us that women should learn in silence with all subjection because Adam was formed before Eve, and the former was not deceived but the latter was (1 Tim. ii. 11–14). This argument would surely be a very weak one even if it were true that Adam was not deceived. And the Book of Genesis gives us to understand that the contrary was the case.

Concerning sexual immorality Paul gives his readers most excellent advice, enjoining them repeatedly in the most emphatic terms to abstain from fornication. Now the horror and shame of prostitution are so great that it would be very comprehensible that a writer might think it unnecessary to give any specific reasons as to exactly why we should avoid sexual immorality. Paul however supplies us with a reason. He enquires if we do not know that he who is joined to a prostitute is one body, "for the two shall be one flesh." "Shall I," he asks, "take the members of Christ and make them the members of a prostitute?" (1 Cor. vi).

Now it is clear that this style of reasoning presents a very real danger. If young people are instructed, on the authority of Paul, that the reason why they should avoid sexual immorality is that what appears to be merely a temporary relationship is really permanent, and that the two persons involved really become one flesh, then if at any later period of their lives they reject Paul's premisses they are likely to reject his conclusions also, and consequently to infer that there is after all no very great harm in sexual licence.

Regarding however the Epistles as a whole, we cannot fail to be struck with the extraordinary robustness of Paul's intellect. He had become a man of one dominating idea—that Christ was everything and everywhere (Col. iii. 11). Consequently he was able to view with indifference those discussions about matters of second-rate importance which have always occupied so much attention on the part of theologians. He tells us:

> If the uncircumcision keep the righteousness of the law, shall not his uncircumcision be counted for circumcision? And shall not uncircumcision which is by nature, if it fulfil the law, judge thee, who by the letter and circumcision dost transgress the law?
> For he is not a Jew which is one outwardly; neither is that circumcision which is outward in the flesh: but he is a Jew which is one inwardly; and circumcision is that of the heart, in the spirit and not in the letter, whose praise is not of men but of God.
>
> (Rom. ii. 26–29.)

As a result of the above reasoning, Paul implies that for the follower of Jesus there is no real difference between Jew and Greek, between barbarian and Scythian, between bond and free, but Christ is everything and everywhere. The externals of religion are valuable to those who believe them to be so. If a Jew, we can imagine him saying, eat food forbidden by the Mosaic code, he does no harm, for the kingdom of God is not meat and drink, but righteousness and peace and joy in the Holy Spirit (Rom. xiv. 17). If on the other hand a Jew refrain from eating such food, again he does no harm. But a point to be remembered is that even if one see no harm in disobeying the Mosaic code, it is better to obey than to offend the susceptibilities of one's neighbours (Rom. xiv. 21). Surely no better advice could possibly be given.

The Epistles deal with a great variety of subjects and include passages of extraordinary beauty, such for example as a well-known chapter (1 Cor. xiii) on what Paul calls ἀγαπη, a word which is, perhaps a little unfortunately, translated as "charity" in the Authorised Version, the meaning being love in its most elevated sense. We also find many excellent maxims of conduct, the general tone of which is that we should strive to do good to all men, including our enemies, so that their evil actions may eventually be overcome by our good ones. We may conclude therefore that although doubtless non-Christians will continue to maintain an attitude of reserve with respect to the ultimate value of Paul's work, nevertheless even hostile critics will be disposed to admit that for the superlative honesty of his sentiments, for the elevation of his principles and for the ability and thoroughness with which he advocated those principles, he is entitled to a very high place indeed among the great teachers of mankind. But his claim on the gratitude of the Christian Church is far more than this. He proved himself to be the supremely great missionary and organiser, who, in laying the foundations of many local Churches, became a pattern for the guidance of all future evangelistic workers. And, centuries after his decapitation at Tre Fontane, when organised Christianity had become so largely a matter of submission to ecclesiastical authority and of acceptance of not very intelligible dogmas, it was the writings of Paul which survived as the chief and unshakable witness to the fundamental principle of the indwelling of Christ in the individual soul.

CHAPTER III

THE SYNOPTIC GOSPELS, ETC.

The word Gospels means "good-spells" or "good-tidings." The term "synoptic" is used of the three Gospels which present many features in common, in contradistinction from the Fourth Gospel, which is of a different character.

It is proposed here to consider:

St. Matthew. Chapter III to end.
St. Mark.
St. Luke. Chapter I, 1 to 4, and III to end, together with the sequel called the "Acts of the Apostles."

It is here assumed, for reasons which will be indicated in a subsequent chapter, that Matt. i and ii and Luke i. 5 to ii. 52 are later additions; and these additions are for the moment ignored.

The three Gospels are strictly speaking anonymous, but are headed "according to" (κατα) Matthew, Mark and Luke. It is doubtless implied that they preserve the different accounts of the life of Jesus handed down by the three converts in question, but the identity of the actual authors is doubtful.

Criticism of the synoptic Gospels can of course be divided into two classes, external and internal. The latter is far the more interesting and fruitful, and scholars have expended an immense amount of time and industry thereon. Many of the inferences which have been drawn must be looked on as highly controversial, but at least it seems clear that the three documents contain passages so similar (e.g. Matt. xxiv. 32–35; Mark xiii. 28–31; and Luke xxi. 29–33) that the reader is forced to the conclusion that either the later evangelists copied from the earlier, or else all three copied from a common source. Moreover the three synoptic evangelists take but little pains to present a connected, consecutive narrative of the life of Jesus, therein comparing unfavourably with the Fourth Gospel; and this fact tends to increase the impression that each of the three documents is the work of two or more writers. Scholars differ widely in their conclusions, but the general trend of modern opinion seems to be that Matthew and Luke both copied not only from Mark but also from an even earlier document no longer extant. This (supposed) document is generally referred to as "Q" (from the German *quelle*, a source).

External criticism has but little basis to go on. As implied in a former chapter, we have no very early manuscript copy of any of the Gospels. Papias, writing probably about 140, tells us that MARK, who was a follower and interpreter of Peter, recorded after the latter's decease the words of Christ and the narratives of his deeds that he (Mark) had heard the Apostle deliver. Peter is believed to have been crucified in 64 or 67, so it is reasonable to think that the Gospel of Mark, very much as we have it now, may have been written shortly afterwards. It is true that some critics call attention to what they regard as evidence of free editing, but the arguments adduced by such critics though weighty can hardly be called conclusive. On the other hand there is every reason for thinking that the last twelve verses (xvi. 9–20), giving an account of posthumous appearances of Jesus, were added early in the second century. Moreover grave suspicion has been cast on the authenticity of the so-called doom chapter (xiii).

As regards MATTHEW, the same authority, Papias, tells us that he compiled the sayings (or oracles, λογια) in Hebrew. A later writer, Eusebius (d. *c.* 349), says that Matthew "after preaching to Hebrews, when about to go also to others, committed to writing in his native tongue the Gospel that bears his name." The (Greek) document which has come down to us as the Gospel according to Matthew can hardly be called a compilation of sayings, neither would it appear to be a translation from the Hebrew. Why should a translator give the original Hebrew, as well as the Greek translation, in xxvii. 46? Surely the inference is that the Gospel was written in Greek for a class of readers who had in general some knowledge of Hebrew. Moreover if the Gospel of Matthew was really written by one of the immediate followers of Jesus, while that of Luke admittedly was not (i. 2), it would be almost inevitable that a comparison of the two narratives would make patent the fact that one evangelist had a more direct personal knowledge of events than had the other. But we fail to find in the Gospel of Matthew any decisive indication of such first-hand knowledge. It is true that Chapter X is fully consistent with the theory that the author really was the tax-receiver of whose call we read in ix. 9. He (the author) relates that Matthew, with eleven other disciples, received from Jesus a commission, reported at very considerable length, to preach the Gospel and to perform miracles. But on the other hand the terms of this commission seem to imply a definite leave-taking (x. 23), or at least an absence extending over a very considerable period (x. 17, 18). And after this leave-taking (xi. 1) nothing further is said about the missionary journey. Very shortly afterwards (xii. 1) we read of "the disciples" as being in immediate attendance on Jesus, but there is no hint as to how many they then were, nor as to whether Matthew was or was not one of the number. It seems most unlikely that a writer who had troubled to report at such full length the circumstances of his dismissal on a journey through "the cities of Israel," should keep complete silence as to the result of this journey, or should fail to let us know when he again got into personal contact with Jesus.

Some passages seem quite unlikely to have been written by an eye-witness. Attention has already been called (p. 21) to xxvii. 51–53, and the inference has been drawn that the statements contained therein are almost certainly untrue. But even assuming the contrary to be the case, the expression "appeared unto many," used without any corroborative detail, seems more likely to have come from the pen of a compiler of oral tradition than of one who had been in Jerusalem on the day in question, and who either had been an ocular witness, or at least had been in direct personal contact with some of those who had been privileged to behold the great prodigy described in the text.

It seems safe therefore to draw the conclusion that in all probability Matthew, the tax-gatherer referred to in ix. 9, was neither the sole author nor the final editor of the First Gospel as we now have it. It is generally thought to have been compiled between 80 and 100.

It may be added that there formerly existed a *Gospel of the Hebrews* of which fragments are still extant. Eusebius tells us that many people regarded this Gospel as authoritative. It is closely related to that of Matthew, and indeed Jerome (*c.* 340–420) gives us to understand that in his day the former was believed by many scholars to be the Hebrew original of the latter. If Matthew's Gospel really is a freely edited translation of the Gospel of the Hebrews, it becomes of interest to note that apparently the latter commenced with an account of the Baptism of Jesus, a fact which harmonises with the conclusion, come to on other grounds (*vide* pp. 36 and 102), that that portion of Matthew's Gospel which deals with matters preceding the Baptism constitutes a later addition.

LUKE, styled "the beloved physician," was a friend and companion of Paul. Assuming that the Gospel bearing Luke's name was really compiled by him, its date is probably about 80. If it be not by him, it may possibly be dated some twenty years later. The first writer known to have attributed its authorship to Luke is Irenaeus (d. *c.* 202).

It will be seen from the above that although it seems likely that there existed a very early "Apostolic tradition," now commonly referred to as "Q," and that this tradition formed a basis of at least two of the three synoptic Gospels, nevertheless we have no ground for thinking that any one of these three records was compiled less than say about thirty-five years after the death of Jesus; and the more elaborate stories, narrating a greater number of miraculous events, are believed to have been compiled considerably later.

In explanation, or at all events in partial explanation of the foregoing, it may be observed that early Christians looked on themselves, not as forming a permanently established Church, but rather as anxious watchers, waiting from day to day for the inevitable return in glory of the Saviour to the earth. In consequence the compilation of formal archives, describing the origin of their faith, would have seemed to the immediate followers of Jesus quite superfluous. But after a few decades had passed the disciples began to ask one another: "Where is the promise of his coming? For since the fathers fell asleep all things continue as they were from the beginning" (2 Peter iii. 4). This feeling of impatience no doubt gradually gave way to resignation, and to a different outlook on the mission of Jesus. It was then that steps began to be seriously taken to commit to writing formal records of the events which formed the basis of the faith.

Commencement of the Gospels

A comparison between the opening sentences of the three Gospels, respectively, is of interest.

Mark commences with the words: "The beginning of the gospel of Jesus Christ." What appears to be a later addition then follows in most manuscripts: *Son of God*, or sometimes *Son of the God*. The Authorised Version translates *The Son of God*. The narrative then goes on to introduce John (*vide infra*) and to describe the baptism of Jesus. We therefore see that the author of the earliest known presentation of the life of Jesus unquestionably looks on the baptism as commencing that portion of the Master's career which is of interest for his disciples. In other words Mark does not merely omit the so-called "birth-stories": his narrative implies that either he never heard of them or he discredited them.

Saint Luke first dedicates his work to a certain Theophilus, and then commences the actual narrative in a very formal manner: "Now in the fifteenth year of the reign of Tiberius Cæsar, Pontius Pilate being Governor of Judea," etc.

Saint Matthew commences with great simplicity "In those days came John the Baptist," the phrase "In those days" (which corresponds to the French *En ce temps-là*) meaning "Once upon a time," or as we should say in modern English "Some years ago." Readers who adopt the traditional opinion that the original Gospel commenced with Chapter I will object that on the contrary the words *In those days* mean *About the time of which we have just spoken*, and are a connecting link between the end of Chapter II and the commencement of Chapter III. But this theory is quite untenable, because if we admit such a hypothesis, we make the accession of Archelaus, the journey of Jesus from Egypt to Galilee and his baptism, follow one another in rapid succession. Now Archelaus succeeded his father in 4 B.C. and was deposed A.D. 7. Jesus was probably baptised A.D. 26.

The Baptism of Jesus

All four evangelists commence their actual narrative by a description of the relationships of Jesus with John the Baptist, a very remarkable character who about A.D. 26 attracted much notice in Judea by preaching the need for repentance and by baptising his converts. The following points strike the reader: (*a*) great importance is obviously attached to an influx of the Holy Spirit received by Jesus in the presence of John. This influx of the Holy Spirit constitutes the true Baptism of Jesus (cf. Matt. iii. 11, Mark i. 8, etc.), and indeed the Fourth Gospel does not make specific mention of the fact that he was physically baptised by water; (*b*) the character of John is introduced with some care, and we even have a description of his dress and personal habits. But the character of Jesus is, one may say, not introduced at all. The authors simply represent Jesus as coming to John to be baptised. Luke, however, unlike the other three evangelists, does something to remedy his lack of introduction of Jesus, for he adds his age and genealogy; (*c*) on the occasion of the Baptism, the Breath

($\pi\nu\epsilon\nu\mu a$) or Spirit of God descended on Jesus and remained on him (John i. 33) so that he became full of the Spirit (Luke iv. 1, 14); and at the same time a Voice from heaven said "*This is my beloved son in whom I am well pleased*" (Matt. iii. 17), or "*Thou art my beloved son in whom I am well pleased*" (Mark i. 11), or "*Thou art my beloved son, this day have I begotten thee*" (Luke iii. 22). The version of Luke is specially noteworthy because it indicates quite unmistakably that the author regarded Jesus as having been re-born on the occasion of his baptism. It consequently seems to have come about that in later ages, when the current conception of the nature of Jesus had become profoundly modified, it was considered expedient to alter the text of Luke so as to bring it into harmony with Matthew and Mark.[1] The matter of this modification of Christian belief is touched on in a later section under the heading of "The Epiphany."

The conclusions which may be drawn are: (i) independently of the very definite statement made by Luke and just referred to, it is clear that even the other three evangelists attach vastly more importance to the baptism than did orthodox Christian theologians from the third century onwards; (ii) it seems impossible to put forward any really plausible theory as to why all four evangelists should have taken more pains to introduce into their narratives the character of John than that of Jesus. But on the other hand it seems reasonable to infer that the fact that the four Gospels in their primitive form tell us so little about the antecedents of Jesus, suggested to two later writers, whom we may for convenience call pseudo-Matthew and pseudo-Luke, the idea of prefacing two of the Gospels respectively by the two series of legends (considered in Chapter VII,) which we call the birth-stories; (iii) it is certain that Luke desires, and it is to be presumed that the other three evangelists desire the reader to understand that it was the influx of the Breath or Spirit of God received by Jesus which definitely sanctified him as the Christ or Anointed One. (It is noteworthy that we do not read that he was ever ceremonially anointed.)

---

[1] Dr. Moffatt translates Luke iii. 22 as follows: and the Holy Spirit descended in bodily form like a dove upon him, and a voice came from heaven, *Thou art my son, the Beloved, to-day have I become thy father*. And Dr. Moffatt makes the following gloss on this passage: Reading $\dot{\epsilon}\gamma\omega$ $\sigma\eta\mu\epsilon\rho o\nu$ $\gamma\epsilon\gamma\epsilon\nu\nu\eta\kappa a$ $\sigma\epsilon$ with D, the Old Latin, Justin, Clement, Tyconius, etc. In the other MSS. it has been altered for harmonistic reasons.

In a former chapter mention has been made of the difficulty experienced by writers on mystical religion when trying to describe matters which transcend ordinary human intelligence. So we are not surprised to find authors using different expressions to indicate what seem to be identical ideas. Thus Paul speaks of Christ being "formed in you" (Gal. iv. 19): the Fourth Gospel speaks of men having "power to become the sons of God" (John i. 12): the Gnostics spoke of receiving the knowledge (γνωσις) of God: the Medieval Rosicrucians spoke of becoming "illuminated," but we may fairly believe that a fundamental idea underlay all these expressions—the entry of the divine Christ Spirit into the human personality. (It may be observed parenthetically that in this treatise no distinction is attempted to be drawn between the designations: *Christ Spirit, Holy Spirit*, and *Spirit of God*. See especially Rom. viii. 9, as also page 84 *infra*). Now we find that similar expressions frequently used in the Gospels are "the kingdom of heaven" and "the kingdom of God." Thus we read that Jesus, shortly after having been baptised in the Jordan and having simultaneously received the gift of the Spirit, says: "Except a man be born of water and of the Spirit he cannot enter into the kingdom of God." We infer therefore that the evangelists wish us to understand that although the entrance into the kingdom of God is free to all who fulfil the necessary conditions, nevertheless Jesus, by virtue of his divine mission and of his own superlative merits, received at his baptism the supernal gift of the Holy Spirit, and consequently became the Messiah or Christ, and in quite a unique sense entered into the kingdom of God.

The Life and Mission of Jesus

After having received the influx of the divine Spirit, Jesus spent some time in solitary meditation, after which he commenced his career as a preacher. He soon collected a devoted band of twelve selected disciples, of whom Simon, a man of exceptional personality, became the leader (or coryphæus). Two other followers, James and John, were also on specially intimate terms with the Master. Jesus seems to have formed the habit of giving nicknames to his personal friends. Simon he called Kephas, meaning "a stone," in Greek Πετρος, which name we anglicise into Peter. James and John, who were brothers, sons of Zebedee, he called Boanerges, meaning "Sons of Thunder," or perhaps more properly "of Tumult." The twelve were despatched on a mission, already referred to,

40 INTRODUCTION TO THE STUDY OF CHRISTIANITY

to preach, to heal the sick, to raise the dead and to cast out devils; but we hear little or nothing as to the result of this mission, and there is no obvious reason to suppose that it was a striking success. (Compare Matt. x. 8 with xvii. 16.)

The records of the work of Jesus himself are crowded with miraculous events. Something has already been said with a view to preparing the reader's mind for a consideration of such occurrences. If we attempt to classify the gospel miracles, we find that the great bulk consists of acts of healing performed by Jesus on sick persons, notably on patients referred to as "possessed of devils," by which we should in general presumably understand sufferers from neurasthenia. Now few educated people would deny that it occasionally happens that very remarkable cures of disease take place either by auto-suggestion or through the agency of some individual apparently possessing what we can only regard as abnormal gifts. And the school of Coué has attempted, not without a certain success, to demonstrate to us that, contrary to what was formerly believed, organic disorders are cured by auto-suggestion at least as readily as functional disorders. So there is nothing at all improbable in the belief that Jesus possessed the gift of healing to an extraordinarily high degree.

But on the other hand it is equally true that if we study carefully the gospel narratives, in several instances we are enabled to verify traces of the growth of a legend. Take for example the case of Malchus. We are told, and the story is common to all four narratives, that, a body of men having come to arrest Jesus, a follower who was carrying a sword struck a servant of the High Priest and cut off his ear (Matt. xxvi. 51, Mark xiv. 47, Luke xxii. 50, John xviii. 10). Now one of the evangelists, and one only (Luke), implies that there was something miraculous about this incident, for he goes on to say that Jesus touched the ear of the servant (Malchus) and healed him. There is no need to suggest that Luke was guilty of deliberately inventing a miracle, but the natural inference is that the legend grew as it were spontaneously.

When dealing with miracles of healing, our attention is naturally drawn to the story of the Gadarene swine (Matt. viii. 28–34, Mark v. 1–20, Luke viii. 26–40), the reason being that half a century ago, when a belief in the verbal inspiration of Scripture was much more frequently professed than is now the case, the opponents of this doctrine used to pour special ridicule on the story in question. The narrative is, very briefly, to the effect that a certain man (or, according to Matthew, two men) was (or were) possessed of evil spirits; that Jesus commanded the spirits to leave him (or them), that the spirits requested permission to take possession of a herd of swine, and on such permission being granted the maddened swine rushed into a lake and were drowned.

The first point that strikes us in the narrative is this. The Gospels speak frequently of the casting out of evil spirits, and it is, as implied on a former page, to be presumed that in the vast majority of such cases the patients were simply neurasthenics. But this explanation will not hold good in the present instance. If we accept the narrative we have to believe (*a*) that the individuality of the patient was, wholly or in part, substituted by that of evil spirits; (*b*) that the spirits left the patient at the command of one possessing supernormal psychic power; and (*c*) that the spirits thereupon obsessed certain animals which consequently went mad and met their death in consequence.

Half a century ago, this story excited undisguised ridicule. But opinion to-day is not only much better informed with respect to psychology, but is also more ready to admit the possibility of the supernormal. Few really educated people would to-day affirm that the events described are absolutely incredible. Enlightened opinion would rather be inclined to suspend definite judgment. But on the other hand we should not overlook the fact that the verbal similarities in the three accounts of the miracle are such that it is difficult to conclude that we have three independent witnesses to the truth of the occurrence.

It has been pointed out with justice that in former ages, when the general level of instruction was lower and when credulity was more common than is to-day the case, the accounts of the miracles of Jesus constituted a potent argument in advancing the claims of Christianity. To-day the Gospel accounts of Jesus as a thaumaturge are felt to be rather a hindrance than a help. But we may well conclude that if we are disposed in principle to admit that the Holy Spirit may illuminate human beings, and if we admit that one particular human being may have been specially illuminated in order to fit him for a unique divine mission, then it is not unreasonable to expect that that man would be endowed to a superlative degree with such powers over the physical and mental health of his fellow-beings as are in every age possessed to a lesser degree by a few abnormally gifted individuals.

So we need not regard as wholly incredible what the poet writes of Jesus:

> He speaks—and listening to his voice
> New life the dead receive,
> The mournful broken hearts rejoice,
> The humble poor believe.
> Hear him, ye deaf; his praise, ye dumb
> Your loosened tongues employ;
> Ye blind, behold your Saviour come,
> And leap, ye lame, for joy!
>
> (C. WESLEY.)

The Teaching of Jesus

The teaching of Jesus as reported in the synoptic Gospels can be conveniently considered under three headings, (i) ecclesiastical, (ii) eschatological and (iii) moral. (i) As regards matters ecclesiastical, the Gospels supply us with but little information. Matthew's account contains it is true a passage, the authenticity of which has been called in question, in which Jesus is represented as speaking of building his Church. But nevertheless we are struck by the absence of any decisive indication that Jesus meant to found a visible permanent organisation. Consequently Dean Inge (*The Indictment against Christianity*) finds himself able to say:

> There is no evidence that the historical Christ ever intended to found a new institutional religion. He neither attempted to make a schism in the Jewish Church, nor to substitute a new system for it.... Institutional Christianity may be a legitimate and necessary historical development from the original Gospel, but it is something alien to the Gospel itself.

(ii) The eschatological teaching of Jesus has been a source of grave difficulty to his followers, and many modern critics, notably Albrecht Schweitzer, seem to consider such teaching as the key-note of the whole of primitive Christianity. Jesus unquestionably taught the imminence of a terrible catastrophe, generally referred to by Christians as "the end of the world," in which sun and moon would be darkened and in which the stars would fall from heaven, and the Son of Man would come in the clouds of heaven with power and great glory. Jesus affirmed that these events would take place in the lifetime of some of his hearers (Matt. xxiv. 29–34), and indeed Luke represents him as associating the great catastrophe with the siege of Jerusalem (xxi. 20–32). Such passages as these impress the reader as being undoubtedly authentic, because we can hardly conceive that a later generation could have invented a prophecy so patently unfulfilled by subsequent facts.

(iii) A study of the moral teaching of Jesus involves us at the outset in considerable difficulty. Several of the precepts laid down are such that if we take them to embody general principles, and attempt to expand such principles into a definite code, the result appears to most of us not merely impracticable but definitely wrong. If we were to base our ordinary conduct, for example, on Luke vi. 29, then it would follow that every time that an evil-disposed person wanted to deprive us of a portion of our substance, we should be obliged to surrender to him more than what he demanded. Society could not be held together if such were the basis of the everyday actions of the bulk of the community. Some writers have believed that the particular precepts above referred to are a result of the eschatological teaching of Jesus, who meant to imply that the end of all things was so near at hand that it did not really matter to a man if he and his wife and family had or had not proper food and clothing. But it would seem more likely that the intention of Jesus was to give emphasis to his teaching by shocking his hearers with what are in effect striking exaggerations: instead of telling them not to be unduly anxious about the material cares of the future, he told them to take no thought for the morrow: instead of telling them not to waste too much time in thinking out means of protection against possible theft, he told them to surrender both coat and cloak to anyone who tried to steal one garment only.

But leaving aside such special precepts as have been referred to above, and turning to the general principles of Christian ethics, it is noteworthy that opponents of the Christian religion have expended an immense amount of time, and very considerable ingenuity, in searching the literature of antiquity with a view to proving that the moral precepts of Jesus had been anticipated, centuries previously, by one or other of the old religious teachers. Now it may at once be admitted that it is impossible to adduce an entirely new ethical principle which shall be at once valid and suitable to the environment in which it is propounded. In the exact sciences, such as astronomy, we always have the possibility of new discoveries, but in the science of ethics there can be nothing comparable, for example, to the location of a new planet. If any teacher had arisen nineteen centuries ago, and had taught an entirely new code of morals, radically different from any existing precepts, it is patent that such code must have been unadapted to the needs of his fellow-countrymen. So it may be conceded that although Jesus did in point of fact give his disciples a new code of morals, nevertheless the general principles of this code were not wholly a novelty to the theologians of his day. What can be reasonably claimed is that the uniform excellence of his doctrine considered as a whole, and the simple and attractive way in which that doctrine was put forward, give him an undoubted claim to occupy absolutely the first place among all religious teachers.

No attempt will be made in this place to summarise the moral teaching of Jesus. It is felt that to do so would merely be to express inadequately what he himself has already expressed adequately, for he said:

> Thou shalt love the Lord thy God with all thy heart, and with all thy soul, and with all thy mind. This is the first and great commandment. And the second is like unto it: Thou shalt love thy neighbour as thyself. On these two commandments hang all the law and the prophets (Matt. xxii. 37-40).

But while it is felt that nothing further need be said about the subject matter of the teaching of Jesus, it may be useful to call attention to the manner. Jesus had a genius for expressing his meaning in short pithy sentences. "The Sabbath was made for man, and not man for the Sabbath." "Whosoever shall receive one of such children in my name receiveth me, and whosoever shall receive me, receiveth not me but him that sent me."

The special feature of Jesus' teaching is however his so-called "parables," or short anecdotes intended to point a moral. These parables have been the subject of much study on the part of commentators, and their extraordinary value can hardly be doubted by anyone who will go to the trouble of attempting seriously to reflect on their meaning. That of the Prodigal Son is perhaps the best known, and has given hope and consolation to many millions of unquiet consciences.

The family connections of Jesus

It has already been observed that three of the evangelists take no pains to introduce the character of Jesus into their narratives, and the fourth, Luke, merely gives us his age and genealogy.

This genealogy makes Joseph, his father or supposed father, a descendant of David, a point of some importance, as the Jews anticipated that the Christ would be "the son of David." But Luke himself (xx. 39–44) makes Jesus appear anxious to prove that the Christ would not be so descended. In this respect Luke is supported by the other synoptic evangelists (Matt. xxii. 41–46; Mark xii. 35–37), and it seems impossible that a later author would have invented this attitude, which is out of harmony with the traditional opinion as to the ancestry of Jesus. Consequently it seems to follow that Joseph was not descended from David, or at least had the reputation of not being so descended.

Another point that the synoptic evangelists bring home to us is that Jesus impressed his fellow-townsmen as being, if not commonplace, at all events not so very different from other human beings. He was unable to make any deep impression on the inhabitants of Nazareth, or to perform important acts of healing in their presence, because they felt unable to regard him as other than the son of a well-known carpenter, and in consequence they refused to take him and his mission seriously (Matt. xiii. 53–58; Mark vi. 3–6). Here again we are struck by the obvious authenticity of the text.

Institution of the Lord's Supper

We now have to consider one of the most discussed incidents in the life of Jesus—the institution of the Lord's Supper, or Holy Communion. This event is narrated by all the synoptic evangelists and also by Paul, whose account is believed to be the earliest. This writer gives us to understand that in his day there existed at Corinth a pagan rite somewhat similar to the Christian ceremony, and that some converts took part in both (1 Cor. x). He therefore says:

> I would not that ye should have fellowship with demons ($\delta\alpha\iota\mu o\nu\iota\omega\nu$). Ye cannot drink the cup of the Lord and the cup of demons. Ye cannot be partakers of the Lord's table and of the table of demons.

He goes on to say that he had received a revelation on the subject from Jesus, who had in the same night in which he was betrayed taken bread, and given it to his disciples saying: *Take eat: this is my body.* Likewise he took the cup saying: *This cup is the new testament in my blood. This do ye as oft as ye drink it in remembrance of me.*

All three of the synoptic evangelists give an account closely harmonising with the foregoing. But the Fourth Gospel, the only one of the four professing to be written by an eye-witness, is silent on the matter, and this is the more remarkable on account of the very great detail in which the author treats of the other events of the evening before the Passion of Jesus. (The synoptic evangelists each devote from fifty to sixty verses to these events, and the Fourth Gospel 182.) It is further remarkable that a perusal of the Fourth Gospel would lead us to infer that the washing of the feet, and not the partaking of bread and of the cup, was the distinctively Christian rite. It has been suggested with some plausibility that the rite of the breaking of the bread may have previously been habitual with Jesus, and that the synoptic evangelists attached special importance to the occasion when, immediately before his tragic death, he performed the ceremony for the last time. This theory, which may be said to derive a certain measure of support from Luke xxiv. 30, 31, 35, would possibly help to account for the omission on the part of the author of the Fourth Gospel.

The meaning of the ceremony may, it is suggested, be best understood by a study of the prayer of Jesus (John xvii. 21): *That they all may be one: as thou Father art in me, and I in thee, that they also may be one in us.* The partaking of the bread and the cup is apparently symbolical of that union with God and with each other possessed by all those who are to a greater or less extent endued by the Christ Spirit.

The expressions: *This is my body: This is my blood* have given rise to much controversy. Perhaps there has been on the part of theologians too great a tendency to assume that the words of Jesus necessarily meant: *By this act I now cause this bread and this wine to become my body and my blood.* It would on the contrary appear that he, at the solemn moment in question, felt himself to be exalted on to the loftiest spiritual plane, and to be wholly one with the Christ Spirit *by whom all things were made* (cf. John i, 3; Heb. i. 2), and whose material body is consequently the whole visible universe. In this mystical sense, not one particular morsel of bread but all matter of whatever kind is the body of Christ.

The Passion of Jesus

The earthly ministry of Jesus was inevitably of a nature to excite the animosity of the temple authorities at Jerusalem.

It is quite likely that they really regarded him as worthy of death as a blasphemer, but in any case they doubtless looked on him as a fanatic, likely to foment disturbances which would inevitably be the cause of repressive measures on the part of the Roman authorities. The priests therefore, after examining Jesus, denounced him to the Roman governor, who after some little hesitation had him tortured and subsequently put to death by crucifixion. The heroic attitude assumed by Jesus throughout his sufferings aroused, we are told, the sympathy of even the Roman officer in charge of the execution.

After the death of Jesus, and his burial in a tomb belonging to a disciple, divergencies between the different authors render the narrative exceedingly difficult to follow. We have four accounts—those of three of the evangelists and of Paul—of posthumous apparitions of Jesus. Moreover we find that the Gospel of Mark in its original form tells us that the tomb of Jesus was found miraculously empty of the body, though it is only in the supplementary twelve verses that anything is said as to any actual appearances.[1] Paul, who is in general unaccountably reluctant to make reference to the acts and sayings of Jesus, cites the largest number (six) of posthumous apparitions, including one to "above five hundred brethren at once" (1 Cor. xv. 6). And singularly enough this particular appearance, which would presumably be the most widely known, is mentioned by Paul only.

Definite conclusions are exceedingly difficult to draw in this matter, but the following seem assured:

(a) The narrators have not taken any pains to compose an artificial and plausible story. For example we find that Matthew (xii. 40) quotes a prophecy of Jesus to the effect that he would be buried for three days and three nights, that is for a period certainly exceeding sixty hours. But Matthew himself gives us to understand that Jesus was actually buried considerably after three o'clock on a Friday afternoon, and rose from the tomb as it began to dawn on the following Sunday morning—the interval being therefore certainly less than forty hours.

[1] It is not probable that Mark actually intended to conclude his work at Chap. xvi. 8. Presumably either he left his Gospel unfinished and a later hand added the last twelve verses, or the original conclusion is missing, and the conclusion we possess was intended to substitute the missing portion.

(b) The earliest detailed version of the Resurrection would seem to be that of Mark, who tells us that very early in the morning certain female disciples approached the sepulchre of Jesus with materials for anointing the body. Seemingly they anticipated no opposition to be made to their so acting, and were only concerned with the problem of obtaining help to remove the stone closing the tomb. They, however, finding the stone already removed, were received by a celestial messenger who told them that Jesus was no longer there, but was going to Galilee, where not only they but the disciples generally and Peter would see him. It is remarkable that neither Mark nor the later writer who completed his Gospel tells us that Jesus did actually go to Galilee. The narrative of Luke indeed, in the final form in which we have it, seems inconsistent with the possibility of Jesus having met his disciples in Galilee between the Resurrection and the Ascension (see especially xxiv. 49).

Matthew's version is very much like that of Mark, but he tells us that Pilate had, with the express intention of preventing the disciples from removing the body, sealed the tomb and ordered "a watch" to guard the spot. On the occasion of the arrival of two female disciples, who came to "see the sepulchre" and apparently had no thought of entering or of anointing the body, there was a great earthquake, the stone closing the tomb was rolled away, the keepers fainted, and an angel told the holy women that Jesus had risen and was going to Galilee, where the disciples would see him.

Notwithstanding the above, Matthew, pseudo-Mark, Luke and John all give (somewhat divergent) accounts of appearances of Jesus to his disciples on the same day, in the immediate vicinity of Jerusalem.

The question of the final appearance of Jesus is one of special interest. Matthew lays the last scene in Galilee, and represents the Master as dismissing his disciples on their missionary labours with the promise *I will be with you alway*. Luke on the other hand finishes his narrative when Jesus is still in the vicinity of Jerusalem, and we are told that *he withdrew from* the disciples (xxiv. 51, Vulg. *recessit ab eis*). A later pen has inserted *and was taken up into heaven*. The sequel to Luke's Gospel, described in the following section, adds considerable detail as to how the Ascension took place (Acts i. 9 and 11). It can hardly be doubted therefore that we have narratives embodying successive additions to the original story.

(c) The disciples retained unimpaired their faith in Jesus even after the bitter disappointment of his crucifixion. Consequently they were apparently disposed to welcome any allegation of the Master's appearance, albeit on not wholly satisfactory evidence. (*Vide* especially Matt. xxviii. 17; Luke xxiv. 16.) And it must be remembered that the early disciples not merely attributed to Jesus himself the power of raising the dead (Luke vii. 15; John xii. 9), but also believed that such power had been delegated by him to his apostles (Matt. x. 8; Acts ix. 40). Hence it seems fair to conclude that there must have been on the part of the disciples an *a priori* disposition, doubtless largely sub-conscious, to believe that Jesus would be restored to them. They could hardly have been willing to convince themselves that he saved others but himself he did not save.

(d) The question of the resurrection of Jesus has, very naturally, been generally treated as a physical one—did or did not the natural body which was laid in the tomb become reanimated and eventually rise and disappear in the sky? But from what Paul tells us of the resurrection of mankind in general we may reasonably infer that the idea of a physical resurrection of Jesus would not have appealed to him. He tells us that "flesh and blood cannot inherit the kingdom of God, neither can corruption inherit incorruption" (1 Cor. xv. 50). Moreover Paul held that true believers are, during their earthly lives, already risen with Christ (Col. iii. 1, Col. ii. 12 and Eph. ii. 5 and 6). And he clearly considered his own vision (at Damascus) as on a par with those of the other disciples (1 Cor. xv. 8), notwithstanding the fact that we are given to understand that on the occasion in question what was visible to the physical eye was a bright light only (Acts ix. 3 and 7, xxii. 9). However this may be, it is plain that to Paul the really essential point was not that the natural body of Jesus had become reanimated, and that corruption had consequently inherited incorruption, but that though Christ had been crucified in his weakness he nevertheless liveth by the power of God (2 Cor. xiii. 4).

For us individuals the essential point is, it is suggested, that the stone of self may be rolled away from our hearts and that the Christ may arise within us.

Events subsequent to the Resurrection

All the evangelists terminate their original narratives with events apparently not more than a few weeks subsequent to the resurrection of Jesus. Luke however supplies us with a sequel, which we term the Acts of the Apostles. In this sequel we observe the commencement of the evolution of the Christian body from a small Jewish sect to a world-wide community. We note also a change in the mental outlook of believers, for whereas the primitive Christians imagined that Jesus would return and that the world would be destroyed by fire almost immediately, we see that as time went on steps were taken to establish a permanent Church order in a manner which would appear unnecessary if Jesus were expected to return visibly to earth at any moment.

Scholars are generally agreed in recognising the great historical value of Luke's account of the early Church, but nevertheless we cannot fail to note that the former part of the treatise is less trustworthy than the latter. It appears that up to chapter xvi, verse 8, Luke is giving us a description of incidents of which he personally was not a witness. Some of these events took place as early as A.D. 29, and Luke's account may very probably have been written after 80, so it is patent not merely that there is abundant scope for error, but that it would be almost miraculous if no error existed. On the other hand from chapter xvi. 10 onwards, Luke writes sometimes as an eye-witness and sometimes as one who at the time seems to be in touch with the principal characters in the narrative. Consequently a comparison of the two sections is of considerable interest. Let us take as an example the incident of Tabitha (ix. 36–41) and compare it with that of Eutychus (xx. 7–12). In the first instance Luke repeats a story to the effect that Tabitha had died and that Peter raised her from the dead. Either this is simply untrue, or a miracle took place. Many readers will accept the former hypothesis. But the circumstances are quite different in the case of Eutychus who met with an accident when Luke, although apparently not actually present, was in close touch with Paul. We are told that the latter fell upon and embraced the body of Eutychus; and this detail naturally reminds us of the manner in which modern

Oriental mystics, when in a trance, are said to be resuscitated by the intimate physical contact of the bodies of their teachers. (See also 1 Kings xvii. 21 and 2 Kings iv. 34.) Paul told the onlookers not to be alarmed, as the patient was still alive, and indeed the latter shortly afterwards recovered. It is clear therefore that we are meant to understand the word νεκρος (*dead*) in verse 9 to mean "in a dead faint," as otherwise the statement of Paul is in direct contradiction to that of the narrator. We see therefore that the latter is dealing with a natural, albeit unusual, event which he tries to describe truthfully, while at the same time there seems a certain desire on his part to make the reader infer that a miracle occurred.

The situation is similar when Luke tells us about the action of the civil authorities, the persecutions inflicted on the saints, and the miracles consequent on these persecutions. In the first section, when Luke is merely writing from hearsay, he tells us (xii. 4) that Peter was imprisoned by Herod and made to pass the night, bound with chains, between two soldiers; that he was visited by an angel; that his chains fell off and that he was released from prison; that the angel accompanied him on his subsequent walk during which a gate opened of its own accord to let the saint pass; and that Peter finally made good his escape, while Herod commanded the gaolers to be executed. Here one can, as in the Tabitha incident, say quite definitely that either the account is untrue, or else a miracle occurred. But in the second section of the work we have a somewhat similar incident related of Paul and Silas (xvi. 19–40). Luke tells us that the two saints were flogged and subsequently imprisoned along with other captives; that in the night there was a great earthquake and "all the doors were opened and everyone's bonds were loosed"; that notwithstanding this fact no one apparently attempted to escape; that the gaoler was consequently converted and that he ministered to Paul and Silas; and that finally on the following morning an order arrived for the release of these two prisoners, who were recognised as being Roman citizens. Luke was apparently in the vicinity when this happened, and it is reasonable to suppose that he is giving a truthful account of the events as known to him: that is to say that there really was an earthquake, the gaoler was afraid that, as a result of the accompanying confusion, his prisoners would attempt to escape, and after he found that they made no attempt to do so, he showed very considerable kindness to Paul and Silas. But Luke seems to wish to give his readers the impression that a miracle took place, although it is difficult to accept this hypothesis, seeing that apparently nothing supernatural occurred either to save Paul and Silas from being flogged or to diminish the period of their captivity.

Luke indeed, when describing experiences of which he has some direct knowledge, seems to have a tendency to give a miraculous aspect to occurrences which are merely unusual. This tendency is seen for example in verses 1 to 6 of the last chapter. We are told that a serpent fastened on Paul's hand, but was shaken off without doing any harm to the Apostle. This incident is of a nature to cause but little astonishment to anyone having personal knowledge of the generally unaggressive habits of serpents. But Luke tells us that the onlookers were so surprised at the fact that Paul was unharmed that they took him for a god.

CHAPTER IV

THE FOURTH GOSPEL

Authorship

THE question of the authorship of the Fourth Gospel is one of the most interesting in the study of ancient literature. Three principal theories have been put forward:

(a) the author was John, a son of Zebedee and one of the more prominent disciples of Jesus. Or, alternatively, what comes to almost the same thing, the work was written by a disciple of John under the latter's immediate direction. This is the view traditionally held, but the tradition can hardly be proved to date from earlier than about 180.

(b) the author was some immediate follower of Jesus, other than John. The name of Lazarus, a friend of Jesus referred to in the Fourth Gospel only, has been put forward in this connection. There is no traditional support for this view, but the internal evidence is worthy of attention.

(c) the work is a late forgery and the author wrote about the middle of the second century, when oral tradition as to the Master's teaching had become corrupted, and a tendency had arisen to complicate the simple precepts of Christianity with Greek or Alexandrian metaphysics.

It is here proposed to make a rapid summary of the Gospel, calling attention to any passage specially bearing on one or other of these theories.

Prologue

The Gospel commences with a Prologue of fourteen verses, the general style of which is not quite like anything else in the Bible. This fact is emphasised by those critics who hold the third theory as to the authorship, i.e. that the work is of late date and the writer was influenced by foreign schools of thought. On the other hand it can hardly be alleged that in the fourteen verses in question there is anything beyond the intellectual capacity of a well-educated Jewish writer contemporary with Jesus.

The Prologue commences: *In the beginning was the Word, and the Word was with*[1] *the God, and God was the Word. The same was in the beginning with the God.*

The exact meaning of these sentences is very difficult to determine. A plausible theory is that the original might have read simply: *In the beginning was the Word and the Word was with the God,* and that a later hand might have inserted in the margin, as two suggested amendments, *and God was the Word* and *The same was in the beginning with the God.* Under these circumstances it would be comprehensible enough that a copyist should have inserted all three sentences, thus giving the text the form in which it at present stands.

It may here be observed that one of the difficulties in the way of an exact comprehension of the New Testament is the fact that the various authors seem to use the definite article (ὁ) somewhat loosely, and there is nothing in the Greek language which exactly corresponds to our indefinite article. In the sentences above quoted there is no very obvious reason why the word *God* should in two instances be preceded by the article *the,* but not in the third.

It may also be remarked that, excepting in the earliest times, the principal language of religious controversy in the Western Church has been Latin, in which tongue there is no article at all, and the passage runs: *In principio erat verbum et verbum erat apud Deum et Deus erat verbum: hoc erat in principio apud Deum.* (In beginning was Word and Word was with God and God was Word: this was in beginning with God.)

The Prologue does not make mention of either Jesus or the Christ, and its general tenor is to set forth the nature of the "Word" and to affirm that the "Word was made flesh." It would appear that the "Word" of the Prologue may be regarded as synonymous with the "Christ," as set forth in the synoptic Gospels and in the remainder of the Fourth Gospel. But it must be observed that although the expression *the Word of God* appears as a title in Revelation (xix. 13), yet so far as we know Jesus never called himself *the Word,* nor did he affirm that he was the Creator of the material universe, as is claimed for *the Word* in the third verse of the Prologue.

We now have to consider a point of great importance. We have already called attention to the uncompromising monotheism of the Hebrews. Did the author of the Fourth Gospel

[1] Possibly "next to" rather than "with" is the real meaning of πρός. The Vulgate translates *apud,* not *cum.*

wholeheartedly conform to this monotheism, or did he, by following the cult of a secondary deity, break away from it? We may reasonably reply that if the Prologue is really by the same hand as the rest of the Gospel, and if verse 15 is consequently to be read as following on verse 14, then the author means to say: Although I have told you that *the Word was made flesh and dwelt among us and we beheld his glory*, you are not to fall into the error of thinking that God thereby became visible to man, because *no man hath seen God at any time*, and the mission of Jesus was not to make God visible to our physical eyes, but to *declare him* unto us (John i. 18).

Commencement of the Narrative and Baptism of Jesus

The author of the Fourth Gospel first mentions Jesus by saying "grace and truth came by Jesus Christ," but the latter is only introduced into the action of the narrative a few verses farther on, where we read "the next day John seeth Jesus coming unto him and saith *Behold the Lamb of God which taketh away the sin of the world*." It will be observed therefore that, as has been remarked in a previous chapter, in its general lines the Johannine narrative agrees with those of Matthew and Mark in this respect: there is no formal introduction of the principal character to the reader. This lack of preliminary information with respect to Jesus is more noteworthy in the Fourth Gospel than in the others, because the author gives us to understand that he himself eventually became on terms of close filial intimacy (xix. 27) with the mother of Jesus, and resided with her after the crucifixion. As a result of this intimacy the mother of Jesus must almost inevitably have related to the evangelist many details as to her son's life, not so much during the three years of his public ministry as during the thirty previous years, when the contact between mother and son would presumably have been much closer. But of these thirty years our author says not a word, and he, like the synoptic evangelists, introduces Jesus into the narrative at the moment when the latter seeks out John the Baptist. The obvious explanation is that our author felt it incumbent on himself to write not all he knew, but all he thought his readers had a legitimate interest in knowing. This forms a ground for concluding with some degree of certainty that he, like the synoptic evangelists, regarded the Messiahship of Jesus as commencing at his baptism.

With reference to this baptism, the narrative of the Fourth

Gospel is perhaps even more striking than those of the synoptic evangelists, for we are told:

> John bare record saying: I saw the Spirit descending from heaven like a dove, and it abode upon him. And I knew him not: but he that sent me to baptise with water the same said unto me: *Upon whom thou shalt see the Spirit descending and remaining on him, the same is he which baptiseth with the Holy Spirit* (i. 32, 33).

In the above passage attention may be called to four points: (*a*) According to the author of the Gospel, the baptism of Jesus was by no means a spectacular function intended to call public attention to the latter's divine mission. On the contrary the text gives us no indication that any onlooker other than John had the vision of the Spirit. (*b*) The Spirit descended *and remained*. Consequently what took place was not a mere manifestation of the temporary and local presence of the divine Spirit, but on the contrary Jesus became in virtue of his baptism, a new creature (cf. 2 Cor. v. 17), in that he was thereby definitely endued with the Spirit, or in other words he became "in Christ." (*c*) Jesus not merely received the divine Spirit himself, but became the medium for conferring that same Spirit on others in the measure of their respective capacities. (*d*) There is no statement that the influx of the Spirit which we call "the Baptism" was accompanied by any physical contact with water.

The Mission of Jesus

We now get an account of the choosing of the disciples, and this account is on the whole somewhat unfavourable to the theory that John, the son of Zebedee, is the author. Matthew and Mark make Jesus choose firstly Peter and his brother Andrew, and next James and John. Luke makes Peter, James and John partners in a fishing-boat, and represents the call of all three as being practically simultaneous. The Fourth Gospel makes the call come first to two disciples, one of whom remains anonymous, but the other of whom was Andrew, who thereupon sought out Peter, saying "We have found the Christ" (John i. 41).

It would seem that the author when describing the call of Peter, may have had in mind Matthew's account of Peter's confession of the Messiahship of Jesus. Matthew makes Jesus eulogise Peter for having affirmed that he (Jesus) was the

Christ. The words are "Blessed art thou, Simon Bar Jona, for flesh and blood hath not revealed it unto thee, but my Father which is in heaven" (Matt. xvi. 17). The author of the Fourth Gospel seems to be countering this affirmation by pointing out that it was in point of fact a human being (Andrew) who informed Peter as to the Messiahship of Jesus.

The above, so far as it goes, is quite consistent with the theory that the author was John the son of Zebedee, because we know from the first two Gospels that John and his brother desired to share the primacy of the Apostles between them (Matt. xx. 20 and Mark x. 35), and hence they would inevitably regard Peter as their rival. But on this understanding how can we account for John, when describing the call to the ministry of Peter whom he subsequently attempts to belittle, saying nothing about the call of his brother James and himself? Moreover, it seems most probable that the author of the Gospel, although an eye-witness, was not one of the twelve. He relates the call of Andrew, Peter and Philip, but not of the other nine, and indeed we do not get any reference to the "twelve" until the end of Chapter VI, after two journeys have been made to Jerusalem.

It will be remembered that these twelve were said to have been sent out at quite an early stage of the ministry of Jesus with very full powers, including even that of raising the dead (Matt. x. 8). It is hardly credible that one who had personally worked on so solemn and extraordinary a mission would have omitted all mention of the fact. Again, Luke (ix. 54) tells us that John and his brother, when accompanying Jesus on a missionary journey, wished to call down fire from heaven to destroy a village which had refused them hospitality. Surely this is not the type of man who would, when subsequently writing an account of events, have maintained complete silence as to his own share right up to the last act of the tragedy.

The Marriage in Cana of Galilee

We now come to consider the first miracle recorded in the Fourth Gospel (ii. 1-11). This took place at Cana, an ancient but unimportant town mentioned in the Old Testament (Josh. xix. 28). It may here be noted how topographically precise is the author of the Fourth Gospel. He not only tells us where the miracle took place, but some time subsequently (iv. 46) he reverts to the subject saying: "So Jesus came again

58 INTRODUCTION TO THE STUDY OF CHRISTIANITY

into Cana of Galilee, where he made the water wine." Mere collectors of legends do not customarily write like this.[1]

The narrative of the changing of water into wine impresses the reader unfavourably in several respects: (a) it does not seem reasonable that the orderly march of the universe should be interrupted merely because a host had underestimated the amount of wine his guests were likely to consume; (b) we are surprised at what seems to be the excessive amount of wine (calculated at about 120 gallons) miraculously called into being to supply the shortage; (c) there was no apparent excuse for the seeming rudeness of Jesus towards his mother when she courteously told him: "They have no wine"; and (d) it is difficult to understand why Jesus said that his hour was not yet come if he intended to perform a miracle.

While no wholly satisfactory explanation has been put forward, it has been suggested that the phrase (ii. 4): "Woman what have I to do with thee?" is a mistranslation, the sentence being affirmative and not interrogative: "Woman in this I have to do with thee." The proposed explanation is that Jesus was at the outset of his career, and had not yet acquired sufficient psychic force to bring about the necessary miracle. Consequently he told his mother that his hour was not yet come, and he appealed to her to join her psychic forces to his own, and they together performed on the assembled guests a feat of what may be called collective hypnotism, as a result of which those present drank water under the suggestion that wine was really being consumed. Readers need hardly be reminded that one of the commonest feats of a mesmerist is to make his patient drink water under the delusion that it is some other beverage.

Again it has been suggested that this story is intended to be allegorical only—that the water represents the Mosaic dispensation and that the wine is symbolical of the new covenant, freely offered by Jesus to all who care to partake. It must be admitted that this latter theory does not sound wholly convincing.

Journeys to Jerusalem

The writers of the synoptic Gospels represent the earthly mission of Jesus as being almost exclusively Galilean: they give us to understand that he visited Jerusalem but once, that

[1] For further topographical details which give an air of verisimilitude to the Gospel *vide*: i. 44, iii. 23, iv. 5, v. 2, ix. 7, xviii. 1.

is to say a few days before his death. But on this understanding the Gospel story is exceedingly difficult to accept literally. The discussions with the scribes and Pharisees are surely much more likely to have taken place at Jerusalem than at various points in Galilee. Matthew appears to feel this difficulty, and seems to try partially to meet it by saying, when speaking of a time when Jesus was at Gennesaret, that there came to him "scribes and Pharisees *which were of Jerusalem*" (xv. 1).

Again several of the details of the final week of the earthly mission of Jesus are only readily comprehensible if we understand that the infant Church had so to speak already begun to take root at Jerusalem. Several passages in the synoptic Gospels seem hardly applicable to the actions of an itinerant preacher coming to a strange city for the first time (Matt. xxi. 1-3, Mark xiv. 13, Luke xix. 37, xxiv. 52, 53). In this respect the Fourth Gospel is much more comprehensible than the other three, for in it Jesus is made to visit Jerusalem on various occasions. Under these circumstances there is in the discussions with the scribes and Pharisees a verisimilitude which is lacking in the earlier Gospels. It is noteworthy that on his first visit to Jerusalem, Jesus was asked for a sign and replied: "Destroy this temple and in three days I will raise it up" (John ii. 19). At his subsequent trial Jesus was accused of saying something very much like this, and Matthew and Mark evidently understood the accusation to be wholly false (Matt. xxvi. 60; Mark xiv. 58). The inference would seem to be that the author of the Fourth Gospel had some special points of contact with Jesus when the latter was at Jerusalem.

Further Miracles

We are now told of the following miracles performed by Jesus: healing, at a distance, of the son of a Capernaum nobleman; healing of an impotent man at Jerusalem; feeding of five thousand followers on a mountain; walking on the water near Capernaum; healing of a blind man at Jerusalem; raising of Lazarus at Bethany.

It will be seen therefore that in the Fourth Gospel we read of seven miracles only, including that of the marriage in Cana, and these are related in a style not quite like that of the synoptic evangelists. The Fourth Gospel tells us nothing about the casting out of devils, and in this respect differs in a striking manner from the earlier ones. And the relatively small number of miracles which are related by our author seem to be introduced largely as a basis for a discourse or a discussion. Thus the healing of a blind man at Jerusalem, with the accompanying discussion, occupies no less than forty-one verses of the text.

Raising of Lazarus

We now come to consider the most interesting and remarkable of the many miracles attributed to Jesus. The story very briefly is this. Lazarus, a friend of Jesus, resident near Jerusalem, had died. Jesus, hearing news of his illness, arrived after the body had been four days in the tomb. Jesus nevertheless caused the stone to be removed from the entrance to the tomb, and then summoned Lazarus to come forth. Lazarus arose and, still wrapped in the grave-clothes, came out of the tomb. As a result of this miracle the chief priests and Pharisees finally determined that both Jesus and Lazarus must be put to death.

The difficulties of accepting this story are considerable. If so marvellous a prodigy were really performed, and "many of the Jews" saw it and believed in Jesus, and if the death of Jesus was a direct result, how can we account for the silence of the synoptic evangelists on the matter? And indeed why should Paul, speaking some thirty years subsequently, refer to Christ as the first that should rise from the dead (Acts xxvi. 23), if Lazarus had a prior claim to the title? And why should the author of Revelation (i. 5) use a similar expression? A wholly satisfactory answer to these questions cannot be given, but the following theory is worthy of consideration.

Theory as to the Lazarus miracle

It is of course well known that the great religions of antiquity had in general two sets of teaching to offer—an esoteric and an exoteric. Now such esoteric teaching was in general so carefully concealed from outsiders that although we know that it existed, the utmost uncertainty surrounds its real nature. Death was the punishment allotted to anyone who should profane the sacred mysteries. To quote a single example of the seriousness with which such questions were regarded, we know that the whole course of Grecian history was modified by an accusation brought against Alcibiades of having at a banquet revealed and burlesqued part of the Eleusinian mysteries. The accused was actually on active service as one of the three joint-commanders of the Sicilian expedition of 415, when a government vessel arrived at Catana from Athens

THE FOURTH GOSPEL

with instructions to take him back in order that he might stand his trial. He escaped at Thurii and took service against his mother city, with the far-reaching consequences which are familiar to students of Grecian history.

The secret of the mysteries in the old religions has, as has already been said, been very carefully kept; and moreover it is to be presumed that the various esoteric schools differed widely one from another both as regards doctrine and practice. There seems however reason for believing that in at least some of the schools the disciple (or neophyte) was given instruction concerning the nature of the Deity and the ties uniting God to man, and men to one another. When his instruction was sufficiently advanced, the neophyte was sometimes caused by some unknown means to fall into a deathlike trance, lasting several days, during which it was believed that the spirit, having left the body, was instructed by higher powers by means of what Paul calls "sacred secrets which no human lips can repeat" (2 Cor. xii. 4).

Now we can hardly doubt that primitive Christianity presented both an esoteric and an exoteric teaching, the former being what Paul calls "the hidden wisdom" (1 Cor. ii. 7). The references made by Jesus himself to his esoteric teaching seem quite unmistakable. (See, e.g., Matt. vii. 6, xiii. 13–17, Mark iv. 11–12, Luke viii. 10, John xvi. 12.) And it is of course clear that the Book of Revelation, whatever its real meaning may be, was intended to be unintelligible to the uninstructed reader. According to the theory now put forward, the three synoptic evangelists purposely avoid any plainer reference to the esoteric teaching of Jesus, or to the spiritual progress of any neophyte.

Lazarus, according to this theory, was spiritually the most highly developed of the disciples of Jesus, so much so that his sisters, when writing to Jesus about him, refer to him simply as "he whom thou lovest" (xi. 3). By this expression we ought presumably to understand not a mere human affection, but rather that the respective souls of Jesus and Lazarus were able to meet and to interact on one another on an exalted spiritual plane.[1] Jesus observed, when he heard that Lazarus was ill: "This sickness is not unto death, but for the glory of God,

---

[1] It is noteworthy that we read in Matt. xix and Mark x of how Jesus instructed a possible neophyte in the way whereby he, after renunciation of his worldly goods, might become "perfect," and on this occasion also we are told that Jesus loved the disciple in question.

that the Son of God might be glorified thereby." This surely cannot mean: "Lazarus has been put to this suffering, and his relatives to this deep sorrow, merely to give me an opportunity of working a miracle and impressing the onlookers with my power." The real meaning would appear to be: "This sickness is not unto death, but for the glory of God, because, during the resultant trance the Christ Spirit, or Son of God, will illuminate Lazarus, who will then become an initiate." It is noteworthy that Jesus is reported as saying: *Our friend Lazarus sleepeth, but I go that I may awaken him out of sleep,* and immediately afterwards: *Lazarus is dead.* To a non-initiate the foregoing is a simple contradiction, but an initiate might conceivably have understood the double statement to indicate the death-like trance accompanying initiation.

It is now to be observed that Jesus then remained where he was for two days (xi. 6), the reason apparently being that he did not wish to arrive at Bethany to awaken Lazarus from his trance until the expiration of a convenient term.

We read that Jesus, just before the actual miracle, "groaned in the spirit and troubled himself," and that he "wept" and "again groaning in himself" came to the grave. These are the phenomena which appear to accompany any extraordinary exercise of psychic power: there would be no point at all in Jesus bemoaning the loss of Lazarus whom he was about to reanimate.

Jesus then made it clear that a great prodigy was being performed publicly so that the onlookers might believe (xi. 42); and afterwards we find that these onlookers reported the matter to the Pharisees, and a council was held and on the advice of the High Priest the death of Jesus was decided on. Later on, it was also thought expedient to kill Lazarus also (xii. 10), though we hear nothing as to the execution of this plan. It is suggested that the reason was that Jesus and Lazarus had, in the opinion of the priests, merited death owing to their having profaned the sacred mysteries, inasmuch as they had done publicly what should only have been done in the most private manner possible.

Continuation of the Narrative

In the chapter (xii) following that narrating the raising of Lazarus, we observe the author's desire to keep the event before the reader's mind. In verse 1 we are told that Jesus came to Bethany, "where Lazarus was, which had been dead, whom he raised from the dead." In verse 2 we read that "Lazarus was one of them that sat at table." In verse 9 we again read that "much people of the Jews . . . came . . . that they might see Lazarus." And in the next verse we get the passage already referred to, where the chief priests "consulted that they might put Lazarus also to death." And when our author describes the triumphant entry of Jesus into Jerusalem, he explains the enthusiasm of the people by saying:

> the people therefore that was with him when he called Lazarus out of his grave and raised him from the dead, bare record. For this cause the people also met him, for that they heard that he had done this miracle[1] (xii. 17 and 18).

From this moment however Lazarus, whom the author so obviously desired to keep well before the reader's eye, drops completely out of the narrative.

In the next chapter we get a picture of Jesus partaking of a final meal with "the disciples," and we read "There was leaning on Jesus' bosom one of his disciples whom Jesus loved" (xiii. 23). Now we are definitely told in another place (xxi. 20 and 24) that this disciple was the author of the Gospel. The question is: Was this disciple named John, according to tradition, or Lazarus, as is here suggested? Attention will be given to this point a few pages later.

The next verse (xiii. 24) affords us an example of a certain tendency on the author's part from Chapter XIII onwards to give himself a prominent share in events, and this tendency was coupled with a special desire to belittle Peter. Why should the chief of the twelve find it necessary to ask the anonymous evangelist to put a confidential question to Jesus instead of putting it himself?

The Passion of Jesus

The narrative, as set forth in the Fourth Gospel, of the closing scenes of the great tragedy is more orderly, and of a nature to inspire greater confidence, than the accounts given in the synoptic Gospels. To mention a relatively unimportant detail, it has already been stated (page 40) that all four evangelists

---

[1] It will be observed how relatively awkward is the narrative of the synoptic evangelists. If Jesus arrived in Jerusalem for the first time on Palm Sunday, why should "a very great multitude spread their garments in the way" (Matt. xxi. 8) and behave generally not as sightseers or enquirers, but as enthusiastic converts?

give an account of the wounding by a disciple of a servant in the ear. The names of the two parties concerned, Peter and Malchus, are given in the Fourth Gospel only. Now there would be nothing surprising if we were to find that a century or so after the death of Jesus, oral tradition had preserved the name of the apostle concerned, and that a literary forger had consequently been able to introduce the name into his narrative. But a forger or late compiler of oral tradition would not be likely to know either the name of the servant in question (xviii. 10), or the wholly unimportant fact that he was a kinsman of a servant who spoke to Peter in the palace of the High Priest (xviii. 26). So we have here further evidence that the author really was an eye-witness; and, if we are comparing the claims of John and Lazarus, the incident perhaps points in favour of the latter, who was a resident of Bethany on the outskirts of Jerusalem, and was therefore more likely to know the names of the domestic servants of the High Priest than would be a Galilean fisherman on a visit to the Holy City.

We then get the scene of Peter's denial. One cannot but feel that there is something approaching to malice in the way the author gives details bearing on Peter's misconduct, omitting however the fact of his remorse (Matt. xxvi. 75; Luke xxii. 62). Moreover it should be noted that Peter, when following Jesus, was accompanied by "another disciple" (xviii. 15) who, being known to the High Priest, was enabled to enter the palace when Peter was left outside, and who subsequently exercised his influence to obtain permission for Peter also to enter. Now this other disciple takes no further part in the action of the tragedy, and such detailed mention of him is inexplicable unless we are to think that the author intends us to infer that he himself is this "other disciple."[1] On this assumption the incident forms another example of the author's desire to exhibit himself in a more prominent and dignified position than that of Peter. It also points to some slight extent in favour of the Lazarus theory, because for the reason set out in the last paragraph Lazarus would be more likely to have influence at the High Priest's palace than would John.

But it is perhaps the various accounts of the crucifixion itself which give us the greatest cause for thought with regard to the authorship of the Fourth Gospel. The synoptic evangelists mention a number of Galilean women, including the mother

[1] In the same way the anonymous disciple of John i. 35-40 may not improbably have been the evangelist himself.

of John, as having accompanied Jesus to Jerusalem, as being present at the crucifixion, and as having taken a considerable part in the subsequent events (Matt. xxvii. 56, Mark xv. 40, 41; Luke xxiii. 55, 56; xxiv. 1). Now it must be pointed out that the mother of John was clearly a woman of strong personality, and we know that shortly before the Passion her son was in close touch with her (Matt. xx. 20). If therefore John were the author of the Fourth Gospel, it would seem that his natural tendency would be to call special attention to his mother's share in the events. On the contrary he says not a word about her. Moreover he tells us that the Mother of Jesus was present, and was commended to his own care and protection with the words "Behold thy Mother." The foregoing seems to form a definite obstacle to accepting the theory that John was the author, as we can hardly think either that he would omit all mention of the part played by his own mother, or that Jesus would ask his (Jesus') mother to adopt John as a son (xix. 26) when John's own mother was not merely living but actually present.

The Commission to the Disciples

The Fourth Gospel is peculiar in giving us details as to a very remarkable occurrence which took place after the resurrection. We read (xx. 19–23) that on an occasion when "the disciples" were assembled with closed doors, Jesus came and stood in the midst of them and said:

> *Peace be unto you; as my Father hath sent me, even so send I you.* And when he had said this he endued them with the Spirit (literally "breathed on them") and saith unto them *Receive ye the Holy Spirit: whose soever sins ye remit they are remitted, and whose soever sins ye retain they are retained.*

The above words, which have proved themselves to be of immense importance in the history of Christianity, have been a serious stumbling-block to countless earnest enquirers. It is indeed evident that it is impossible to grant a commission to any group of human beings without incurring the possibility of one or more members of the group exercising his or their function unworthily. It consequently follows therefore that the words of Jesus force us to contemplate the possibility, and indeed probability, of some penitent sinner being desirous of reconciliation with God, but being unable to approach the divine mercy-seat owing to the ill-will of one of the holders of the commission granted in virtue of the utterance in question. If on the other hand it be admitted that the penitent sinner is pardoned, and that the impenitent is punished, irrespective of any intervention of another human being, then it appears that the work of the commissioners is reduced to a mere fiction. They can merely proclaim the fact that God pardons the penitent and will punish the impenitent. Such proclamation is useful and indeed necessary, but is very far removed from what at first glance appears to be promised by Jesus in the text under discussion.

It unfortunately happens that the sacerdotal system of the Christian Church has been bound up, with the most unhappy results, with a literal interpretation of the words in question. It was argued that Jesus created commissioners forming a priestly caste, having the same authority as that enjoyed by himself, including the right of appointing new members with similar powers, so that a permanent supply of such commissioners might be assured. Many of the commissioners so appointed fell, as was indeed inevitable, into the obvious temptation of abusing the spiritual powers claimed by them, and thereby obtained all sorts of temporal advantages for themselves and for their caste. This matter will be touched on in a subsequent chapter dealing with Christianity as an Institution. It is for the moment enough to say that the lamentable failure of organised religion in Europe seems to be largely due to a miscomprehension of the passage under discussion, as also of a somewhat similar passage in Matthew xvi. The passage in Matthew will be discussed in a subsequent chapter: we are now concerned with the interpretation of John xx. 21–23.

It must firstly be remembered that we are dealing with the Fourth Gospel, in which the most exalted spiritual truths are expressed in a manner incomprehensible to anyone who has not commenced to lift his heart God-wards. It must further be observed that the evangelist represents Jesus, at the close of his earthly ministry, as carrying out the function proclaimed by the Baptist at its commencement: *Upon whom thou shalt see the Spirit descending and remaining on him, the same is he which baptiseth with the Holy Spirit* (John i. 33). So the words *As my Father hath sent me, even so send I you. Receive ye the Holy Spirit, etc.* would appear to mean:

> As the Father baptised me with the Holy Spirit, causing me to be made both Lord and Christ (Acts ii. 36; x. 38),

so I now baptise you with this same Spirit, thereby causing you also to partake of the Christ nature. Being raised, as you henceforth are, on to an exalted spiritual plane, it becomes part of your function to assist to remove the shortcomings of those brethren who are capable of progressing God-wards. But on the other hand, those who are by their sins rendered unable to react to the influence of the Holy Spirit, as irradiated through you, will suffer the inevitable consequences of their wrongdoing, or in other words their sins will be retained.

It is evident therefore that in the ministry instituted by Jesus as described above, there is nothing external and formal. The minister's function is exercised solely on an exalted spiritual plane, to which he can only attain if he be endued with the Holy Spirit, or in other words, made to partake in the Christ-nature. In this sense there can be no such thing as an unworthy minister. A minister is one who is, by means of his lofty spiritual attainments, able to assist the divine purpose, and so to facilitate the spiritual progress of his fellow-beings. One who does not so assist the divine purpose is simply not a minister (in the sense in which the word is here used) whatever may be the ostensible profession he follows on earth.

Concluding Chapters

The author's desire to exhibit himself in a favourable light when compared with Peter, is again shown in xx. 4, where our attention is even drawn to the unimportant detail that the author was the better runner of the two.

The original work apparently terminated at the end of Chapter XX, the following chapter being however quite probably a postscriptum by the same hand. In this final chapter the former tendency to underrate the position of the chief of the apostles seems to have disappeared, and Peter and the author are clearly on excellent terms.

The Gospel, as added to, ends with a hint that possibly the evangelist would not die before the return of Jesus. In so far as this hint may affect the question of the authorship it is perhaps an argument, albeit not a very strong one, in favour of Lazarus. Obviously it might appear to be somewhat futile to perform the prodigy of restoring a dead man to life if the only result were to be that he would continue a mute, inglorious existence; and a few days, a few months or a few years subsequently would succumb to some commonplace ailment. Hence there might not unreasonably arise in the minds of the disciples an idea that Lazarus, having (apparently) died once, would have some special destiny allotted to him, and would be no more subject to death, but would remain on earth until the (early) return of Jesus.

Conclusions as to authorship

The foregoing considerations enable us to form from purely internal evidence the following conclusions:

(a) If we suspend our judgment concerning the first fourteen verses, written as they are in a style quite different from the remainder, we infer that the Fourth Gospel is in all probability not a late literary fabrication, but is a genuine account of the life of Jesus, written by an eye-witness, and is, as regards its structure, logic and orderly sequence, superior to the First and Third Gospels.

(b) The author was probably not one of the twelve apostles, and was almost certainly not John the son of Zebedee.

(c) While all positive theories as to the authorship present difficulties, it seems easiest to believe that Jesus had specially intimate relationships with a disciple named Lazarus, in the vicinity of Jerusalem; that this disciple was instructed by Jesus in those truths which it was not desirable to preach publicly; that, as the culminating point of this esoteric teaching, Lazarus fell into a death-like trance, during which he received psychically his final instruction; that this trance Jesus explained as being not a sickness unto death, but a mere preliminary to the manifestation of the divine power in Lazarus; that finally the promised manifestation of the divine power took the form of the compilation of the Fourth Gospel, with its matchless discourses on the higher truths of Christianity.

(d) Any theory which may be formed has necessarily to be reconciled with certain peculiarities of the text, notably that Chapters XI and XII lay stress on the affection of Jesus for Lazarus, and keep the latter in the foreground as much as possible, while Chapters XIII to XXI similarly stress the affection of Jesus for the anonymous evangelist. Moreover the author shows an obvious desire to belittle Peter, of whom he is doubtless jealous, and he further manifests a special animus against Judas.

Now if we reject the Lazarus theory, we find that the following difficulties result from the peculiarities above set forth:

(i) Jesus had a very special affection for two different individuals—the author of the Gospel and Lazarus. But if the former was by disposition distinctly inclined to jealousy, how do we account for the obvious pleasure he takes, throughout two chapters, in indicating Lazarus as a special object of this affection?

(ii) We find that the sisters of Lazarus used the phrase "he whom thou lovest" as a kind of pseudonym for their brother. The anonymous author uses practically the same pseudonym for himself (xiii. 23; xix. 26; xx. 2; xxi. 20). How do we account for this? It may be replied that Jesus loved both men, and that there was no objection to saying so. This however is not quite the point. We are here dealing not with the fact of the affection of Jesus but with the choice of a pseudonym. Why should the author, after having so consistently kept Lazarus before our notice, confuse the narrative by choosing for himself the same pseudonym as had just been used for Lazarus?

(iii) The narrative from Chapter XI onwards forms a harmonious and logical whole, and as regards its structure compares very favourably with the synoptic Gospels, composed as they largely are of disconnected paragraphs. But this narrative, good as it is, has from a literary point of view, one great defect. It introduces the character of Lazarus, tells us a good deal about him and then, when our attention is still concentrated on him, suddenly drops him. Immediately afterwards a new character, the author himself, suddenly appears without any introduction whatever, and our attention is thenceforward directed in a marked manner to the author, exactly as had previously been the case with Lazarus. Now if Lazarus and the author be not the same person, why did the latter write as he did? Why should the author give us details as to the call of so relatively unimportant a person as Andrew, and say nothing about the call and early career of the one person—that is himself—whose prominent position he at the end of the narrative so clearly desired to emphasise?

70 INTRODUCTION TO THE STUDY OF CHRISTIANITY

(e) If on the other hand we accept the Lazarus theory we are faced with this difficulty. In xxi. 20 the author is indicated by the relatively insignificant circumstance that he had leaned on Jesus' breast at supper, and not by the more important circumstance that he had been raised from the tomb. Why is this? It may be suggested that if Lazarus had said definitely "I who was raised from the tomb wrote this gospel," he would have created a precedent, and thereby possibly have been indirectly the cause of other disciples of the esoteric school writing details of their supernormal spiritual experiences, and *ex hypothesi* this could not be permitted. One fact however is clear, and that is that the writer deliberately withheld such information as would enable us to identify him with certainty. A reason can be suggested why Lazarus should have done so, but why should John have so acted?

(f) If we are disposed to accept the theory that it was as a spiritual experience that Lazarus fell into a death-like trance and was raised therefrom, and further that he subsequently wrote the Fourth Gospel, the question of the attitude of the synoptic evangelists has to be considered. We are then forced to conclude that these evangelists, desiring to omit any reference to the esoteric school of doctrine, deliberately suppressed any mention not only of Lazarus personally, but of the visits of Jesus to Jerusalem, in or near which town Jesus may be supposed to have carried on his esoteric teaching. (Bethany, the residence of Lazarus, is about two miles from Jerusalem.)

It may be noted that in John vii. 10 we get a specific admission of the artificial secrecy made to surround a visit of Jesus to Jerusalem. (It is clear that the reason alleged for this secrecy is not the true one. Cf. vii. 1 with vii. 14.) Moreover a trace of the suppression of incidents connected with such visits is presumably to be seen in Luke x. 38. If we compare this passage with John xi we get the impression that Luke originally wrote something of interest, but subsequently decided to mutilate what he had written, by deleting all reference to Lazarus. We are consequently left with a colourless paragraph about Jesus coming to a certain village and being

THE FOURTH GOSPEL

received by a certain woman named Martha into her house. Surely the inference is that Luke had some special reason for mentioning neither Martha's brother Lazarus (presumably the chief of the family and the householder) nor the visits of Jesus to Jerusalem.

Similarly the omission, on the part of the synoptics, of all mention of the presence on Calvary of the mother of Jesus can perhaps be explained by the assumption that she said or did nothing of special interest, and consequently that the only way in which she could be truthfully brought into the narrative would be to relate her being entrusted to Lazarus, and this the synoptic evangelists were *ex hypothesi* unwilling to do. It is admitted that the situation as set forth above is difficult to understand, but the suggestion is that any other theory presents even greater difficulties.

External Evidence

We find that Polycarp (d. 156) in his epistles to the Philippians gives frequent quotations from the synoptic Gospels, but makes no allusion to a Fourth Gospel. As Polycarp was the most intimate disciple of John, this fact carries considerable weight as against the Johannine authorship. There are passages in the works of Justin (d. *c.* 163) which indicate that he may possibly have been acquainted with the Fourth Gospel, but even if this be a fact the attitude he assumes makes it clear that he did not think the Gospel authoritative. (It is Justin who tells us that John wrote the Book of Revelation.) The existence of the Gospel cannot be conclusively proved prior to about 170, when it was undoubtedly regarded as possessing considerable authority. Theophilus of Antioch, writing about 180, seems to be the first to affirm definitely that John was the author. Irenaeus, probably writing very shortly after Theophilus, accepted this statement as an undoubted fact.

The position therefore seems to be the following. Internal evidence makes us think that the author was an eye-witness; external evidence fails to prove that the work was generally known before about 170. This is consistent with the theory enunciated above, that the Gospel deals with the Christian mysteries, and it is therefore comprehensible that it should have been for a considerable time reserved exclusively for the use of pupils of the esoteric doctrine. If however we finally conclude that the Gospel in question was written by a contemporary of

Jesus, the following difficulty presents itself. There seems some reason for thinking that the author of the Fourth Gospel intends to correct certain statements made by the synoptic evangelists (see page 57.) But as modern scholars are inclined to put the date of both Matthew and Luke as not much earlier than 80 and possibly later, it is not probable that an eye-witness of events which took place from 26 to 29 would have written a book rectifying any errors which those two evangelists might have made. A possible solution of this difficulty seems to be that errors may have occurred in the (supposed) document (customarily referred to as "Q" and mentioned on page 33), which many scholars believe to have formed a partial basis of Matthew and Luke, and possibly to some extent of Mark also. That is to say that "Q" may have come first, then the Fourth Gospel, and finally the synoptic Gospels. But the subject is too obscure to permit of a definite conclusion to be drawn.

The Johannine Discourses

It may very possibly be objected to all that has hitherto been said anent the Fourth Gospel, that no consideration has been given to the discourses therein put into the mouth of Jesus. In reply it must be admitted that we have not hitherto discussed the principal argument against the authenticity of the Fourth Gospel, i.e. the alleged unnatural and artificial nature of the long speeches stated to have been delivered by Jesus. The synoptic evangelists represent the doctrine of Jesus as something individual and personal: hostile critics have deprecated the value of this doctrine, but have nevertheless recognised the strong individuality of Jesus, which caused his discourses to be quite unlike the speeches or writings of any other religious teacher. "But," say in effect the hostile critics, "in the Fourth Gospel we meet with an entirely new situation. The discourses therein given do not impress us as being speeches at all, but as literary compositions, written by some author who had never been under the personal influence of Jesus, and who was unacquainted with both his doctrine and his mannerisms." Renan goes so far as to say:

> If Jesus spoke as Matthew tells us, he could not have spoken as John tells us. Between the two authorities no critic has hesitated or will hesitate. . . . It is not by pretentious, heavy and badly written tirades (*des tirades prétentieuses, lourdes, mal écrites*) appealing but little to the moral sense, that Jesus has founded his divine work (*Vie de Jésus*, Introduction).

THE FOURTH GOSPEL

In answer to this criticism we may commence by calling attention to the well-known analogy existing between the respective biographies of Socrates and of Jesus. Socrates left no written works, but his discourses are known to us by the writings of two disciples, Xenophon and Plato. The former gives us a well-written narrative, the latter puts into the mouth of Socrates long and elaborate speeches, which may very probably represent the Socratic line of thought, but which most assuredly can never have been uttered word for word in the form in which they are presented to us. But nevertheless, after twenty-three centuries have elapsed, the work of Plato is far more highly esteemed than that of Xenophon.

Similarly we get biographies of Jesus in the synoptic Gospels and in the Fourth Gospel. In the former we get one account of his teaching and in the latter another. The records of the synoptic evangelists evidently deal with a very real and human teacher: the discourses of the Fourth Gospel are, as we have already seen, called by Renan *des tirades prétentieuses, lourdes, mal écrites*. Why then is it that after the lapse of so many centuries the latter are, by a large body of Christians, so much more highly esteemed than are the records of the synoptic evangelists?

Before trying to answer this question it may be well to recall the words of Paul: "If any man be in Christ, he is a new creature: old things are passed away: behold all things are become new and all things are of God" (2 Cor. v. 17, 18). The discourses contained in the Fourth Gospel were, it has already been suggested, probably committed to writing for the benefit of an esoteric school, consisting of disciples who had already begun to be in Christ. These discourses, suitable as they are for study by those to whom all things are become new and to whom all things are of God, are practically meaningless to the casual reader. But even the casual reader, unable or unwilling though he may be to enter into their spirit, may nevertheless feel a greater disposition to treat them with respect if it is explained to him that the spokesman Jesus is understood to be identified with the Christ, and that the Christ is understood to have entered to a greater or less degree into the being of each individual reader or hearer. Consequently the discourses may be regarded as being uttered by the Christ or Higher Ego, and to be addressed to the "new creature," or natural man in course of becoming regenerated.

A comprehension of these discourses is greatly facilitated by a study of the Bhagavad Ghita, already referred to on page 24.

74 INTRODUCTION TO THE STUDY OF CHRISTIANITY

In this work the god Chrishna is supposed to have taken the form of a chariot-driver, and it is while attending his master Arjuna at the commencement of a battle, that Chrishna is represented as uttering the speeches attributed to him. These speeches merely excite our ridicule if we suppose that an actual chariot-driver did really address his employer in the words contained in the poem. But if we attempt to interpret the Ghita in the manner we have already suggested with respect to the Johannine discourses, and if we regard Chrishna as personifying the Higher Ego, and Arjuna as the "new man" who is in process of becoming "in Christ," we cannot fail to be struck by the essential identity of the teaching. A few passages are selected from the Ghita for the purpose of comparison, and these passages will be found in Appendix A, page 295.

IN the following four chapters the development and progress of Christianity will be dealt with under the following headings:

Chapter V. The Christians as a Jewish sect.
Chapter VI. Christian propaganda, the influence of paganism, the formation of traditional Christianity and the crystallisation of dogma.
Chapter VII. Christianity as an institution.
Chapter IX. Christianity of to-day.

It is obvious that the history of Christianity cannot conveniently be cut up into well-defined sections dealing with separate periods of time. Thus as regards Chapters V and VI, there continued to be Christians in Palestine who regarded themselves as still belonging to the Jewish body long after Christians in Rome had come under the influence of paganism. It may however be said roughly that Chapter V deals with events commencing about the time of the Passion of Jesus (A.D. 29), while Chapter VI may be said to commence with Paul's missionary labours.

CHAPTER V

THE CHRISTIANS AS A JEWISH SECT

It may be interesting if we take the suppositious case of some inconspicuous citizen of Jerusalem, a convert to the teaching of Jesus, living a few years after the crucifixion, and if we ask ourselves what his real religious convictions are likely to have been, or in other words, how would he have answered the questions: what was the nature of the mission of Jesus? and in what way, if any, was the relationship between God and mankind modified by the execution of this mission? It seems not too much to say that the course of human history for nineteen centuries would have been considerably altered if unequivocal records had existed enabling us to answer these questions with certainty. Let us for a moment consider the case of Stephen (Acts vi. 8 to vii. 60). He was accused of claiming that the effect of the mission of Jesus would be to change the Mosaic customs. He consequently had an opportunity given him of proclaiming publicly what his convictions on that point really were. But we find that he delivered, or at least the author of the Acts represents him as having delivered, a speech consisting of no less than fifty-two verses in which he, following the time-honoured custom of accused persons, said a good deal which does not seem to have any very direct bearing on the indictment, and terminated by accusing his hearers of having murdered the Just One. But as to Stephen's actual convictions with reference to the nature and office of the Just One we gather very little.

It seems that we are justified in concluding that among the very early Christians the faith was a matter of inward fervour rather than of intellectual conviction. The convert who felt the Christ Spirit working within him believed himself to be a new creature, and for him all things had become new (2 Cor. v. 17). And the inference that, as regards the early Christians, religion was much more a matter of the heart than of the intellect, helps us to understand certain phenomena of which the New Testament tells us. Thus we read in Acts ii. 13 of how the disciples, after an exceptionally powerful influx of the Divine Spirit, were so affected physically as to appear to unsympathetic spectators to be under the influence of strong drink. And again Paul gives us to understand that in his day the Spirit used to manifest itself by causing gifted disciples to speak in a manner unintelligible to their hearers, and apparently sometimes even unintelligible to themselves also. (*Vide* 1 Cor. xiv, a chapter which is full of difficulties, but which nevertheless seems to bear out the foregoing statement. In verse 23 the apostle even warns his readers against the possibility of an outsider concluding that the whole assembly had gone mad.)

Phenomena analogous to the foregoing take place to-day: indeed the name Quaker is said to have been given on account of the behaviour of some of the members of the Society of Friends when under the influence of religious excitement. And it will be found that while people who outwardly exhibit physical symptoms of their spiritual fervour are usually very ready to talk about their belief, they do not generally give any reason satisfactory to an unprejudiced auditor as to exactly why such belief is held by them.

So in our examination of the theological position of our imaginary convert to Christianity, of whom mention was made at the commencement of this chapter, we must be prepared to find considerable obscurity with respect to various points. We can however feel confident that he would unquestionably have regarded himself as a Jew, and would indeed have been unable to conceive of any religion acceptable to the Deity and not founded on the Jewish law. Jesus, the Messiah or Christ, was a Jew, and the eleven left to carry on his work were also Jews—they would have enjoyed no confidence whatever among the inhabitants of Judea if they had not been. So our imaginary convert would have continued to entertain the most profound respect for the Law (*Thorah*) delivered once for all by Jehovah to Moses—that Law which the Messiah had declared that he had come not to destroy but to fulfil. But on the other hand we may reasonably suppose that the influence of Christian sentiment caused at quite an early date Jewish converts to become somewhat less strict as regards the actual application of some of the precepts of the Mosaic code. While this code would still be considered as theoretically binding, a feeling would doubtless soon arise that many of its dispositions had become less important than they had been in the past. An illogical sentiment of this sort may be traced in our own days. The Jewish Law enjoined a man whose brother had died leaving a childless widow, to contract an alliance with the widow, so as to produce a child on behalf of his deceased brother, independently of the widow's inclinations or of his own domestic ties (Deut. xxv. 5, Mark xii. 19, Luke xx. 28). Now there are to-day millions of excellent and intelligent Christians who would be deeply shocked if they heard anyone either (*a*) deny that this disposition had divine sanction or (*b*) affirm that it should be acted on. The early Christians were probably as inconsistent as their twentieth-century brethren; so we are not surprised that notwithstanding the respect for the Law professed by the first followers of Jesus, one of them was, as we have just seen, early accused of boasting that "Jesus of Nazareth shall change the customs which Moses delivered us" (Acts vi. 14).

But on the other hand the question of changing, or not changing, the customs enjoined by the Mosaic code probably assumed in the minds of the immediate followers of Jesus a position of only secondary importance. The conviction of the very early Christians was, as has already been noticed, that the departure of Jesus from the earth would only be for quite a short period, and that when he returned there would be some tremendous cataclysm and the twelve apostles would seat themselves on twelve thrones to judge the twelve tribes of Israel (the Jews taking but little interest in what happened to the rest of humanity). And as the day of the Lord would come as a thief in the night, the believer's whole outlook on life became radically affected. One very natural result of the belief in the close proximity of the end of this dispensation was, as already mentioned, the lack of contemporary records. In the firm conviction that within a very few years at most the Lord would descend from heaven with a shout, and with the voice of the archangel, and with the trump of God, the Christian had but little temptation to pass his precious moments in writing useless books for a generation which would never grow up to read them.

Another result of belief in the imminent return of Jesus was the establishment of the communal system. Disciples, so soon as they became converted, sold their worldly goods and offered the proceeds to a common fund. We have no details as to the length of time for which this custom lasted, nor as to the difficulties which caused it to be abandoned. It is to be presumed however that no very long period elapsed before the impracticability of this system made itself evident.

A further matter concerning which the early Christians differed widely from the bulk of the Jewish teachers is that of encratism. The Mosaic Code was compiled for a warlike race, endued with an extraordinarily strong nationalistic spirit, and for this race the injunction to "be fruitful and multiply" was founded on obvious necessity. But the teaching of both Jesus (e.g. Matt. xix. 10–12) and Paul (e.g. 1 Cor. vii. 7–9) lends itself to the interpretation that physical relationships between the sexes are of an essentially sinful nature, and that the higher life demands rigid continence from the disciple. This doctrine, which the Essenes had already made familiar to Jewish ears, met with most surprising acceptance when Christianity was subsequently preached as an international religion in the overcrowded cities of Asia Minor, Greece, Italy, and Egypt, where the question of lack of population did not arise, and where bad government inclined thinking men and women to extreme pessimism. The practical effect of Christian encratism has been *inter alia* (*a*) the affirmation of the perpetual virginity of the Blessed Virgin Mary and (*b*) the regulation that men devoted to the religious life should remain celibate—two subjects which will be touched on in a subsequent chapter.

We now come to consider the opinion as to the personality of Jesus retained by the early disciples. The founder of the Christian religion was called by his followers "Master" and "Lord," but there are in addition two titles specially associated with his name: "Son of Man" and "Son of God." Now it might at first glance be concluded that the second title is so incomparably more dignified than the first, that we should specially find it in those passages of the Gospels in which the evangelist seeks to impress us with the divine nature of the Messianic mission. But in point of fact we observe that this is not the case, and that Jesus is referred to by the title "Son of Man" in circumstances in which an orthodox Christian theologian of a later age would undoubtedly have considered that the title "Son of God" was more appropriate. Take for example the following:

> The Son of Man is Lord even of the sabbath day (Matt. xii. 8).
>
> The Son of Man shall come in the glory of his Father with his angels: and then shall he reward every man according to his works (Matt. xvi. 27).
>
> The Son of Man hath power on earth to forgive sins (Matt. ix. 6).
>
> I see the heavens opened and the Son of Man standing on the right hand of God (Acts vii. 56).

The title *Son of Man* has been interpreted by many critics, including Renan, to imply *the Messiah*. Renan adds that this title *exprimait sa qualité de juge*, but it is not very clear why this should be so. Indeed to give a quasi-technical meaning to the term *Son of Man* involves us in considerable difficulty. The prophet Ezekiel represents Jehovah as calling him *Son of Man* on several occasions in circumstances in which it is clear that the phrase simply means *Man* (cf. Ps. viii. 4). Again we must remember that the synoptic evangelists write of Jesus as exercising considerable reticence as regards calling himself *the Messiah* (Matt. xvi. 20, Mark viii. 29, 30, Luke ix. 20, 21), and there would be no point in such reticence if *Messiah* and *Son of Man* were equivalent terms, seeing that Jesus is quoted as freely referring to himself, from the early days of his Ministry, by the latter title (Mark ii. 28, etc.).

The title *Son of Man* seems to imply: "the man specially indicated as representative of the human race." In the use of the title there is perhaps something of the idea which prompted Walt Whitman to write the *Song of Myself*:

> I celebrate myself, and sing myself
> And what I assume, you shall assume,
> For every atom belonging to me as good belongs to you.
>
> Stop this day and night with me and you shall possess the origin of all poems.
> You shall possess the good of the earth and sun (there are millions of suns left),
> You shall no longer take things at second or third hand, nor look through the eyes of the dead, nor feed on the spectres in books,
> You shall not look through my eyes either, nor take things from me,
> You shall listen to all sides and filter them from yourself.

But nevertheless the Christian concept of the *Son of Man* goes considerably deeper than what is suggested by Whitman. Jesus according to the former idea is something more than a type of humanity at its highest: he is more than the first-fruits of our race: he is the representative and architypical man whom God chose to fulfil a certain mission, that of being a vehicle for the reception of the Christ Spirit, for the direct association of the Christ Spirit with physical life and physical death, and for the diffusion of that same Spirit among mankind. "Upon whom thou shalt see the Spirit descending and remain-

THE CHRISTIANS AS A JEWISH SECT

ing on him, the same is he that baptiseth with the Holy Spirit" (John i. 33).

Notwithstanding the frequency of the title *Son of Man* in the Gospels, it is only used once in the remaining books of the New Testament (Acts vii. 56). In later years, when Jesus began to be thought of as "Very God of Very God," the title was doubtless felt to be inappropriate, and seems to have been disused altogether.

The other title: *Son of God* also calls for careful examination. The word *Son* seems to have been used by the Hebrews in a very elastic sense, and frequently had nothing to do with actual generation. Thus biblical authors use the word in an unfavourable sense when speaking of "Sons of the wicked one" (Matt. xiii. 38), "Sons of Belial" (1 Sam. x. 27), "Son of hell" (Matt. xxiii. 15). So we are not surprised to find the title *Son of God* used in the Bible with some freedom. In Old Testament days the expression was sometimes used to mean a heavenly being, not partaking of the divine nature, but probably corresponding to some extent to medieval ideas of an archangel (cf. Gen. vi. 2 with Job i. 6). Considerable light is shed on the title *Son of God* in John x. 35, 36, where Jesus himself is represented as saying to the Jews:

> If he called them gods unto whom the word of God came . . . say ye of him whom the Father hath sanctified and sent into the world *Thou blasphemest* because I said *I am Son of the God* (Ύἱος του Θεου ειμι).

Now a critic may possibly be sceptical as to whether Jesus actually used the words here attributed to him. The synoptic evangelists do not represent him as calling himself *Son of God*, and we find that he charged his immediate disciples to keep secret the fact that he had a claim to the title (Matt. xvi. 16–20). And although the author of the Fourth Gospel puts the words above quoted into the mouth of Jesus, we do not attach to the fact the importance that we might otherwise do, seeing that, as we have already seen, this author probably rather laid himself out to indicate the more recondite truths of Christianity than to reproduce with verbal accuracy exactly what he had heard Jesus say. Consequently we cannot be certain that the words above quoted were actually used by Jesus in his discussions with the Jews, but nevertheless we at least know that they represent the opinion of that writer who is most frequently appealed to in support of the traditional doctrine of the nature of Jesus. And it is quite clear that this opinion is that the reason why Jesus could claim to be *Son of God* was that the Father had sanctified him and sent him into the world.

And in harmony with the foregoing, we find that Paul seems to apply the title *Son of God* to any man endowed with the Christ Spirit. "As many as are led by the Spirit of God, they are the Sons of God" (Rom. viii. 14). The expression in the Fourth Gospel (i. 12) "He gave power to become the Sons of God" would appear to have a similar meaning. But in other places the same phrase probably means simply what in more modern English we should call "a godly man." For example Matthew and Mark make the Roman centurion on the occasion of the crucifixion of Jesus say "Truly this man was Son of God" (not *the* Son of God), and Luke makes him say "Certainly this was a righteous man." The natural inference is that in these cases the expressions *Son of God* and *righteous man* have an almost identical meaning.

As regards the doctrine taught by Jesus about his own person, much difficulty has arisen owing to the apparently contradictory nature of the various utterances attributed to him. Even the Fourth Gospel quotes him as saying: "The Son can do nothing of himself, but what he seeth the Father do" (John v. 19), "My Father is greater than I" (John xiv. 28). Such passages seem to be in disaccord with other parts of the Johannine discourses, wherein Jesus, feeling his soul to be exalted on to the highest spiritual plane, and wholly identified with the Christ Spirit (or Higher Ego), utters such phrases as:

> All things which the Father hath are mine (xvi. 15). Whatsoever ye shall ask the Father in my name, he will give it you (xvi. 23): The Father himself loveth you, because ye have loved me, and have believed that I came out from God (xvi. 27).

But while the greatest weight must be given to such passages as those above quoted, it must not be forgotten that the early disciples were taught that the high spiritual dignity possessed by Jesus might equally be attained by themselves: "I am in my Father, and ye in me and I in you" (John xiv. 20), "As thou Father art in me and I in thee, that they also may be one in us" (John xvii. 21). This fact is of vital importance to the right understanding of the sayings of Jesus.

The general outlook of the disciples on the much vexed

THE CHRISTIANS AS A JEWISH SECT

question of the nature and mission of Jesus is well exemplified in the great speech made by Peter (Acts ii) on the day of Pentecost. The orator is reported as saying:

> Ye men of Israel hear these words: Jesus of Nazareth, a man approved of God among you by miracles and wonders and signs . . . being delivered by the determinate counsel and foreknowledge of God, ye have taken and by wicked hands have crucified and slain. . . . This Jesus hath God raised up, whereof we are all witnesses. . . . Therefore let all the house of Israel know assuredly that God hath made that same Jesus, whom ye have crucified, both Lord and Christ.

The above is of great interest as setting forth the attitude of the primitive Church with regard to the position held by Jesus. It will be observed that Peter gives no hint of regarding him as a kind of secondary Deity, existing co-eternally with God. On the contrary Peter speaks of "Jesus of Nazareth, a man approved of God," who for certain reasons which seemed sufficient to the divine mind, was made by God both Lord and Christ. The natural interpretation of Peter's words is that although Jesus of Nazareth may doubtless have been foreordained to his exalted mission, nevertheless he was actually born into the world as a human being, and that this human being was at some period subsequent to his birth made by God both Lord and Christ. This is entirely consistent with what would appear to be the belief of the evangelists that Jesus became the Christ at the time of his baptism.

It is noteworthy that Peter is represented as explaining (Acts x. 38) how "God consecrated (or more literally *christened* ἔχρισεν) Jesus of Nazareth with the Holy Spirit and with power." The word ἔχρισεν is, here as elsewhere, translated "anointed" in the Authorised Version. This is of course the primary meaning, but obviously what Peter desired his hearers to understand was "endued with the Christ Spirit," so "christened" seems more appropriate than "anointed." Similarly in 2 Cor. i. 21 and 1 John ii. 20 we get passages in which the Authorised Version gives "anoint" and "unction," but in which the respective authors obviously had in mind "endue with the Christ Spirit."

Another point on which the belief of the primitive Church is of great interest is that of the mission of the Paraclete (Παρακλητος). This word seems to have more than one meaning, perhaps "witness favourable to one's cause" is the original one. It may be variously translated: advocate, helper, consoler, etc. It is used with reference to Jesus by John in his first Epistle (ii. 1): "If any man sin we have a Paraclete with the Father, Jesus Christ the righteous." The Vulgate here translates *Advocatum habemus apud Patrem*, and our Authorised Version, following the Vulgate, gives "advocate." The same word is used three times in the Fourth Gospel, and this fact has been stressed by those critics who believe that the Fourth Gospel and the Epistles attributed to John are by the same hand. The three passages are:

> I will pray the Father, and he shall give you another Paraclete (xiv. 16).
>
> But when the Paraclete is come, whom I will send unto you from the Father, even the spirit of truth (xv. 26).
>
> If I go not away the Paraclete will not come unto you, but if I depart, I will send him unto you (xvi. 7).

In these three instances the Vulgate makes no attempt to translate, but gives simply *Paracletus*, whereas our Authorised Version translates by *Comforter*.

In the next chapter, when touching on the crystallization of dogma, mention will be made of the traditional opinion as to the nature of the Paraclete. We are here however concerned with the opinion which the primitive Church might have been expected to have held. It would, as has already been said, seem to have been a fundamental belief of the early Christians that an emanation, or manifestation of the Deity, descended on Jesus at his baptism, thereby causing him to become the Christ. This emanation the Evangelists call the *Holy Spirit* (literally *Holy Breath*), but Paul, who generally says *Spirit* or *Holy Spirit*, also says *the Spirit of his* (God's) *Son* (Gal. iv. 6), or *Spirit of Christ* (Rom. viii. 9). Similarly in the first Chapter of Peter's First Epistle we find the expressions: *the Spirit, the Spirit of Christ, the Holy Spirit*, all having apparently the same meaning (verses 2, 11, 12). In the present treatise it has been thought convenient to say generally *Christ Spirit*. The meaning of the words of Jesus in John xvi. 7 (quoted above) may it is suggested have been somewhat as follows:

> The Christ Spirit or Paraclete is present within my heart, and has so identified himself with me that I am become *the* Christ. This Christ Spirit however should be received by you into your own hearts, so that you in turn may be one with Christ. Your spiritual development is now advanced to such a point

that it is more suitable for you to receive the influx of this same Spirit in the normal way, than in the supernormal way which has during the last three years been made possible by my physical presence and oral teaching.

The disciples believed that this promise of Jesus was specially fulfilled by means of a manifestation or outpouring of the Holy Spirit which we are told took place seven weeks after the Resurrection. It was as a consequence of this outpouring of the Spirit that Peter was moved to make the speech to which attention has already been called.

Commencement of Conversion of the Gentiles

We have to wait for a considerable time, probably for more than a decade after the crucifixion, for any evidence of a formal change of attitude on the part of the Christian community in the direction of discarding Hebrew exclusiveness and fraternising with members of other races (or "Gentiles," as the Jews called them).

Jesus himself seems to have been in principle as exclusive as his fellow-countrymen (see especially Matt. x. 6 and xv. 24), and the passages in the Gospels which appear to point to the foundation of a world religion are very probably late additions.[1] But we find that Peter, while on a visit to Joppa (possibly about 41), had a vision and was simultaneously commanded to slay and to eat unclean animals, and, on refusing, was told "What God hath cleansed, that call not thou common." Immediately afterwards Peter was approached by a certain Cornelius, "a devout man" but not a Jew, whom Peter welcomed with what was clearly intended to be perfect courtesy, saying: "Ye know how that it is an unlawful thing for a man that is a Jew to keep company or come unto one of another nation, but God hath showed me that I should not call any man common or unclean" (Acts x. 28).

Peter then expounded the gospel to Cornelius, and we read that "they of the circumcision which believed were astonished because that on the Gentiles also was poured out the gift of the Holy Spirit" (Acts x. 45). And when Peter had returned to

---

[1] The passage *To be a light to lighten the Gentiles* is from the series of so-called "birth-stories" prefixed to Luke's Gospel, and the injunction to *go into all the world and to preach the gospel to every creature* is from the twelve verses added to Mark probably in the second century. The passage in Matthew, commanding the disciples to *teach all nations*, is discussed on page 115 *infra*.

86 INTRODUCTION TO THE STUDY OF CHRISTIANITY

Jerusalem "they that were of the circumcision contended with him saying: *Thou wentest in to men uncircumcised and didst eat with them*" (Acts xi. 2, 3). So it will be seen that the early Christian community was unquestionably for some years as exclusive in its Judaism as were the orthodox Jews themselves. The practical difficulty so raised seems to have been accentuated by some Jewish Christians who hindered Paul's work in Antioch by telling his disciples that unless they were circumcised they could not be saved (Acts xv. 1). [Paul was indeed destined to suffer much annoyance in this respect. We find him a few years subsequently expressing a wish that the Judaisers who continued to insist on circumcision might be subjected to a far more unpleasant operation themselves (Gal. v. 12).] But the step immediately taken by Paul was to repair to Jerusalem, where a formal Church council was held to consider the community's attitude towards the non-Jewish world. This fact is of itself of importance as showing that the community was already, perhaps semi-consciously, beginning to feel that possibly after all the coming of Jesus was not so imminent as had been supposed, and that it behoved the Church therefore to take a definite attitude with respect to the urgent problems which were presenting themselves. Hence the decision to convoke a general council, whose resolutions were to be considered as permanently binding on the whole of the body.

The proceedings of this council (Acts xv) are of great interest. "When there had been much disputing Peter rose up" and defended the attitude already assumed by him. Paul and an immediate follower named Barnabas followed to the same effect. James (traditionally the Lord's brother) acted as president, and pronounced final sentence. It is interesting to note that James stated that he was influenced in his opinion by the consideration that "Moses of old time hath in every city them that preach him, being read in the synagogues every sabbath day." In view of this fact it was decided that "no greater burden" should be laid on non-Jews than to enjoin them to abstain from (i) meats offered to idols: (ii) blood: (iii) things strangled and (iv) fornication. Formal letters to this effect were consequently issued in the name of "the apostles and elders and brethren," and the four prohibitions in question seem to have constituted a definite code, which is again referred to at a later date (Acts xxi. 25).

In the above incident there are several points of interest:

THE CHRISTIANS AS A JEWISH SECT

(a) We note the reluctance of the community to break away from Jewish customs in the direction of entering into any kind of fellowship with non-Jews. This reluctance is patent even in cases where non-Jews were able to convince the Jewish Christians that they had received the gift of the Christ Spirit. This seems to prove conclusively that if Jesus ever intended to found an universal Church which should be independent of the Mosaic Code, he failed to make his immediate disciples understand his wishes.

(b) The council allowed its conscience to be quieted by the fact that, whatever action it might take, the Law would none the less continue to be expounded in the synagogues.

(c) The conditions under which the council was prepared to extend the right hand of fellowship to non-Jewish co-believers are a little unexpected. To put fornication on a par with eating a fowl which has had its neck wrung seems to modern ideas to show a certain lack of proportion.

* * * * *

It is now convenient to consider two documents called respectively THE EPISTLE TO THE HEBREWS and THE EPISTLE OF JAMES, which documents are specially associated with the early Jewish-Christian Church. They are of considerable interest, and this interest would be intensified if we could be certain as to their date and the authority which was attributed to them in the first and second centuries. As regards the latter point, we know that some considerable time elapsed before either was regarded as possessing canonical authority, and the documents indeed are of a controversial nature, one being apparently written in answer to the other.

The Epistles to the Hebrews opens in a style somewhat reminiscent of the first fourteen verses of the Fourth Gospel. We are told that God hath spoken to us by his Son, whom he hath appointed heir of all things, by whom also he made the world, who being the brightness of his glory and the express image of his person and upholding all things by the Word of his power, sat down on the right hand of the Majesty on high. It will be observed by comparing the two passages that while the terminology is different, the ideas are undoubtedly similar. The Fourth Gospel tells us that all things were made by the

Word (Λογος): the Epistle to the Hebrews says that God made the world by the Son.

But this Epistle is perhaps chiefly notable on account of the emphasis it puts on what we may call the theory of the sacrificial nature of the mission of Jesus. This theory, hinted at by other writers but more plainly set forth herein, may be very briefly summed up as follows: God demands the shedding of blood as a sacrifice, for otherwise there can be no remission of sins (ix. 22). Until the death of Jesus the necessary sacrifices were rightly offered in the Jewish Temple. Now however that the blood of Jesus has been shed on Calvary there is no further need of any sacrifice of animals.

> For if the blood of bulls and goats and the ashes of an heifer sprinkling the unclean, sanctifieth to the purifying of the flesh, how much more shall the blood of Christ, who offered himself without spot to God, purge your conscience (ix. 13, 14).

Our author argues that the temple sacrifices were enjoined by the "old covenant" which, being decayed and waxed old, is ready to vanish away (viii. 13). Consequently it is implied that the carrying on of the temple sacrifices is useless.

On the general subject of sacrifice a few remarks may be not out of place. There seems to be a deep grounded human sentiment that it is sometimes proper to offer gifts of no appreciable value to the receiver, such gifts, which cost something considerable to the donor, being made as an outward sign of the sincerity of his sentiments. On this principle costly and almost wholly useless presents, such for example as white elephants, have often been offered to royal personages. And we find that in almost every quarter of the world a custom either exists or has existed, to a greater or less degree, of slaughtering animals as an offering to the Deity. The gift is obviously quite useless to the higher powers, but the fact that the donor has deprived himself of something valuable is thought to be a pledge of his sincerity. Hence the belief that sin can be atoned for by the blood of animals, and hence the eventual belief that the offering of Jesus as a sacrifice on the cross was a substitute for existing sacrifices, which were thenceforward rendered unnecessary.

This doctrine, as set forth in the Epistle to the Hebrews, may be said to form the key-note of medieval and indeed of much modern Christianity. The Prayer Book of the English Church speaks of Jesus having offered on the cross "a full, perfect and

THE CHRISTIANS AS A JEWISH SECT

sufficient sacrifice, oblation and satisfaction for the sins of the whole world." The Roman Catholic office for Good Friday reads: "We adore thy Cross (*Crucem tuam adoramus*) O Lord . . . because on account of the wood joy came to the whole world." And, a little further on in the same office: "The Lamb is lifted on the Cross to be immolated."

Now it is of course true that this theory of the office and mission of Christ is not only expounded in the Epistle to the Hebrews, but is fully consistent with much that we find in other parts of the New Testament. But on the other hand it is important to notice the distinction existing between the word "sacrifice," used in its technical sense to mean the putting to death of some animated being in order to propitiate the wrath of the Deity, and the same word used in its more familiar sense to imply a surrender of one's life, interests or pleasures. Thus in the former sense the writer of the Epistle to the Hebrews (x. 12) speaks of Jesus having offered one sacrifice for sins for ever, and in the latter sense Paul (Rom. xii. 1) enjoins his readers to present their bodies as a living sacrifice, holy, acceptable unto God. And it is to be noted that, outside the Epistle to the Hebrews, there are many scriptural passages which have been adduced in favour of the medieval theory of the sacrificial mission of Jesus, but which nevertheless are in fact more consistent with the idea of his earthly career being a "sacrifice" in the more familiar sense of the word. Let us take for example the exclamation of John the Baptist: "Behold the Lamb of God, which taketh away the sin of the world" (John i. 29). These words taken by themselves may unquestionably be understood as harmonising with the medieval theory. But we should note that John goes on to say: "The same is he which baptiseth with the Holy Spirit." So it would appear that what John really means is that the taking away of the sin of the world was to be brought about, not necessarily by the offering of Jesus as a sacrifice (in the same way as lambs were sacrificed in the Temple), but by the irradiating of the Holy Spirit among human souls.

To take another example. Paul tells us (1 Cor. v. 7) that "Christ our Passover is sacrificed for us," a phrase which seems of course in entire harmony with the medieval conception of the mission and death of Jesus. But if we read the context, we see that Paul is not meaning primarily to impart doctrine, but is enjoining the Corinthian converts to rid themselves of evil companions in the same way as, at the Passover, they were accustomed to rid their houses of leaven. He seems to urge them to make their whole lives a Passover feast, free of the leaven of malice and wickedness, and to let their thoughts be centred round Christ even as, throughout the Mosaic rite, their thoughts were centred round the Paschal lamb.

This subject is eminently one anent which we may remember profitably the words of Matthew Arnold (*Literature and Dogma*):

> The Bible language is not scientific, but the language of common speech or of poetry and eloquence, approximative language thrown out at certain great objects of consciousness which it does not pretend to define fully.

This quotation may serve to prepare us for a consideration of Paul's general attitude towards the doctrine of the sacrificial nature of the death of Jesus. It is clear that several passages (e.g. Rom. iii. 24, 25) are written to a greater or less extent under the influence of this doctrine. But here we are met with a very real difficulty. Paul, not in one or two phrases only but consistently, makes it clear that he believes that the redemption of man is brought about by the indwelling of the Christ Spirit. Thus in the Epistle just referred to we read:

> You are not in the flesh, you are in the Spirit, since the Spirit of God dwells within you. Anyone who does not possess the Spirit of Christ does not belong to him. On the other hand, if Christ is within you, though the body is a dead thing owing to Adam's sin, the spirit is living as the result of righteousness (Rom. viii. 9, 10).

Now it would be an overstatement to say that this doctrine is wholly incompatible with the proposition that the redemption of man is brought about by the acceptance, on the part of God the Father, of the death of Jesus as a sacrifice and satisfaction for the sins of mankind. But it is at least certain that no one can regard the two doctrines as equally fundamental. Thinkers of the mystical type, among whom are for example many Quakers, tend to emphasise the importance of the inner light, and of union of the Christ Spirit with the individual soul. Thinkers of the evangelical school emphasise the merits of the blood of Jesus as alone acceptable in the eyes of the Divine Father. And while many Christian theologians profess in the utmost good faith the truth of both the propositions involved, nevertheless it is difficult to see how anyone can in his innermost conscience believe them to be equally essential. When we take the case of Paul we can hardly feel any hesitation. We know that for him what was really fundamental was that for the true believer Christ is everything and everywhere (Col. iii. 11).

On the subject of the sacrifice of Jesus on the cross the language of the Epistle to the Hebrews is definite. When the writer says that "this man offered one sacrifice for sins for ever" he obviously wishes to be interpreted literally. But the language of Paul is different: he sees an analogy where the former writer sees identity. We must remember that the doctrine, as expounded in the Epistle to the Hebrews, of the substitution of the Temple sacrifices by the one great sacrifice of the crucifixion, was primarily one intended for Jewish auditors. If therefore Paul really whole-heartedly believed what the writer of the Epistle to the Hebrews believed, the former in his speeches to Jewish audiences could hardly have failed to have emphasised the fact. We cannot imagine a modern evangelical preacher, if called upon to give a short account of his theological position, failing to say in effect that he looked for salvation through the acceptance, on the part of the Divine Father, of the precious blood of Jesus offered as a sacrifice for his (the preacher's) sins. But we find that while the Acts of the Apostles represents Paul as making several speeches before Jewish audiences in defence of his general position, nothing is said about such sacrifice. These speeches are stated to have been delivered at the Synagogue at Antioch (xiii. 16 to 41), before the public at Jerusalem (xxii. 3 to 21), before Agrippa, an Idumean by race but "one expert in all customs and questions which are among the Jews" (xxvi. 2 to 27), and to the Roman Jews (xxviii. 17 to 28). But neither in these speeches nor in those of Peter and of Stephen to their fellow-countrymen (ii. 14 to 40, iii. 12 to 26, iv. 8 to 12, vi. 8 to vii. 53) do we read of the death of Jesus being a sacrifice. The language attributed to Peter and Stephen indeed indicates that they believed the murder of Jesus to be simply an atrocious crime. The foregoing is of course not adduced as conclusive evidence of what Paul, Peter and Stephen actually did say; because only those theologians who accept the verbal inspiration of the Scriptures can believe that the speeches given in the Acts of the Apostles are literally and accurately reported. But if we have no decisive evidence as to exactly what the three speakers said, we have at least decisive evidence of how Luke believed them to have spoken, and the omission of any reference to a sacrifice made by Jesus is almost as noteworthy in the one case as in the other.

It seems therefore reasonable to infer that the passages in the Pauline Epistles which have been adduced in support of the sacrificial doctrine are what Matthew Arnold calls "approximative language thrown out at certain great objects of consciousness which it does not attempt to define fully."

We are now able to summarise the principal facts relative to the doctrine that the death of Jesus was a sacrifice for our sins, acceptable in the eyes of God:

(*a*) It was originally a tenet of the Jews that the wrath of God could be appeased, at least partially, by the sacrifice of animals. As however the nation advanced in civilisation the tenet lost its importance. Thus centuries before the Christian era we find the Psalmist exclaiming: "Thou desirest no sacrifice else would I give it thee, but thou delightest not in burnt offerings."

(*b*) The mission of Jesus was from the first associated with purging from sin, it being taught that Jesus was "he who baptiseth with the Holy Spirit," or in other words was he through whose agency the Holy Spirit entered the hearts of men to purify and cleanse them.

(*c*) Paul gloried "in the cross of our Lord Jesus Christ" because scoffers saw only disgrace therein, and Paul had the insight to understand that it was only with the accompaniment of intense suffering that the new Adam could attain the summit of spiritual development. As Musset expresses it: "*Rien ne nous rend si grands qu'une grande douleur*" (vide Appendix B, p. 297).

(*d*) As and when the primitive Church began to wean itself from Judaism, it was inevitable that differences of opinion should arise as to the attitude which Christians ought to assume with respect to the Mosaic code. (We know for example that, as has already been explained, considerable conservatism was shown by many converts with respect to non-fellowship with uncircumcised Gentiles.) It seems highly probable therefore that in the course of the discussions which took place, those who advanced the general proposition: *The life and death of Jesus rendered unnecessary all Jewish ceremonial observances* should have followed it up by the further proposition: *The death of Jesus was a sacrifice substituting and rendering unnecessary all the Jewish ceremonial sacrifices*. The author of the Epistle to the Hebrews carried this proposition to its logical conclusion, and

THE CHRISTIANS AS A JEWISH SECT

his tenets have been very generally adopted by Christians; so much so that the doctrine forms the basis of much popular theology, and has tended to force into the background the Pauline teaching as to the indwelling of the Christ Spirit in the human soul.

After dealing with the question of sacrifice, the author of the Epistle to the Hebrews treats at length of that of faith. It is perhaps a little unfortunate that he does not explain as clearly as he might what he means by the word "faith." He says: "Faith is the substance of things hoped for, the evidence of things not seen" (xi. 1). But many readers would be inclined to think that the substance of things hoped for may be the object of faith, and the evidence of things not seen may be its cause, but it is difficult to see how either can be faith itself. The author tells us that without faith it is impossible to please God (xi. 6), and in support of this statement he cites a number of Hebrew historical characters who, as recorded in the Jewish sacred writings, performed various laudable actions, which actions our author attributes in each case to faith. It is here that the Epistle of James joins issue with that addressed to the Hebrews. The point of controversy between the two writers may be summed up as follows:

Both authors seem to understand, though they do not clearly say so, by the expression "faith" a conscious impulse taken God-wards by the human soul. The writer of the Epistle to the Hebrews argues that if a man perform good works unaccompanied by this endeavour to approach the Deity, his action is not pleasing to God. James replies in effect that if a man have a mere impulse to rise God-wards, and this impulse be not strong enough to translate itself into action and so to affect the man's life, then the impulse becomes dead. In other words James argues that the essential thing is that a man's upward striving should be sufficient to bring about good works; and the author of the Epistle to the Hebrews thinks that the spiritual condition conducive to good works is what really matters. Most readers will be inclined to think that there is no real question of principle at stake between the two writers, but that nevertheless on the whole James had the best of the argument.

It may be objected that we do not know as a fact that James was replying to the Epistle to the Hebrews, and the contrary may have been the case. It seems however much more likely that the Epistle of James is considerably the later of the two, and modern scholars indeed put the probable date of Hebrews about 60–65 and of James about 100–120. It is noteworthy that the Epistle to the Hebrews specially points out sixteen characters who it is said gave practical effect to their faith. These sixteen include Abraham, the patriarch of the Jewish race, and, singularly enough, Rahab, a disreputable woman inhabiting Jerico, who betrayed her own people by facilitating the escape of two Jewish spies. James in his Epistle cites two cases only—those of Abraham and Rahab—of people who were justified before God by their good works. Now it seems unlikely that James would have picked out these two particular names as those of people whose actions were specially creditable, if he had not been replying to an adversary who had already instanced them. It would be as if a modern Frenchman, wishing to choose two typically heroic characters in French history, had put forward in the same breath Joan of Arc and Clément, the Dominican friar who assassinated Henri III.

The two principal points of doctrine set forth in the Epistle to the Hebrews—the death of Jesus considered as a sacrifice for our sins, and the necessity of faith accompanying our works—were in later years the cause of acute controversies. These controversies will be touched on in a subsequent chapter: we here merely record the fact that the language of the Epistle has lent itself to certain very unfortunate interpretations.

Further progress of the Jewish Christian Church

After the sack of 70 Jerusalem ceased to be the recognised centre of the Christian cult. And it was presumably not very long after that date that Rome, the world focus, began gradually to assume the position which Jerusalem had lost.

When the Holy City fell before the army of Titus, Jesus had been dead for about forty-one years. It is evident therefore that most of those who had been actively associated with his earthly mission would, if still alive, have been too old to take a very active part in missionary work. As an exception, it is recorded that John the son of Zebedee lived to a very advanced age, but he appears to have left Palestine and to have resided in Ephesus.

Concerning the organisation and work of the Church which survived in Palestine after the final defeat by the Roman army we really know very little, and the greater part of what we do know we learn from the pens of hostile critics. It is clear however that when pagan ideas and pagan customs began to influence Christianity, many of the Jewish Christians opposed these innovations with that dogged tenacity which has so consistently characterised their race.

It is probable that many readers of this treatise will be able to recall the strong opposition aroused both in England and in Scotland when public opinion gradually turned away from the strict observance of Sunday as a counterpart of the Jewish Sabbath, and tended to make it more a day of rest and recreation. It is reasonable to suppose that similarly in Palestine many of the Jewish Christians were found to adhere strictly to the form of religion taught by Jesus and his immediate followers, and to reject modern innovations. Now, as has been said above, it unfortunately happens that what we know about the conservative Jewish Christians, resident in Palestine after 70, is chiefly what their opponents have written about them. Many of them called themselves "Poor Men" (*Ebionites*), thus anticipating the similar title (*Les Gueux*) assumed by the Flemish Protestant patriots who resisted Philip II. We know that, just like the certain men which came down from Judea to Antioch (Acts xv. 1), the Ebionites continued to regard circumcision as obligatory. Hence they considered Paul as an apostate from the Mosaic law, and denied any authority to his Epistles. Origen (185–254) divides them into two classes, according as to whether they did or did not accept the doctrine that Jesus was supernaturally born of a virgin. All of them however seem to have rejected the doctrine that Jesus had from all eternity been identified with "the Word."

The foregoing may attract the sympathy of some readers, who will recognise that the Ebionites, for a time at least, adhered closely to the simple apostolic faith. But about the beginning of the third century their creed commenced to develop along other lines, and they accumulated a considerable amount of superstition. Their views lingered on in a modified form for many years, and it was not till the seventh century that the remnants of the body were finally absorbed by Mahometanism.

CHAPTER VI

CHRISTIAN PROPAGANDA, THE INFLUENCE OF PAGANISM, THE FORMATION OF TRADITIONAL CHRISTIANITY AND THE CRYSTALLISATION OF DOGMA

It is possible that some readers of this treatise may in their early youth have derived their impressions of a missionary from an account, written probably many years ago, of the arduous labours among the heathen undertaken by some pious and enthusiastic Dominican or Jesuit. We very naturally get a picture of a man vastly more cultured and intelligent than the less favoured beings among whom he is working. When he wants fire on a sunny day he can take a small object, like a piece of round crystal, out of his pocket, hold it for a few seconds over a dry leaf, and, miraculously enough, the leaf catches fire. Or again, he is sometimes able to announce that on the night of the next full moon an extraordinary darkness will be observed, even though the night may be quite cloudless.

These qualities, exhibited by the missionary, very properly convince his neighbours that he really is what he professes to be, far wiser than they are. So when the missionary begins to explain that he is himself subject to the orders of the supreme earthly ruler, who holds his court in a city called Rome, and who is by a supernatural disposition preserved from all error when teaching humanity, there is nothing surprising in the result that the uncultured savage not infrequently believes whatever his instructor may see fit to teach.

But when we look back on the earliest Christian missionaries we see that their position was radically different, because they when preaching could hardly profess to be on the whole more highly cultured than their audiences. It is of great interest therefore to reflect on what would probably be the gospel, or good tidings, offered to pagans during the first century of the Christian era. It fortunately happens that by means of the account of Paul's speech on the Areopagus (Acts xvii) we have an insight into the attitude which he personally adopted. Paul, very properly, commenced by an item of local interest. He called attention to an altar in the vicinity dedicated to the

"Unknown God," and said: "Whom therefore ye ignorantly worship, him declare I unto you." He then went on to speak of that man whom God had ordained and had raised from the dead.

Now it is difficult to see what there could have been in this speech which could have appealed to the average Athenian. The hearer would, we presume, have replied that Paul's argument rested on the allegation that the unknown God had raised a certain man from the dead. How was this proved? Paul would possibly reply, as he did elsewhere (Acts xxii. 6, 7), that he had on a certain occasion had a vision. This however would hardly sound very convincing to an Athenian, who would doubtless feel justified in answering that the fact that an unknown visitor from Tarsus alleged that when in or near Damascus he had had a vision, was no reason why an Athenian should believe that a certain native of Palestine had been ordained by God and raised from the dead. We are not surprised therefore to find that Paul's Athenian preaching was looked on as no more than a partial success (xvii. 32).

Anatole France has written a very attractive work of fiction (*Sur La Pierre Blanche*) in which Paul's difficulties at Corinth (Acts xviii. 12–17) are expanded into a short story. We are told that in U.C. 804 Junius Annaeus Novatus (surnamed Gallio after his adoptive father), Pro-Consul of Achaia, while entertaining some guests, related to them a case which he had just tried in the judgment-hall of Corinth. The Pro-Consul is represented as saying:

> On entering the pretorium, I found it full of a miscellaneous troop of those Jews who sell to sailors, at the port of Kenkrees, in those sordid booths of theirs, carpets, cloth and trifles of gold and silver. They began by filling the air with their strident cries and with a horrible smell like a ram's. I had difficulty in guessing the meaning of what they said, and I had to make an effort before understanding that one of these Jews named Sosthenes, who called himself the chief of the Synagogue, accused of impiety another Jew named Paul or Saul, a man from Tarsus, strikingly ugly, crooked-legged and sore-eyed, who has been here at Corinth for some time working as a carpet-maker. They talked all at once in very bad Greek. I managed to understand however that this Sosthenes made it out to be a crime on the part of Paul that he had come into the house where the Corinthian Jews meet every Saturday, and had made a speech tending to seduce his fellow Jews and to persuade them to serve their God in a manner contrary to

their law. I had no wish to hear anything further. After having with some difficulty made them keep quiet, I told them that if they had come to complain to me of any injustice or of any violence which they had suffered, I would have listened patiently and with all necessary attention, but that seeing that the matter was only a dispute about words, and a difference about the terms of their law, the case had no interest for me and I could not judge it. So I sent them away saying "Settle your quarrels among yourselves as best you can."

After Gallio had related this incident to his friends, a discussion took place as to the future development of religion throughout the empire. Gallio remarked that he had been told that there existed a Syrian sect whose members met together to worship an ass's head, and he suggested that Paul might possibly belong to this body. But he went on to ask:

What possible importance can the religion of this Jew have for us? ... His God will never reign except over those fortune-tellers, usurers and sordid hucksters who swindle sailors in every port. The most he could do would be to make adherents, on the outskirts of the large towns, of a few handfuls of slaves.

Few readers will be disposed to deny that the attitude which Gallio is made to assume in Anatole France's work of fiction is a natural and reasonable one. Exactly wherein therefore did the former err? In other words: We have seen the unattractive side of Paul's preaching, and in so far as it was unsuccessful we can understand the lack of success. But we know that taken as a whole Paul's preaching was marvellously successful, and we naturally enquire the reason. This of course opens up a question which different classes of readers will answer in different manners. The sceptic will very probably say that the causes of all important social phenomena are so complex that it is impossible to give an explanation, at once logical and accurate, as to how such phenomena have come about. No one, for example, could explain the military successes of Alexander and of Genghis Khan, or could tell us why Paris came to be the chief city of France. But a more satisfactory answer seems to be that Paul's teaching was successful because the message he delivered was a true one: he taught, in a form peculiarly adapted to the hearers' needs, the doctrine of the union between God and man, and very many of his hearers were able to put the doctrine to the test and to become convinced of its essential truth. And while it is suggested that the foregoing is the real key to Paul's success, nevertheless it is of interest to point out the advantage afforded to the early Christian missionaries by the existence of important Jewish communities in the chief cities of the Empire.

Paul indeed in the course of his Epistles indicates more than once the harsh treatment meted out to him by the Jews with whom he came in contact on his various journeys. But after a perusal of other New Testament writings we are on the whole rather surprised at the tolerance with which Jews both inside and outside Palestine regarded early Christian propaganda. We gather that Jesus himself was allowed to preach habitually in the synagogue at Nazareth (Luke iv. 16). And in connection with Paul's residence at Ephesus (Acts xix) we see an example of the attitude of tolerance which he himself experienced. "He went into the synagogue and spake boldly for the space of three months, disputing and persuading the things concerning the kingdom of God." When he thought it expedient to separate himself from the synagogue he did so, and disputed "daily in the school of one Tyrannus. And this continued for the space of two years." And as regards the Gallio incident referred to above, it is worthy of remark: firstly that the origin of the trouble seems to have been the fact that Paul was permitted to expound Christian doctrines in the Synagogue every sabbath (xviii. 4), and secondly that after the contending factions had come to actual blows, it was Sosthenes, the ruler of the Synagogue, and not Paul who got the worst of it (xviii. 17).

It would not be right to infer from these facts that the Jews of the first century were necessarily extraordinarily broad-minded and tolerant. But they were both highly intelligent and eager to hear anything new. So when they were told that an unknown rabbi was shedding fresh light on the Hebrew scriptures, they were anxious to hear what he had to say. To appreciate their conduct properly we have but to imagine the case of a Protestant preacher asking to be allowed to occupy the pulpit of Toledo Cathedral on a Sunday morning in the time of Philip II. Even to-day it is to be imagined that such a request would be received by the Cardinal Archbishop without cordiality.

So, though we are told that the founder of Christianity compared his missionaries to lambs being sent out among wolves, it will be seen that the lambs had in fact a very real advantage in the reception—practically useful rather than sympathetic—which they received from the local Jewish wolves in the various cities they visited. Consequently it is evident that the first Christian missionaries to preach at Antioch and Salonika were in certain respects in a much more favourable position than were those who, many centuries later, first visited Canton and Yeddo.

We have already indicated an example of how Paul presented the case of Christianity to the pagan world. To find anything which can be compared with Paul's speech at Athens we have to wait for nearly a hundred years, and even then the comparison is far from being a close one. In the middle of the second century Justin, a Samaritan resident at Rome, wrote an *Apologia* for Christianity. From this *Apologia* we give the following extract:

> If then we hold some opinions near of kin to the poets and philosophers in greatest repute among you, why are we unjustly hated? For, in saying that all things were made in this beautiful order by God, what do we seem to say more than Plato? When we teach a general conflagration, what do we teach more than the Stoics? By opposing the worship of the works of men's hands, we concur with Menander the comedian; and by declaring the LOGOS, the first-begotten of God, our Master Jesus Christ, to be born of a Virgin without any human mixture, and to be crucified and dead, and to have risen again, and ascended into heaven, we say no more in this than what you say of those whom you style the Sons of Jove.
>
> For you need not be told what a number of sons the writers most in vogue among you assign to Jove. There is Mercury, Jove's interpreter, in imitation of the LOGOS, in worship among you. There is Æsculapius, the physician, smitten by a thunderbolt, and after that ascended into heaven. There is Bacchus torn to pieces, and Hercules burnt to get rid of his pains. There are Pollux and Castor, the sons of Jove by Leda, and Perseus by Danae. Not to mention others, I would fain know why you always deify the departed Emperors, and have a man at hand to swear that he saw Cæsar mount to heaven from the funeral pile. As to the Son of God, called Jesus, should we allow him to be nothing more than man, yet the title of the *Son of God* is very justifiable upon account of his wisdom, considering you have your Mercury in worship under the title of the WORD and Messenger of God.
>
> As to the objections of our Jesus being crucified, I say that suffering was common to all the aforementioned sons of Jove, although they suffered another kind of death. As to his being

born of a virgin, you have your Perseus to balance that. As to his curing the lame, and the paralytic, and such as were cripples from their birth, this is little more than what you say of your Æsculapius.

The first thing which strikes us about this extract is that it is not quite what we are looking for, because Justin seems to be attempting not so much to convince his readers that they ought to become Christians, as rather that there is nothing reprehensible in Christianity, which is, he implies, after all a religion in innumerable ways greatly resembling paganism. It is this last point which is of special importance. The early Christians did not in all probability, when they found themselves in touch with pagans, specially emphasise the difference between the creeds but rather their essential similarity. And this fact presumably accounts, at least in part, for the readiness with which pagan beliefs and pagan ritual were, within the first few centuries of our era, incorporated into the Christian cult. But on the other hand it does not account for the conversion of pagans to Christianity. One can hardly convince a man that he ought to change his religion merely by telling him that the new religion is fundamentally the same as the old. And the Christian missionary started with the initial disadvantage that his own body was primarily a Jewish sect, and Judaism was so radically different from paganism that those arguments which had been found useful in making converts among the Jews were almost meaningless to pagan audiences. We have already considered the Epistle to the Hebrews, with its emphasis on the merits of our Great High Priest who has entered within the veil, and also on the sacrificial shedding of blood as the result of a divine command given to the Jews. But it is not easy to see how this line of thought could appeal to a pagan, who would presumably take but little interest in any doctrine based on the assumption that the Hebrews had been for many centuries the special recipients of divine wisdom and divine favour. The real kernel of the message which Christianity had to offer to the world was *Sursum corda!* (Hearts upwards.) Do not be overdistressed at whatever unhappy material conditions may surround you. Seek union of your soul with God, and believe such union to be the only real and lasting benefit you can receive, and believe that separation from God is the only real evil. Believe that you have not to go far to look for God, because he himself has already sent the divine Christ Spirit among you, and this

Christ Spirit is always ready and waiting to enter into each individual soul, and to be a bond of union or mediator between such soul and God himself.

It will be observed that here there is but little room for argument, or for intellectual conviction. If the hearer has no wish to unite himself with God the message falls on deaf ears. But it has so happened that millions of hearers have actually tested the truth of the gospel tidings, and have obtained the conviction that neither tribulation, nor distress, nor persecution, nor famine, nor nakedness, nor peril, nor the sword could separate them from the love of Christ. It is quite open to the sceptic to say that this conviction is a mere self-delusion. Logically it may be impossible to prove the contrary.[1] But to tell the believer himself that he is the victim of a priestly fraud would be as futile as it would be to try to persuade a thirsty man that his thirst is a mere subjective illusion and he does not really want to drink.

In the above paragraphs it has been attempted to place before the reader the real kernel of Christianity. But world religions are not formed of kernels alone, and the Christian faith came in time to include very much more than is summarised above. It was indeed inevitable that the early pagan converts should incorporate into their new creed many of their old beliefs. Among the earliest of such beliefs to be incorporated are the so-called "birth-stories" discussed below.

The Birth-Stories

We now have to examine the first two chapters of the First and Third Gospels respectively. The authors of these chapters, whom we may for convenience call pseudo-Matthew and

---

[1] The attitude of modern physical science towards the problem raised in the above paragraph is well summed up in the subjoined extract from Mr. C. E. M. Joad's *Philosophical Aspects of Modern Science*. The extract is specially noteworthy because it is quoted with entire approval by Sir Arthur Eddington in *New Pathways in Science*.

> I should hold then that the researches of the scientist are, equally with the perceptions of the plain man, the moral consciousness of the good man, the sensitivity of the artist and the religious experience of the mystic, revelatory of reality. Epistemologically they stand on equal terms. Such arguments as there are for supposing that any of these forms of experience is merely subjective, apply also to the others; but equally if any of them gives information about a world external to ourselves, so also do the others.

pseudo-Luke, had apparently two objects in mind: (*a*) to embody into the Christian sacred writings certain non-Jewish legends which had presumably been learnt from non-Jewish converts, and which were considered to be both appropriate and edifying; and (*b*) to meet the objection raised against the Messiahship of Jesus that he was not born in Bethlehem, and, in the case of pseudo-Matthew, to prove that Jesus was descended from David.

The necessity for the above is patent from the following incident narrated in the Fourth Gospel:

> Some said: *Shall Christ come out of Galilee? Hath not the scripture said that Christ cometh out of the seed of David, and out of the town of Bethlehem, where David was?* So there was a division among the people because of him (John vii. 41).

Now the above passage seems quite conclusive in proving that the writer of the Fourth Gospel, the evangelist who was in specially close touch with the mother of Jesus, had no reason to believe that he was born in Bethlehem. And in order to understand the situation it is not necessary to assume that pseudo-Matthew and pseudo-Luke deliberately invented what they wrote. Legends, as has been implied in an earlier chapter, tend to grow naturally. The Fourth Gospel tells us that the Bethlehem difficulty caused a division among the people: it is not impossible therefore that a partisan of Jesus may have replied to an opponent: "For anything you know, he may have been born in Bethlehem," and the legend may have gradually arisen in this manner.

If we compare the two sets of birth-stories with one another, we find that they agree in saying that Jesus was born at Bethlehem, without a human father, and that he was the son of Mary, wife of Joseph, a descendant of David. Here however all agreement ceases, and the details are wholly different. Pseudo-Matthew gives us to understand that Joseph was a resident at Bethlehem, that after the birth of Jesus he was compelled to fly into Egypt with Mary and her child; and that only after the death of King Herod did they return to Palestine and, turning aside into the parts of Galilee, come and dwell in a city called Nazareth.

On the other hand pseudo-Luke makes Mary, and presumably Joseph also, residents of Nazareth in the first place. Some weeks after his birth at Bethlehem, Jesus was taken to Jerusalem, and when the usual ceremony of purification had been performed the family returned to Nazareth.

The device employed by pseudo-Luke to take Joseph and Mary from Nazareth to Bethlehem is not a very ingenious one. The author tells us that, a census having been decreed, Joseph, being "of the house and lineage of David," had to leave Galilee and to go with his pregnant wife to Bethlehem, the city of David in Judea, in order to register. This is very much as if on the occasion of a census a resident in the State of New York were compelled to go to Plymouth in the State of Massachusets to register, because some centuries earlier his ancestors had landed from the *Mayflower* at Plymouth.

It may be noted that pseudo-Matthew speaks of "the house," implying obviously the habitual residence of Joseph and Mary; but pseudo-Luke on the other hand makes Jesus to be placed in a manger immediately after birth, there being no room at an inn where admittance had been applied for.

The two sets of birth-stories are wholly unlike in style. That of pseudo-Luke is incomparably the more interesting and poetical. One gets the impression that this version had originally been written as a sacred drama, and was subsequently re-cast in narrative form, the poetical speeches of the characters remaining as originally written. These poetical speeches are of great beauty, and the longer ones have been incorporated into the daily offices of more than one branch of the Christian Church.

The work of pseudo-Matthew on the other hand relies but little on dialogue. The author introduces for example a charming legend of certain wise men ($\mu\alpha\gamma\omicron\iota$ Vulg. *magi*, magicians) who visited Jesus at Bethlehem. But their function was apparently limited to bringing gifts and offering worship: we are not given any hint as to what they said to Joseph and Mary. If pseudo-Luke had been telling the story, we should doubtless have had an admirable speech from each individual *magus*.

It has been observed that the story of pseudo-Luke is reminiscent of the legends which have accumulated round the name of Gautama Buddha. Gautama is said to have been born, without a human father, of Maya while the latter was on a journey. The name Maya is etymologically connected with Mary. Moreover pseudo-Luke (ii. 25–35), describing the meeting between Simeon and Jesus, is reminiscent of a similar story told with respect to Gautama. On the other hand the account given by pseudo-Matthew recalls the legend of Chrishna, whose parents had to remove and to hide him, immediately after his birth, from the persecution of King

FORMATION OF TRADITIONAL CHRISTIANITY

Kamsa, who had been warned by a voice from heaven that the newly-born child would kill him, and who in consequence actually caused the slaughter of various infant children.

An interesting example of the growth of myth may here be mentioned. Pseudo-Luke tells us that on the occasion of the birth of Jesus, some shepherds heard a multitude of angels "praising God and saying *Glory to God in the highest: and on earth peace: good will towards men.*"

Seventeen centuries afterwards a Christian poet incorporated this incident into a hymn commencing:

> Hark, how all the welkin rings!
> "Glory to the King of Kings,
> Peace on earth and mercy mild,
> God and sinners reconciled."
>
> C. WESLEY.

But some years subsequently a less-known author thought that he could improve the hymn by transferring the homage of the angels from God to the child Jesus, and in consequence he made the verse read:

> Hark! the herald angels sing
> "Glory to the new born King."

whence we get the hymn in the form in which it is best known to-day.

Pseudo-Luke gives a further anecdote, which may be regarded as supplementary to the birth-stories, to the effect that Jesus, when a boy twelve years old, was lost by his parents for three days, and was eventually found by them in the Temple. We are not well impressed by the indifference of Jesus to his parents' natural anxiety (ii. 49), but nevertheless the story may very possibly be true. It has been pointed out however by Mr. J. M. Robertson (*Christianity and Mythology*, quoting Lactantius *Div. Instit.* i. 21) that in Egypt there used to be enacted a mystery drama in which the Goddess Isis was represented as bewailing her lost male child, whom she eventually found. Mr. Robertson suggests that as the whole drama was enacted in the Egyptian temples, the finding would of course take place in a temple, and this may be the basis of the legend as we find it in pseudo-Luke.

We are given two genealogies of Joseph and these are, with respect to ancestors subsequent to David, wholly different. Luke makes Joseph the son of Heli, who was descended from David through his son Nathan. Pseudo-Matthew on the other hand makes Joseph the son of Jacob, who was descended from David through his son Solomon. The fact that the two genealogies are so patently irreconcilable makes it a little difficult to understand how the early Church could have come to regard them as equally authoritative. It seems reasonable to infer that in the first and second centuries of our era comparatively little importance was attached to many of the details of the earthly mission of Jesus. This inference is of course in general harmony with the conclusions come to in other parts of this treatise.

Blaise Pascal, who from a purely intellectual standpoint is probably the most eminent of the Bible critics who unreservedly support the claims of traditional Christianity, is hardly at his best when he touches on the subject of the genealogies. He writes:

> All very apparent weaknesses are really sources of strength (*Toutes les faiblesses très apparentes sont des forces*). Example: the two genealogies of S. Matthew and S. Luke: what is clearer than the fact that they were not made in collusion (*de concert*)?
> *Pensées* 578.

The answer is of course two-fold. Firstly, if in this particular case one evangelist had copied from the other, no inference unfavourable to the authenticity of the narrative could be drawn, as no one supposes that Matthew and Luke could have had first-hand personal knowledge with respect to the sons, grandsons, and later descendants of David. Secondly, the merely negative fact that in this instance there was no collusion does not affect the positive inference, drawn from other passages of the two Gospels, that either one evangelist copied from another, or else that both availed themselves of a common source.

It is to be noted that both writers give us the parentage of Joseph and not of Mary, whence it would appear that the desire to prove that Jesus was descended from David antedated the belief that the former had no human father, as otherwise there would be no point in giving the genealogy of Joseph. It is also noteworthy that Luke tells us (iii. 23) that Jesus was "as was supposed" the son of Joseph. Now we are led to believe that in the opinion of Luke (iv. 22) as of the other evangelists (Matt. xiii. 55, John vi. 42) Jesus really was the son of Joseph, so the natural inference is that the words "as was supposed" are a later insertion. This inference is supported by the fact that different manuscripts give a different arrangement of the words of the text, some documents reading και αυτος ην 'Ιησους αρχομενος ωσει ετων τριακοντα ων υιος ως ενομιζετο 'Ιωσηφ and some 'Ιησους ωσει ετων τριακοντα αρχομενος ων ως ενομιζετο υιος 'Ιωσηφ, thereby increasing the presumption that the original manuscript has been added to.

A point which strikes us about the "birth-stories" is that if they be true the evangelists give us a wholly false view of the life and mission of Jesus. All four make it abundantly clear to us that Jesus went about his "Father's business" as a human being working among his neighbours and fellow-countrymen, and enjoyed the advantages, and experienced the disadvantages of such position. "Is not this the carpenter's son? Is not his mother called Mary? And his brethren James and Joses, and Simon and Judas? And his sisters are they not all with us?" (Matt. xiii. 55; *vide* also Mark vi. 3, Luke iv. 22, John vi. 42). The picture that all four Gospels give us is that of a man, fore-ordained and chosen by God to fulfil the mightiest work ever confided to a human being, and who to that end was raised to an unique dignity, being "christened with the Holy Spirit and with power" (Acts x. 38); and "God made that same Jesus both Lord and Christ" (Acts ii. 36). Of the gospel Jesus we feel that, like the hero of Isaiah's poem, he trod the winepress alone and of the people there was none with him; he looked and there was none to help and he wondered that there was none to uphold, therefore his own arm brought salvation unto him and his fury it upheld him (Isa. lxiii).

But all this is profoundly modified if we are to regard Jesus as a "wonder child" having a history which follows the same general lines as those of the "wonder children" of mythology. We should have to suppose that Joseph, the carpenter of Galilee, on an occasion when his wife was in the last stages of her miraculous pregnancy, was obliged to take her to be registered at Bethlehem in Judea, that there she gave birth to the divinely conceived child, that there arrived certain *magi* who had previously consulted with King Herod and who, pursuant to his directions, came to Bethlehem and there offered symbolic gifts. We should have further to suppose that Herod in consequence of this consultation desired to put Jesus to death, and did actually kill all the children under two years old in and near Bethlehem; and that, notwithstanding this somewhat excessive precaution on the King's part, Joseph was able to escape with Jesus into Egypt and to remain there till Herod's death.

It is clear that the reasons for believing all this are by no means self-evident. And if we do decide to accept the veracity of the narrative, we are met by the insuperable difficulty that it is quite impossible that Joseph can have come back to Nazareth, after his Bethlehem and Egyptian adventures, and can have quietly resumed his calling as a carpenter, and can have given Jesus a normal education, without his neighbours looking on the whole family as being very remarkable people, and expecting some very wonderful events to accompany the life of the child whom Herod had persecuted. But what we actually find is that the work of Jesus was positively hampered by the fact that his neighbours, knowing his antecedents, looked on him as being, so far as his origin was concerned, a somewhat ordinary individual.

And of course it is clear that if Luke wrote iii. 22, definitely affirming that it was on the day of his baptism that Jesus was God-begotten (*vide* p. 38), he could hardly have written i. 35. And again if Luke really were the author of the first two chapters of the Gospel which bears his name, Paul, his friend and companion, would presumably have written of Jesus in a manner very different from that which he actually adopted. Paul tells us for example that Jesus was "made of the seed of David, according to the flesh" (Rom. i. 3), and moreover that "God sent forth his son, made of a woman, made under the law, to redeem them that were under the law that we might receive the adoption of sons" (Gal. iv. 4, 5). By the expression "made of a woman, made under the law," Paul clearly means "made in the same manner as we are and subject to the same natural laws," and there would be no point in either of the two statements above quoted if Paul had believed that Jesus did not have a natural conception and birth.

Concerning the question of the virgin birth, it may be observed that it by no means follows that pseudo-Matthew and pseudo-Luke, when telling us that Jesus was born of the operation of the Holy Spirit, wished us to believe that he was actually God. Mythology supplies us with several examples of children (e.g. Minos) with divine fathers and human mothers. And Diogenes Laertius commences his *Life of Plato* with a (somewhat confused) account of how Ariston, the reputed father of the great philosopher, was warned by Apollo to abstain from familiarity with his wife, Periclitione, until she had been delivered of her son. The similarity of this legend with Matt. i. 20–25 is obvious. (It is true that Diogenes Laertius is believed to have written in the first half of the third century of our era, but he quotes as his authority Speusippus, a nephew of Plato, who wrote several hundred years before Matthew.)

Notwithstanding the foregoing we do in fact find that the theological dogma of the divinity of Jesus seems to have arisen not long after the genesis of the legend as to his virgin birth. The first Christian writer, other than pseudo-Matthew and pseudo-Luke, to mention this virgin birth is Ignatius, Bishop of Antioch, concerning whom an immense amount of controversy has taken place, but it is now generally believed that the Epistles properly ascribed to this writer can be dated not earlier than 110 nor later than 150. Now Ignatius tells us (Eph. xix): "Hidden from the prince of this world were the virginity of Mary, and her child-bearing, and likewise also the death of the Lord, three mysteries to be cried aloud." And again he speaks of "one only physician, of flesh and spirit, generate and ingenerate, God in man, true life in death, son of Mary and son of God" (Eph. vii). But, weighty as the above passages undoubtedly are, it would not be right to infer that Ignatius accepted the doctrine of the divinity of Jesus as it was taught in a later age. Ignatius for example tells us in his epistle to the Church at Trallis (a city not far from Ephesus): "Respect is due to the bishop as to God, to the presbyters as the council of God and the college of apostles, to the deacons as to Jesus Christ."

It is of course quite conceivable that the doctrine of Ignatius as regards the respect due to a bishop was, doubtless subconsciously, influenced by his own profession; but however this may be, he makes it clear to us that the respect due to Jesus Christ is considerably less than that due to God himself, an opinion diametrically opposed to that taught by the dominant party in the Church two centuries later. Ignatius therefore forms as it were one of the milestones by which we measure the gradual evolution of Christian dogma as regards the person and mission of Jesus; and, with reference to this evolution, one of the first points which strikes our attention is this. We infer that the earliest Christians were taught that Jesus received the Holy Spirit at his baptism, and they attached the very utmost importance to this fact. Not only do all four evangelists give a detailed account of the event, but we find that Peter, when indicating that period of the life of Jesus when he "went in and out among us," uses the expression: "Beginning from the baptism of John unto that same day that he was taken up from us" (Acts i. 22). But later generations arose which were taught that Jesus was "Very God of Very God" from the moment of his miraculous conception. On this understanding it is difficult to see what occasion there was for the baptism of Jesus. At most, a believer could say that Jesus submitted to the formality of baptism just as he had in the plenitude of his divine wisdom submitted to the formality of circumcision. But here there is an obvious distinction. Circumcision was a formal rite enjoined by the Law: acceptance of the Johannine baptism was a response to a call to a "new mind" ($\mu\epsilon\tau\alpha\nu o\iota\alpha$, translated "repentance" in the Authorised Version). If we try to evade the difficulty by saying that the baptism, like the public raising of Lazarus, was effected so as to give occasion for a manifestation of supernatural power, and that its object was to convince the Jews of the divine approval awarded to the mission of Jesus, then we are met by the objection that none of the evangelists mentions any spectators. The language of Luke is, it is true, quite consistent with the possibility of the vision being seen by third parties, but Matthew and Mark say that it was Jesus who saw the Holy Spirit descend, and the Fourth Gospel states that it was the Baptist.

It was inevitable therefore that as the Christian community came to accept the doctrine of the Incarnation of Jesus, as understood in later days, it should have come to regard the Baptism as an incident which can be only partially explained, and which it is desirable to keep in the background. In consequence we can trace the following steps: (i) the Baptism is commemorated as one of the two chief feasts of the year, there being however, more or less vaguely connected with this festival, commemorations of the physical birth of Jesus, the Adoration of the Magi and the marriage in Cana of Galilee: (ii) a new feast called Christmas is instituted specially to commemorate the physical birth, and steps are taken to make this feast more important than that of the Baptism: (iii) the day of the feast of the Baptism, which has already been made commemorative of the Adoration of the Magi and of the marriage in Cana of Galilee, becomes in popular religion commemorative of the Adoration of the Magi only, and in consequence in Roman Catholic countries the day is now known as "The Kings" or "The Magi Kings" simply. This subject, which is of importance to students desirous of examining the growth of Christian dogma, is discussed in the following section.

The Epiphany

The word Epiphany means a "shining forth" or manifestation. We first read of the feast of the Epiphany in Clement of Alexandria who, writing about 194, says that the Basilidians, a Gnostic body, used to feast the day of the Baptism of Jesus, devoting the whole night preceding it to reading the Scriptures. By about 300 the feast was already widely in vogue throughout the Church.

In 354 the Roman Church commenced to observe December 25th as the birthday of Jesus. There seems no doubt that the date was chosen as being the traditional birthday of the Sun God, who, being supposed to have been dead throughout the winter solstice (December 22nd–24th), is reborn on the following day and then commences his progress northwards through the heavens. Thus Augustine tells us: "We celebrate Christmas, not as do the heathen, in commemoration of the birth of the sun, but in commemoration of him by whom the sun was created." And again John Chrysostom says: "In the sense of allegory this holy day of the Lord's Birth is known as the day of the Sun's birth, and harmony is established between the conception of the ancient mysteries and that of Christianity."

We find that the *Ordo Romanus*, dated about 800, under the heading of the Vigil of the Theophany says that "the second birth of Christ, being distinguished by so many mysteries, is more honoured than the first" (i.e. Epiphany is more honoured than Christmas). And again St. Hilary tells us that Jesus "was born again through baptism, and then become Son of God." And Hilary adds that the Father cried, when Jesus had come up out of the water: "Thou art my beloved Son: this day I have begotten thee" (*vide* p. 38) And Hilary goes on to say: "On that occasion he himself was re-born unto God to be perfect Son; as he was Son of Man, so in baptism he was constituted Son of God as well."

But on the other hand the inconsistency between the solemn commemoration of the baptism and later ideas as to the incarnation of Jesus, was clearly recognised at least as early as the middle of the fifth century. We find that the Sicilian Churches used customarily to baptise neophytes on January 6th, "because baptism conveyed to Jesus and to them one and the same grace." Leo the Great, writing to the Sicilians about 447, protests against this custom saying: "The Lord needed no remission of sins, no remedy of re-birth."

In modern popular theology any connection between the baptism of Jesus and the feast of the Epiphany is reduced to a minimum. In the Roman Church the baptism of Jesus is, it is true, the subject of the Gospel for the octave of the Epiphany, but this is a day which passes quite unnoticed by the bulk of the laity. The feast of the Epiphany itself is popularly considered as commemorating the adoration of the Magi only. A very well-known French dictionary (*Petit Larousse*) defines *Epiphanie*:

> Manifestation du Christ aux gentils, et particulièrement aux Mages. Fête de l'Église le 6 janvier qui rapelle cet évenement, nommée aussi Jour des Rois.

In the above respect the Church of England follows the same general lines as the Church of Rome.

Doctrine of the Blessed Trinity

Readers of the older portions of the sacred literature of the Hebrews cannot fail to notice that the authors represent the Deity as exercising the government of the material universe especially in two manners—by the spoken Word and by the Breath. Thus at the commencement of the Pentateuch we are told that God said "Let there be light" and there was light. It is noteworthy that it seems by no means to be implied that God spoke by way of conveying an order to any inferior deity or being. On the contrary it would appear that we are meant to understand that in some manner transcending human intelligence the spoken Word formed the means whereby God gave effect to his will that light should come into being. And in the same way the writer goes on to imply that the remainder of creation was brought about by the power of God's Word (Gen. i. 3 *et seq.*). In the next chapter on the other hand we read that God breathed into man's nostrils the breath of life, and man became a living soul (Gen. ii. 7).

Various references to these twin creative powers of the Deity —the divine Word and the divine Breath—are found in the Book of Psalms, e.g.:

> By the Word of the Lord were the heavens made and all the host of them by the Breath of his mouth (Psa. xxxiii. 6). He

FORMATION OF TRADITIONAL CHRISTIANITY

uttered his Voice, the earth melted (Psa. xlvi. 6). The Voice of the Lord maketh the hinds to calve (Psa. xxix. 9). Thou sendest forth thy Breath and they are created, and thou renewest the face of the earth (Psa. civ. 30). The Voice of the Lord breaketh the cedars (Psa. xxix. 5).

And coming down to a considerably later date, we find that very similar language is used in the Book of Wisdom. For example we read: (i. 7) "The Breath of the Lord filleth the world, and that which containeth all things hath knowledge of the Voice." And again (ix. 1): "God ... who hast made all things by thy Word."

And if we follow the progress of Hebrew thought in post-Christian times we find not merely that the doctrine of the creative power of God's Word is fully developed, but also that each individual letter of the alphabet came ultimately to be looked on as playing its own share in the formation of the universe. Thus in the *Sepher Yetzira* we read:

> The twenty-two sounds and letters are the Foundation of all things.... He hath formed, weighed and composed with these twenty-two letters every soul and the soul of everything which shall hereafter be....
> From the empty void he made the material world, and from the inert earth he brought forth everything that hath life. He hewed as it were vast columns out of the intangible air, and by the power of his name made every creature and everything which is: and the production of all things from the twenty-two letters is the proof that they are all but parts of one body.

Now we are told that on the momentous occasion when Jesus was baptised in Jordan, God manifested himself both by his Word and by his Breath. The Voice of God was heard saying: "This is my beloved Son in whom I am well pleased." And simultaneously the divine Breath was seen to descend in bodily form on Jesus. It is to be observed that the Greek word meaning *breath* ($\pi\nu\epsilon\upsilon\mu\alpha$) is in the Authorised Version translated into English by *spirit* and also by *ghost*. Neither translation is quite satisfactory. *Ghost* is open to the objection that the usual meaning of the word in modern English is "a spirit visible to the human eye," or in other words "a vision." *Spirit* is open to the objection that the sacred writers, while speaking of "$\Pi\nu\epsilon\upsilon\mu\alpha$ of God," tell us that God himself is a spirit (John iv. 24), so if we say "Spirit of God" we are really saying "Spirit of a Spirit." The difficulty is of course an example of the impossibility of finding language to express transcendental ideas.

But laying aside the question of the exact translation which should be given to the word πνευμα, it is clear that God was associated in the minds of both Jews and Christians with two divine powers, emanations, or methods of manifestation, the Word and the Breath. So we are not surprised to find that at some uncertain date an unknown writer interpolated into the First Epistle of John (v. 7) the words: "There are three which bear record in heaven, the Father, the Word and the Holy Breath, and these three are one."

Now in the above passage there is nothing which is necessarily contrary to the monotheism which Christianity inherited from Judaism. We read about the Father and about the divine Word and the divine Breath, but we are also told that "these three are one," so apparently we are not meant to conclude that there are three separate entities, but rather that the second and third are emanations from (or functions of) the first. On the other hand we are met with the fact that Christianity in its earlier years passed through a phase (of which the *Apologia* of Justin cited on page 100 forms a striking symptom) during which there existed a strong tendency to stress the points of resemblance with other religions. The consequence of this tendency was inevitable—Christian doctrine became modified by, and adapted to paganism.

So in the early days of Christian propaganda it will sometimes be found that when missionaries have congratulated themselves on their success in converting the pagans, it was to a large extent these latter who, by bringing about the adaptation into the Christian cult of alien legends and symbolism, converted the missionaries. This fact is specially noteworthy as regards Egyptian mythology, whence Christianity has apparently derived not only the cult of the boy-God resting in his mother's arms, but also that of the Trinity.

The Egyptian Trinity consisted of Osiris, Horus and Isis: or Father, Son and Mother. The Christian cult seems from quite early times to have been based on the existence of the All Father with his two emanations or manifestations, the Word (Λογος, masculine) and the Breath (Πνευμα, neuter). The second member of this Trinity, the Word or creative power (John i. 3) became specially identified with Jesus, who was called the Son of God; and in the birth-stories we are given to understand that the third member, without being the Father of Jesus, nevertheless played an active part in bringing about his conception (Matt. i. 18, Luke i. 35). So we find a

Christian Trinity consisting of Father, Son (or creative Word) and Holy Spirit (or Breath, who brings about the conception of the Son). It will be seen how nearly the foregoing corresponds to the Egyptian Trinity of Father, Son and Mother.

At the end of Matthew's Gospel we find that Jesus is said to have enjoined his eleven disciples to "teach all nations, baptising them in the name of the Father and of the Son and of the Holy Spirit" (xxviii. 19). It seems difficult to accept the foregoing as a genuine saying of Jesus. Firstly, the words are alleged to have been spoken at the post-Resurrection visit of Jesus to Galilee, an incident which is as has already been pointed out (page 48) inconsistent with the narrative of Luke. If the directions stated to have been given by Jesus really were authentic, they must have been recognised by his immediate followers as being of the utmost importance, seeing that not only do they purport to shed a flood of light on the nature of the Deity, but also they prescribe the sacramental formula necessary for a valid reception into the new community. But the other three evangelists make no mention of these directions, and it seems inconceivable that all three should have thought them unimportant.

Secondly, as has already been pointed out, after about two decades had elapsed the question of the reception of Gentiles into the Christian community was treated as an entirely new problem by the apostles and elders assembled at Jerusalem, and these apostles included Peter and probably several other members of "the eleven" referred to in Matt. xxviii. 16. The obvious inference is that the apostolic band, as existing on the occasion of the Council of Jerusalem, knew nothing as to any instructions given by Jesus to baptise all nations in the name of the Father, and of the Son and of the Holy Spirit.

Thirdly, Paul seems to have been quite ignorant of the doctrine of the Blessed Trinity. Almost all his Epistles contain in the first few verses the same form of greeting: *Grace and peace to you from God our Father and the Lord Jesus Christ.* There is nothing whatever to lead us to infer that Paul either (*a*) attributed the Godhead to Jesus, or (*b*) worshipped the Holy Spirit as one of the Persons of the Deity. It is indeed quite inconceivable that Paul would have consistently given such prominence to his formula if he had accepted the doctrine embodied in the formula current in our own day: *The blessing of God Almighty, the Father, the Son and the Holy Ghost be amongst you and remain with you always.* The teaching of Paul was most unquestionably that *there is one God and one mediator between God and men, the man Christ Jesus* (1 Tim. ii. 5). He also taught that God manifests himself by the operation of his Breath or Spirit. But Paul gives us no hint that this Holy Spirit is in any sense an independent entity or Person. On the contrary, just as the Psalmist says "With his own right hand and with his holy arm hath he gotten himself the victory" (Ps. xcviii), without implying that God's hand and arm have any independent volition, so Paul similarly says:

> "God, who hath given unto us his Holy Spirit" (1 Thess. iv. 8). "God, who hath given unto us the earnest of the Spirit" (2 Cor. v. 5). "We have received, not the spirit of the world, but the Spirit which is of God" (1 Cor. ii. 12), etc., etc.

Consequently we can hardly doubt that the doctrine of Paul was that God is one, and is the Saviour of all men (1 Tim. iv. 10, Tit. iii. 4, 5); that God may be said to manifest himself by means of his Breath or Spirit; and that this Spirit illuminated in a very special sense the man Jesus, who consequently became the Christ, our Lord.

A point which will probably occur to the reader is the following. While each of the four Gospels gives us a biography of Jesus, it is remarkable that none of the very early writers gives us any summary of the fundamental doctrines of the faith. Indeed it would appear that in the primitive Church teaching and dogmatising occupied only a secondary place. It will be remembered that, as described in chapter vi, the Council of Jerusalem, when faced with the situation created by the fact that on some of the Gentiles "was poured out the gift of the Holy Spirit," decided to "lay no greater burden" on the new converts than to ask them to abstain from certain acts regarded by the Jews, reasonably or unreasonably, as immoral. We get no indication of such converts having been called upon to subscribe to a formal creed.

But on the other hand it was inevitable that the question should frequently be asked: "Exactly what is Christianity?" and it was consequently desirable that some definite statement of belief should be drawn up and recognised as authoritative. Such formula would of course be based partly on well recognised facts connected with the earthly life of Jesus, and partly on the doctrine as to the nature of the Deity held by such of the early Fathers—Peter, James, John, Paul and Jude—as were recognised as being privileged men of specially keen spiritual insight.

Evidence of the existence of a formal creed is to be found in the writings of some of the earliest of the post-apostolic Fathers (Polycarp and Clemens Romanus), and indeed Irenaeus, writing about 180, gives us what appears to be a paraphrase of such a document. But it is not till much later that we find the actual text of what is thought to be the earliest of the Christian creeds. This confession of faith was called the "Apostles' Creed," the title being due to a tradition that it was actually compiled by the Apostles themselves. The following is a literal translation of the form used in Rome in 390:

> I believe in God the almighty Father and in Jesus Christ his unique Son our Lord, who was born by the Holy Spirit of the Virgin Mary, crucified under Pontius Pilate and buried. The third day he rose again from the dead. He ascended into the heavens. He sits on the Father's right hand, whence he is about to come to judge living and dead. And in the Holy Spirit, the Holy Church, the remission of sins, the resurrection of flesh.

In comment on the above it may be observed:

Firstly: we are now dealing with a Latin document. The Christian canonical writings were, at least as regards the greater part, written in Greek, and as regards the doubtful minority (such as the Epistle to the Romans) the Greek form is the earliest known to us. Irenaeus, Bishop of Lyon, wrote in Greek. But when we come down to 390, Latin is the recognised language of the Western Church, and the above creed is given in Latin. In consequence the Holy Spirit is now called *Spiritus* instead of $\Pi\nu\epsilon\upsilon\mu\alpha$ as in the Gospels, and is masculine instead of neuter. Hence it was taught that Jesus at the same time was the Son of the divine Father and was conceived by the Holy Spirit (also masculine). It is possible that the reaction caused by this anomaly did something to prepare men's minds for the cult of the Mother of Jesus. This cult will be touched on in a later section.

Secondly: the Apostles' Creed in no way seems to imply that Jesus is God. It inculcates belief firstly in the Almighty Father, our God, and secondly in Jesus, his Son, our Lord. Clearly therefore the writer desired to establish the same distinction between the terms "God" and "Lord" as is adopted in the Pauline phrase: *The grace of the Lord Jesus Christ and the love of God, etc.* (2 Cor. xiii. 14).

Thirdly: Jesus is spoken of as *unicum Filium ejus*, which has here been translated *his unique Son* rather than *his only Son*. (Thus Livy speaks of *unicus dux* meaning *an unrivalled leader*, not *the only leader*.) All Christian writers seem to agree that all men either are or may become Sons of God, so the translation *his only Son* is not appropriate.

Fourthly: Jesus is spoken of as being *born* by the operation of the Holy Spirit. So the Apostles' Creed, while plainly pointing to a supernormal manner of birth, nevertheless gives us to understand that Jesus was a human being. There is no suggestion of a previously existing deity having formed for himself or taken on a human body, as might be inferred from the prologue to the Fourth Gospel.

In fine therefore, it may be said that the Apostles' Creed harmonises in all respects with the synoptic Gospels in the form now extant, or in other words with the three original Gospels together with the birth-stories. Consequently it seems reasonable to infer that the Apostles' Creed had probably come to be considered as authoritative before the Prologue to the Fourth Gospel had come to be so considered (say about 170).

With reference to the expression "made flesh," contained in this Prologue, it is instructive to note that for a long period, especially during the second and third centuries of our era, the doctrine that Jesus had no human body was very widely accepted. About 137 one Cerdo, a Syrian, established a school at Rome, where he taught that Jesus was a divine Being sent into the world to combat evil, that he had no natural body and that he was consequently incapable of physical suffering. What was seen by the disciples was, Cerdo taught, a mere phantom.

Marcion, who founded a community in Rome about 144 and who came under the influence of Cerdo, based his teaching chiefly on the Pauline Epistles, which Marcion studied very deeply, and indeed it seems fair to say that he was the earliest critical student of the New Testament canon and text. He founded his distinctive doctrines largely on the antithesis, as emphasised by Paul, between the Law and the Gospel. He believed in the existence of a lower deity who had laid down the Mosaic law, and whose chief characteristic was justice with a leaning towards severity, and he taught that a higher Deity, a God of love, had finally intervened to take the government of the universe out of the former's hands. This beneficent Deity sent his Son, clothed in a visionary body and having the appearance of a man of some thirty years of age, down to earth to redeem mankind. The twelve Apostles, with their

Judaising tendencies, were unwittingly servants of the inferior deity, and Paul is the sole orthodox evangelist, because his keen spiritual insight raised him above their errors and enabled him to worship the higher God and to declare the true gospel of the Christ.

A disciple (or ex-disciple) of Marcion named Apelles taught his pupils that Jesus really possessed a human body, but that this body was not born of a woman. The doctrine of Apelles was that Jesus as it were materialised, or in other words that he was a divine being who in order to manifest his presence on earth took on him a human body miraculously drawn from the surrounding elements. It was further taught that on the occasion of the so-called "Ascension" of Jesus this miraculous body disintegrated, and Jesus, without a body, went back to his place at the Father's right hand. Apelles never seems to have had any important number of followers, but his teaching is interesting because it is not unlike the theories of modern spiritualists with respect to the formation of temporary bodies out of ectoplasm. Moreover the teaching of Apelles seems to harmonise better with the prologue to the Fourth Gospel ("the Word was made flesh") than do the traditional "birth-stories."

The Marcionites became a body of very considerable importance, and long constituted a serious rival to the main Christian body. It so happens that the earliest known inscription on a Christian place of worship is Marcionite. (The date is 318 and the inscription was found on a stone which had been built into a house in a Syrian village.) From about 300 onwards the Marcionites began to die out, but their existence can be traced as late as the seventh century.

The Marcionites are regarded as a branch of the Gnostics, and it is, in our survey of the development of the doctrine of the Blessed Trinity, desirable now to say something about the general teaching of the latter sect.

The observation has frequently been made that orthodox Christianity differs from Gnosticism primarily because the former attaches immense importance to faith in the divine revelation to mankind, while the latter rather aims at leading the neophyte to the knowledge (γνωσις, hence the name "Gnostic") of God. To this it may with a certain plausibility be replied that here there is a distinction without a difference. The orthodox Christian puts forward one set of propositions concerning the nature of the Deity, and believes that he knows them to be true. Hence he claims to possess faith in God. The Gnostic puts forward another set of propositions, and similarly believes that he knows them to be true. Hence he claims to possess knowledge of God. At first sight it would appear therefore that the distinction is a mere verbal one, and the two attitudes are really identical. But on further examination it will be seen that an important difference does in point of fact exist. But to grasp this difference it is necessary to understand the nature of "faith," as the word is generally used in popular theology.

We have already (p. 93), in describing the divergent views of James and of the author of the Epistle to the Hebrews, called attention to the fact that although neither writer gives us a clear definition of "faith," nevertheless we are apparently to understand that what is meant is a conscious attempt on the part of the human individual to raise his spiritual being towards God. But this is not quite the meaning which theologians customarily assign to the word, and for that reason some further examination is necessary. Let us suppose that a history student has been taught some phrase in an unknown tongue, and that it has been explained to him that the translation is doubtful, but that the words probably mean *Rome was founded by Romulus in B.C.* 754; what would be his attitude? He might, if he was intelligent, possibly say that he was not convinced that Rome really was so founded, because (*a*) it was admitted that the translation was doubtful, and (*b*) the historical evidence for the statement is exceedingly weak. But if on the other hand our imaginary student were to say that he was fully prepared to believe unquestioningly that Rome really was founded by Romulus in 754, he would be getting very near to what is called "faith" in popular current theology. In point of fact theologians submit propositions which (*a*) were originally written in a foreign language, there being very frequently a doubt about either the accuracy of the translation or the authenticity of the text, (*b*) were originally written by an unknown author at an unknown date and (*c*) appear to many of us to be inherently incredible. The acceptance of such propositions is frequently called "faith," and such faith is inculcated by orthodox theologians as the one indispensable virtue: "Except a man believe faithfully he cannot be saved."

But it is here suggested that the only kind of "faith" which can be looked on as a real virtue is something quite different, and this will be made somewhat clearer if we study such a

FORMATION OF TRADITIONAL CHRISTIANITY

text as: "Believe on the Lord Jesus Christ and thou shalt be saved." It is reasonable to suppose that the meaning is somewhat as follows:

> Salvation, or in other words union with God, can only be brought about by the mediation of the divine Spirit, whom we call Christ, whom God sends forth to enter into human souls, thereby becoming to each soul so entered the Way, the Truth and the Life. To avail ourselves of this divine gift we must have faith, that is to say there must be a conscious and strenuous uplift of our being in the direction of Christ, with confidence that they who seek him shall find him.

But unfortunately it has happened that (partly through an unintelligent interpretation of the Epistle to the Hebrews) many Christians have understood that there was a kind of magic virtue in merely saying, orally or mentally, "I believe in Jesus Christ." Now faith is not a mere assenting to a proposition, and it is difficult to see that there is any more real virtue in simply uttering the words "I believe in Jesus Christ" than there is in saying: "I believe that Rome was founded by Romulus." Such mere assent to a proposition, unaccompanied by a genuine attempt to raise one's soul upwards and to seek God, falls short even of what James calls "faith without works," seeing that it cannot properly be called faith at all.

Now on this subject the Gnostics seem to have avoided the error fallen into by so many Christians. As has already been said, the former aimed at bringing their disciples to the knowledge of God, and mere unintelligent acquiescence in theological formulæ would not have appealed to them—any more than it did to James—as being the exercise of a cardinal virtue. In consequence the Gnostic took a view of his own as regards such legends as, e.g. the Deluge, which legends the Gnostics accepted in an allegorical sense only; while the orthodox Christians were taught that it is an exercise of the cardinal virtue of faith to believe that they are literally true. Consequently we find in Gnosticism exactly what we should expect to find: firstly that it attracted the class of people whom we should now call "intellectuals"; secondly that it tended to split up into a number of small sects, each of which offered its own teaching; thirdly that many if not all of such sects professed to teach esoteric doctrine, the exact nature of which is now unknown; and fourthly the Gnostics lacked what so many

Christians possessed, that energy and enthusiasm which frequently results from unquestioning belief in a dogmatic system.

It may assist us to judge how Gnosticism fell short of the aspirations of mankind if we contrast two relatively modern opinions as to the nature of the Deity. We have already seen (p. 17) that Cardinal Newman appears to have mentally visualised the Deity as a being who miraculously brought about "the liquefaction of the blood of Saint Januarius at Naples and the motion of the eyes of the pictures of the Madonna in the Roman States." Let us compare the Cardinal's belief with an extract from Jean Martet's *Biography of Camille Desmoulins*. Camille is speaking to his fiancée shortly before their marriage.

> "What do you think of God?" he asked.
> "I do not know what that word means" said she, with that air of false candour which was fashionable in 1790. "It often happens that I meditate on life and death, and I can swear to you that I never find God."
> She was silent for sufficient time to collect her thoughts.
> "I meet with a being endowed with all the attributes of divinity" she said. "But I do not call him, I will never call him God."
> "What name do you give him?"
> "The Indefinitive Being, my dear." ("*L'Être Indéfinitif, mon ami.*")
> This reply afforded Camille the most intense satisfaction.

Now notwithstanding the "most intense satisfaction" with which Camille received his fiancée's profession of faith, it requires no very profound knowledge of human nature to be assured that for every human being whose thoughts would aspire to the "Indefinitive Being" as confessed by the future Madame Desmoulins, there are a thousand disposed to adore the Deity as preached by Cardinal Newman. As to whether Newman's ideal is a lofty one, a difference of opinion is permissible. But as to whether it is a popular one, there is no doubt whatever.

For the Gnostics God was unknowable and unapproachable. This remote Deity manifested himself by means of emanations, called Eons, and Christ was held to be a superior Eon who descended into the world to combat the local Eon, who had created the material universe, including mankind, but had attempted to prevent man from acquiring the knowledge of good and evil.

It has already been said that Gnosticism attracted the class of people whom we now call "intellectuals," and in this respect it was of incalculable service in bridging the gulf between primitive Christianity—a Jewish system, originally taught by apostles of quite humble origin—and the elaborate philosophies current at Alexandria, Athens and other centres of learning. But we ought by no means to infer that all those who upheld the tenets of orthodoxy as against their Gnostic opponents were men of second-rate intellect. On the contrary, two exceptionally acute and accurate thinkers, Tertullian (*c*. 150–*c*. 230) and Origen (*c*. 185–253) made themselves especially noteworthy in combating Gnosticism. But the long controversy between the two schools of thought seems to have been influenced, on the side of orthodoxy, by the growing tendency, to which reference has already been made, to consider as a virtue unreasoning acquiescence in theological propositions.

It may perhaps make the situation clearer if an attempt be made to summarise the position as between Gnosticism and orthodoxy.

The primitive gospel, as preached immediately after the death of Jesus, is well summed up in Peter's great speech in Acts ii. It is to the effect that Jesus of Nazareth was a man approved of God by miracles and wonders and signs, that this Jesus was raised up by God and was exalted by God's right hand, wherefore the house of Israel should know assuredly that God hath made this same Jesus who was crucified both Lord and Christ.

And further, in the Fourth Gospel we get a series of discourses in which the Christ Spirit is represented as speaking by the mouth of Jesus and uttering such phrases as: "I came forth from the Father and am come into the world" (John xvi. 28), etc., etc.

Now the latter quotation (from John) is wholly in accordance with the teaching of the Gnostics that Christ is an emanation from God. But the former quotation, to the effect that Jesus was a man approved of God, is not in accordance with their doctrine, as they denied that Jesus possessed any real humanity. They looked on him as divine, and regarded a human birth, childhood, adolescence and manhood as beneath the dignity of so exalted a being. Thus Faustus, a follower of Manes (*c*. 215–*c*. 276) quotes his master as even going so far as to say *Absit ut Dominum nostrum Jesum Christum per naturalia pudenda mulieris descendisse confitear*. Now extravagant ideas of this sort might with propriety have been combated by the orthodox party by means of arguments based on common sense, the apostolic tradition and the Pauline epistles. But, as we have already said, Christians attached immense importance to the virtue of unquestioning belief, and seem to have been anxious to show that so far as dogmatising is concerned they were able to surpass the Gnostics. A well-known passage in Tertullian (*de Spectaculis*) brings this point out clearly:

> I maintain that the Son of God died; that is wholly credible because it is absurd. I maintain that after having been buried he rose again; which I take to be absolutely true, because it is manifestly impossible.

So what eventually happened was that the doctrine of the orthodox party became profoundly modified by their desire to show that in love and respect for Jesus Christ, and in unquestioning belief in him, they fell no whit behind their opponents. Consequently we find the Church tending more and more to claim unreservedly that Jesus was actually God. What may be looked on as the decisive triumph of this doctrine took place in 269, when a synod held at Antioch deposed for heresy the Patriarch of that city, Paul of Samosata, who seems to have preached the earlier theology as set forth by Peter in Acts ii. As in the case of so many other writers who have been accused of heretical teaching, we possess no actual treatise written by Paul, but the following fragments attributed to him are quoted in a work by Athanasius:

> Having been consecrated by the Holy Spirit he received the title of the Christ, suffering in accordance with his nature, working wonders in accordance with grace. For in fixity and resoluteness of character he likened himself to God, and having kept free from sin was united with God, and was empowered to grasp as it were the power and authority of wonders. By these he was shown to possess, over and above the will, one and the same activity (with God) and won the title of Redeemer and Saviour of our race.
>
> . . . . .
>
> The Saviour became holy and just; and by struggle and effort overcame the sins of our forefather. By these means he succeeded in perfecting himself, and was through his moral excellence united with God, having attained to unity and sameness of will and energy with him through his advances in the path of good deeds. This will he preserved inseparable (from the divine)

and so inherited the name which is above all names, the prize of love and affection vouchsafed in grace to him.

·   ·   ·   ·   ·

It was in virtue of love that the Saviour coalesced with God so as to admit of no divorce from him, but for all ages to retain one and the same will and activity with him, an activity perpetually at work in the manifestation of good.
Wonder not that the Saviour had one will with God. For as nature manifests the substance of the many to subsist as one and the same, so the attitude of love produces in the many an unity and sameness of will which is manifested in unity and sameness of approval and well pleasingness.

One remarkable thing about the sentence of deposition pronounced on Paul is that it seems to have been left without practical effect until late in 272, when the Emperor Aurelian, having defeated Zenobia and being anxious to impose on Syria the dogmatic system current in Rome, took steps to enforce the occupation of Paul's see by the rival patriarch. The last word therefore, on this momentous question vitally affecting the future of Christianity, seems to have rested with the pagan civil authority.

It has been well observed that the "teachings of Paul of Samosata form the high-water mark of Christian speculation," and his condemnation was an event of far greater significance than is generally recognised. Thenceforward orthodoxy, while never ostensibly repudiating the teaching of the Apostles' Creed, found itself definitely committed to the additional belief that Jesus is God.

Now a study of comparative religion shows us that it is a common thing for a God to be represented as having dealings with mankind under some material form—such form being generally but not always human. Jupiter for example is said to have manifested himself as a swan. Again it is readily comprehensible that man, when he has attained a certain stage of spiritual development, should come to believe that God has inspired some specially chosen human being so completely as to cause the will of such being to be identified with the divine will: this was the teaching of Paul of Samosata and of other mystics. But the position taken by the fathers of the Church in the third and fourth centuries was not quite in accordance with either of these two alternatives. In their disputes with the Gnostics they, in accordance with the primitive Christian tradition, insisted on the perfect humanity of

Jesus. But on the other hand they concurred with their Gnostic opponents in ascribing to him the Godhead, i.e. they affirmed not that the divine spirit had entered into him, but that he was himself actually God. Consequently they found themselves in the position of affirming that he had two natures, being at the same time perfect man and perfect God.

But this conception of a being at once perfect God and perfect man is altogether too recondite to be understood by the great mass of mankind, and it consequently came about that the doctrine of the humanity of Jesus, while always formally propounded by the Church, soon came to be practically ignored, and Christians were and still are generally made to believe that Jesus was God incarnate in a human body. So while theologians subscribe to the doctrine of the dual nature of Jesus, in actual practice the Christian community has for many centuries held a belief not very far removed from that of the inhabitants of Lystra, who on being visited by Paul and Barnabas thought that the gods were come down in the likeness of men (Acts xiv. 11).

It followed therefore that after the condemnation of Paul of Samosata the Church found itself faced with the difficulties of explaining the relationship of Jesus to the Father, and at the same time of reconciling the new theology with the traditional monotheism of the early Jewish Christians. These difficulties led in course of time to the great Arian controversy.

Arius was, early in the fourth century, a priest in charge of one of the larger Churches in Alexandria, who became involved in friction with his bishop, Alexander, and his archdeacon, Athanasius, who accused him of heresy. Arius seems to have been animated with a sincere desire to reconcile the two dogmas: *Jesus Christ is God* and *There is but one God*. He taught that the Son was before all time begotten by the Father, and was perfect God, not being "one among things created." But on the other hand, while the Son fully shared the Father's divinity, being of like essence with him, some measure of inferiority, the nature and extent of which are very difficult to understand, seems to have been attributed by Arius to the Son.

It may be convenient in this place to point out the extreme difficulty felt by a modern reader in understanding some of the terms used in early theological controversies. It is simple enough to look up these terms in a dictionary, but it is quite another thing to understand exactly what shade of meaning they conveyed to the disputants who used them sixteen centuries

FORMATION OF TRADITIONAL CHRISTIANITY

ago. It may however make matters clearer if something be here said about the words "essence" and "substance," which will be used more than once in the next few pages.

The word ESSENCE means "being." Thus Locke (*Human Understanding*) says: "Essence may be taken for the being of anything, whereby it is what it is." The corresponding word in Latin is *essentia* (from *esse*, to be) and in Greek οὐσια.

The word SUBSTANCE means "that which stands underneath something." Thus Locke (*Human Understanding*) says: "Of substance we have no idea of what it is, but only a confused obscure one of what it does." The Latin equivalent is *substantia* and the Greek ὑποστατις, a word which is anglicised into *hypostatis*.

Now it came about that the controversy between Arius and his bishop became, for reasons which will be touched on in the next chapter, the cause of the convocation of a general Church Council at Nicea in 325. Athanasius not being a bishop was not a member of the council, but he journeyed to Nicea for the occasion, and seems to have exerted himself by means of unofficial conferences to bring about the condemnation of Arius.

Eventually the Council (under the influence of Eusebius of Cæsarea, who apparently took the most prominent part in the proceedings) decided to draw up a profession of faith, taking as a basis the form of the Apostles' Creed then in use in Cæsarea. The creed as modified at Nicea consequently ran as follows:

> We believe in one God the Father Almighty, the maker of all things visible and invisible.
> And in one Lord Jesus Christ the Son of God, begotten of the Father, only begotten, that is of the essence of the Father, God of God, Light of Light, very God of very God, begotten not made, of one essence with the Father by whom all things were made, both those in heaven and those on earth: Who for us men and for our salvation came down and was incarnate, was made man and suffered, rose the third day, ascended into heaven, is coming to judge quick and dead.
> And in the Holy Spirit.

The reader will notice the absence of any mention of Pontius Pilate or of the Virgin Mary. Moreover the composite nature of the document is very evident. It commences with an affirmation of the unity of God. But immediately afterwards Jesus is called "Son of God," in accordance with the old theology, and a little later "God of God," in accordance with the new. In the first paragraph the Father is stated to be the Creator, while in the second, whether by accident or design, the reader is left in doubt whether the Creator is the Father or the Son. If we construe the Creed as one would a legal document, we understand that Jesus is of one essence with that Father by whom all things were made. But if we construe it as a series of semi-independent propositions, we understand that Jesus is of one essence with the Father, and also that by Jesus all things were made. The interpretation generally adopted is the latter one, harmonising as it does with John i. 3, though not of course with the first paragraph of the Creed. Thus in a translation into English, printed in 1530, we get: "Of one substaunce wyth the father. By whome all thynges are made, whiche for us men and women, and for oure helthe cam downe from heuens."

The phrase "of one essence (*or being*) with the Father" was not accepted by Arius, who was in consequence excommunicated and banished. The orthodox teaching among Greek-speaking Christians thus became that Jesus was of the same essence as God the Father, albeit of a different substance (or *hypostasis*). But Latin-speaking Christians held that Jesus was of the same essence and of the same substance (or *substantia*), but was a different *Persona*.[1] The word *persona* primarily means *a mask*, but a secondary meaning is *an actor* (i.e. the wearer of a mask) or *the part played by an actor* (as in the well-known phrase *dramatis personæ*). The English equivalent is, according to the meaning we desire to give, *person* or *parson*.

The Greeks, not unreasonably, took exception to the term *persona*, as they pointed out that it tended to what had come to be called "Sabellianism." Sabellius, who lived in the latter part of the second century and early in the third, was a Roman priest excommunicated by Calixtus I (Pope, 218–222) for holding that God is one, but that God manifests his divine power in three different ways: firstly as the All Father, the Creator of the world; secondly as a Being who came into intimate contact with matter in order to become the Redeemer of mankind; and thirdly as the Illuminator and Sanctifier of the

---

[1] This point comes out clearly in the proper preface for Trinity Sunday as given in the Roman missal, where we read:

Unus es Dominus, non in unius singularitate personæ sed in unius Trinitate substantiæ . . . et in personis proprietas et in essentia unitas et in majestate adoretur æqualitas.

human soul. It is clear that nothing could be more favourable to the Sabellian theory than the use of the expression "*three persons*," which may be taken to liken God to an actor who plays three different parts. But it happened that the discussions arising out of the highly-important differences between Greek and Latin phraseology seem to have led to but little ill-feeling, while the difference between Arianism and orthodoxy, which difference is not readily comprehensible to the majority of mankind, occasioned a most serious schism in the Church.

It is by no means easy for the modern student to sympathise with the fourth-century theologian, or to understand exactly why men felt it their duty to profess such absolutely certain knowledge concerning matters which wholly transcend human intelligence. But in the fourth century as at other times theologians believed that, in accordance with the promise of Jesus *I will be with you always*, the Church was under the direct guidance of the Holy Spirit, and consequently a sentence of a General Council should be considered as an utterance of God himself. Moreover many ecclesiastics seem to have adopted the attitude that, unquestioning belief being a cardinal virtue, the weaker the logical basis of a generally accepted theological proposition the greater the merit of adopting it. Consequently it came about that the Church was eventually, with a greater or less degree of difficulty, able to crush those so called heresies which brought into prominence any lack of logic in the position taken up by the orthodox party. We have already mentioned the Sabellians, who said in effect: "You tell us that God is one, therefore he cannot be three." The followers of Eutyches (*c.* 380–*c.* 456) said in effect: "You tell us that Jesus was only one person, he could therefore have but one nature." The followers of Nestorius (d. *c.* 451) said in effect: "You tell us that Jesus was God and that he was man. He must therefore have had two different personalities." The followers of Apollinaris (d. 390) said in effect: "You tell us that Jesus did not have two different personalities. He cannot therefore have been both perfect God and perfect man." The Monothelites (a school of thought flourishing in the seventh century) said in effect: "You tell us that Jesus was only one person, he can therefore have had no more than one will."

Now all these heresies have been severely condemned by the Church, which has been unwilling to recognise that the cause of such heresies has been the laying down of dogmas concerning matters which God has not revealed to mankind,

130 INTRODUCTION TO THE STUDY OF CHRISTIANITY

and which indeed, as has already been remarked, wholly transcend human intelligence.

In the course of the fourth century the Creed of Nicea became modified by certain additions, one of which expresses belief in the divinity of the Holy Spirit, who it is stated "proceedeth from the Father, and who with the Father and the Son is worshipped."

Consequently it was thenceforth definitely established that the Holy Spirit (or Paraclete) was by no means to be considered as a function or manifestation of God (in somewhat the same way as a man's will is a function of the man himself). On the contrary it was held in the Greek Church that the Holy Spirit actually was God, and was of a substance (*hypostasis*) different to that of the Father. The Latin Church, accepting apparently the same general idea but using a different terminology, held that the Holy Spirit was of the same substance (*substantia*) as the Father, but was a different Person (*Persona*).

About the sixth century the Western Church added the word *filioque* (*and the Son*) after the phrase *proceedeth from the Father*. This interpolation is sometimes stated to have been made by a local Council held in Toledo in 589, but the affirmation lacks evidence, and indeed it seems probable that the insertion was originally a mere copyist's mistake. (This mistake, if mistake it be, is rendered readily explicable by the fact that in the clause immediately following we read that the Holy Spirit, with the Father *and the Son*, is worshipped.) The Eastern Church strongly objected and still objects to the interpolation, both on doctrinal grounds and also on the general principle that no local Church has a right to modify a creed without the consent of the remaining Churches.

The doctrine of the Blessed Trinity, as now understood in the Western Church, may be regarded as having become more definitely fixed by the adoption of a third Creed, called from its opening words *Quicunque vult*. This Creed takes the form not so much of a profession of faith as rather of a solemn warning of the fearful consequences which will inevitably overwhelm the reader who fails to keep whole and undefiled the doctrine therein expounded. This doctrine consists of the new theology superimposed on the old, that is to say we are told that the Father is God, the Son God and the Holy Spirit God; the Father is incomprehensible, the Son incomprehensible and the Holy Spirit incomprehensible; but yet on the other hand the

Creed reaffirms the monotheistic doctrine that there is but one God and one incomprehensible. The author's tone indicates that no attempt ought to be made to reconcile these opposing statements. It is possible that he had in mind the famous saying, already quoted, of Tertullian to the effect that a certain theological doctrine was to be believed because it was impossible.

It has been suggested with some plausibility that the author of this Creed was Victricius, Bishop of Rouen who, having been accused of heresy, may have composed it in order to rebut the charges brought against him. The tone of the document is indeed suggestive of the author being anxious to affirm his faith in any doctrine, however unreasonable, which might be considered orthodox. According to the above theory the Creed was dedicated by Victricius to Anastasius I (Pope 398–402), and there is evidence of its having been occasionally called the "Creed of Anastasius," and it is suggested that the title "Creed of Athanasius," by which it is now popularly known, is a copyist's error. In any case there seems no doubt that the Creed is of Gallican origin and that Athanasius had nothing to do with it.

The Creed has never been adopted into the public offices of the Eastern Church, and is indeed but little known to the bulk of the Roman Catholic laity. On the other hand the prominence given in the Prayer Book of the English Church to this unfortunate document has done immense harm in alienating thoughtful people from Christianity.

It is now convenient to summarise the above conclusions relative to the development of the doctrine of the Blessed Trinity:

(i) The earliest converts to Christianity were Jews, who retained the monotheism of their original religion. As however propaganda commenced among non-Jewish nations, two factors combined to modify this monotheism: (a) the theories of certain philosophers to the effect that God is unknowable and unapproachable, but manifests his power in creating and ruling this earth by means of emanations or Eons; and (b) the mythology of certain pagan nations, some of which worshipped a Trinity of Father, Mother and Son, and some of which were familiar with the idea of a semi-divine being having a human mother but no human father.

(ii) The earliest gospel preached by the followers of Jesus after his Ascension is summarised in Acts ii, and is to the effect that Jesus of Nazareth was a man approved of God, and that therefore God had made him both Lord and Christ.

(iii) At some unknown date, but almost certainly after all four Gospels had been compiled, a legend became generally accepted to the effect that Jesus had no human father. The Apostles' Creed (although the actual form now in use dates back no earlier than the eighth century) is the oldest of the Creeds, and represents the stage of Christian dogma when the doctrine of the Virgin Birth of Jesus had already found general credence, but that of his essential divinity had not. It is a very remarkable thing that what is still regarded by so many millions of Christians as *the* Creed should represent a stage of belief so long out of date.

(iv) The doctrine of the divinity of Jesus seems to have gained ground early in the second century, and by the latter part of the third it must have been generally current, because the Synod of Antioch held in 269 condemned Paul of Samosata for denying it. At the Council of Nicea in 325 the doctrine was accepted by both the opposing parties.

(v) The doctrine of the divinity of the Holy Spirit was sanctioned in an addition made to the Creed of Nicea under circumstances which are not fully elucidated.

(vi) In the *Quicunque Vult* we get the complete doctrine, in its final form, of the Trinity, as consisting of three co-equal, co-eternal Persons, each being perfect God, there nevertheless being but one God. This doctrine, which was imposed on believers by the most awful punishment being threatened to anyone who failed to accept it, was supported by the forging of an addition, favourable to the doctrine, to the first of the Epistles (v. 7) attributed to St. John.

(vii) In order to secure acceptance of the new doctrines, the Church found itself compelled to condemn alike those who, like Paul of Samosata, refused to accept them altogether, and those who, like Nestorius and Eutyches, carried certain of them to their logical conclusion.

The Arians after the Nicean Council

Instead of the reputation of Arius having diminished as the result of his condemnation in 325, on the contrary it seems to have increased. He was recalled from exile in 330, while his rival Athanasius, who had in the meantime become Bishop of Alexandria, was banished to Trèves in 335. In the Eastern Church Arianism may then be said to have gained the upper hand, and this preeminence it retained for some time. In the West the Arian doctrines were less popular, though St. Vincent of Lérins (d. *c.* 450) tells us that "almost all the Latin bishops were contaminated." St. Hilary, Bishop of Poitiers (d. *c.* 368), who was subsequently honoured with the title of Doctor of the Church, and his disciple St. Martin of Tours (*c.* 316–*c.* 400) were forced to go into exile as a result of their opposition to Arianism. And describing the situation so created, St. Jerome (*c.* 340–420) tells us, possibly with a trace of exaggeration, that the whole earth groaned with surprise at finding itself Arian (*ingemuit totus orbs et arianum se esse miratus est*) and no hope remained (*nihil jam superat spei. Adv. Lucif.*).

It is remarkable, when we consider the importance of Rome as an ecclesiastical centre, that the Roman theologians seem to have taken so relatively small a part in the controversy. We hear most about Liberius, who was Pope from 352 to 366, and who in 355 very properly refused to sign a condemnation of Athanasius imposed by imperial command on all the Western bishops. Liberius was in consequence banished to Thrace, but at the end of two years was allowed to return to his see on subscribing to an Arian formula and receiving the Arians into communion. After the death of Constantius in 361 Liberius showed evidence of more orthodox tendencies, but he was to the end a man of moderate views, doubtless inspired by a sincere desire for peace and by an indisposition to dogmatise concerning doubtful points of doctrine. Needless to say he has in consequence been severely criticised both by Roman Catholic writers and by their opponents.

The Arians in the East after having long had the upper hand seem to have gradually diminished in importance, and to have eventually disappeared without having exercised much real influence on Christian thought. In the West, the Goths, Vandals, Swabians and Burgundians all adopted Arianism and involved the orthodox party in considerable difficulties, but the medieval Church was eventually successful in effecting the conversion of all these tribes.

A remarkable feature about the Arian controversy is this. The orthodox party frequently accused their opponents of denying the divinity of Jesus altogether. This accusation was not merely untrue, or at least untrue as applied to Arius and his immediate followers, but was from the orthodox point of view a tactical error. Before the accusation was made, the doctrine of the divinity of Jesus had already become common to the two parties, and it was therefore to their joint interest that such doctrine should not be again called in question. But as a result of the accusation, the term Arianism came to be by no means limited to what was taught by Arius, but was indeed applied to any form of religion which teaches the divine mission of Jesus, but denies his essential divinity. Thus Voltaire (*Dict. Philosophique*) speaking of "Unitarians" makes it clear that he regards the term as identical with "Arians," and says: "This party, after three centuries of triumph and twelve of oblivion, has sprung again from its ashes."

The Cult of the Blessed Virgin Mary

In a former section of this chapter a rough outline has been sketched of the development of the doctrine of the Trinity. It is now proposed similarly to outline the evolution of Christian sentiment with regard to the Blessed Virgin.

The first point which strikes us is that in none of the Gospels, assuming always that the birth-stories are late additions, is there any direct statement as to the name of the Mother of Jesus. On the other hand the natural interpretation of Matt. xiii. 55 and Mark vi. 3 is that the Mary therein mentioned did in fact have several children, and that these children included Jesus, James and Joses. But in Matt. xxvii. 56 and Mark xv. 40 this same Mary is described as "the Mother of James and Joses" without any reference to Jesus; and it seems very highly improbable that both writers should have identified the mother of the subject of their biography by calling her not "the Mother of Jesus" but the mother of two very minor characters in the story.

It may be that we possess a clue to the difficulty in the contention of Jerome (*Against Helvidius*) that James and Joses were the sons of Mary, sister of the Mother of Jesus, mentioned in John xix. 25. It seems indeed quite possible that owing to domestic matters of which we are ignorant, Jesus had been in such close contact with his aunt and cousins that he was frequently referred to as the son of the one and the brother of the others. [It is to be noted that Matthew and Mark (*loc. cit.*) do not actually say that Mary was the Mother of Jesus, but tell us that people enquired whether his mother was not called Mary.]

The above theory seems to be consistent with the attitude of the writer of the Fourth Gospel, the evangelist who was on terms of close filial intimacy with the Mother of Jesus but who gives her no name, telling us merely that she had a sister called Mary. He might have known quite well that the name of the former was not Mary, but he might nevertheless have been unwilling to upset an established tradition, and it might have been on this account that he refrained from telling us what her name was. The (possibly unfounded) tradition that the name of the Mother of Jesus was Mary may have become firmly established by the factor which caused the doctrine of the Blessed Trinity to have been formed, i.e. by a combination of Jewish ideas with pagan myths.

There seems to have been a Hebrew tradition that the Old Testament character Joshua was the son of Miriam,[1] or, giving the names their anglicised forms, Jesus was the son of Mary. The name Mary is etymologically connected with Maya and Maia. Maya was the mother of Gautama Buddha, and Maia in Greek mythology was the mother of Hermes, whose father was Zeus. The etymology of these names (Mary, Miriam, Maia, and Maya) is obscure, but a very plausible suggestion is that they come from a root meaning *illusion* or *mist*, the names being considered as specially appropriate to the mother of the Sun God, who is as it were born out of the morning mist.

Although there are, as has been pointed out, certain details as to the family relationships of Jesus which remain obscure, it is at least certain that if he was an only son, the very early Church attached no theological importance to the fact. *Vide* Matt. i. 25, xiii. 55, 56; Mark vi. 3; Gal. i. 19. Both Origen and Tertullian call attention to these passages when arguing (against the Gnostics) that Jesus had a human nature and consequently underwent the material process of physical birth. By the fourth century however, as the result of certain extravagant opinions as to the essentially sinful nature of human generation (*vide* p. 79), the doctrine had become current that Mary lived and died a virgin, and some later writers, including Jerome, even go so far as to affirm that Joseph also led a life

[1] Mr. J. M. Robertson (*Christianity and Mythology*) cites the "Chronicle of Tabari" in support of this statement.

of perpetual virginity. Consequently we find that some theologians argue that the "brethren" mentioned in the Gospels must have been Joseph's children by a former marriage, and some that they were the cousins of Jesus. The Council of Chalcedon (451) formally proclaimed the perpetual virginity of Mary, and this doctrine has ever since been current both in the Eastern Churches and in the Roman communion.

Mary seems to have been given the title "Mother of God" not originally with the intention of doing her any very extraordinary honour, but rather of combating the Nestorian school by emphasising the tenet that she was the mother of the God-man Jesus Christ, and not merely the mother of his human body. There are even instances of early writers having similarly called David the "Father of God," and James the "Brother of God." But as time progressed, two factors united to bring about what non-Roman theologians are accustomed to call "Mariolatry," or the ascription of quasi-divine honours to the Mother of Jesus. In order to make these factors clear it is necessary to say something about the mission of Jesus considered as a Mediator between God and men.

As we have already noticed in former sections of this work, the higher truths of Christianity are intensely difficult to express in words, but we gather, chiefly from the Fourth Gospel, that the supreme aim of the human individual is, or should be, union (or atonement) with God. That attribute of God which renders him approachable in the above sense, we call the Holy Spirit, or Christ Spirit. The Fourth Gospel gives us to understand that the Christ Spirit specially endued Jesus in such manner that the will of the latter became identified with the divine will, and he was consequently enabled to act as the mouthpiece of the Spirit and to say "I am the Way: no man cometh to the Father but by me."

But such doctrine, here so very inadequately expressed, was too recondite to be preached with advantage to the bulk of mankind in the first few centuries of our era. In other words Christianity, like other religions, necessarily had its exoteric and its esoteric teaching. In consequence, among the majority of Christians a conception different from the foregoing arose as to what was meant by the office of Christ as Mediator. People did not in general think of a divine Spirit coalescing with the human soul, and forming a binding link between man and God. Rather on the other hand did they conceive of an Advocate, pleading before God the spiritual and material interests of humanity. And as we have already seen, in harmony with this view the word παρακλητον in 1 John ii. 1 is translated *advocatum* in the Vulgate, whence we get the well-known reading in the Authorised Version: "If any man sin we have an Advocate with the Father."

So it will be seen that the majority of Christians, when regarding Christ as a Mediator, did not think of a Way (John xiv. 6) or means of approach to God, but rather of an Advocate or Intercessor, whose function it is to influence the Deity in a manner favourable to mankind. Now it is of course evident that any idea such as this presupposes the existence of two different wills, that of the Advocate and that of the Judge. We cannot think of an Advocate without thinking of the Judge before whom he pleads, and if the Judge from the outset takes the same view as that set forth by the Advocate, the latter's function ceases to have any practical utility. So the bulk of the early Christians, while thinking of God as a Judge who, like the Jewish Deity, had a marked inclination towards severity, came to think of Jesus as an Advocate whose mission it was to attempt to mitigate such severity by consistently appealing to the divine sense of mercy.

But when the doctrine became current that Jesus was perfect God, of the same essence as the Father, it inevitably came about that popular ideas as to his function as a Mediator were modified. It would of course be an over-statement to say that having regard to the generally accepted identification of Jesus with God, Christians ceased to look on the former as a Mediator. But it does seem true that, in view of the new doctrine, Christians began to regard Jesus as a Being far away and unapproachable, and hence they became attracted by the idea of a Mediator between mankind and Jesus, in the same way as an earlier generation had been attracted by the idea of Jesus as a Mediator between mankind and God. Now it is obvious that she whom we know as Mary, the Mother of Jesus, was specially indicated as the human being most likely to have influence over her Son; and consequently she in course of time came to occupy, at least in part, in men's minds that position of Mediator which earlier Christians had attributed to him.

When once the idea had been adopted that Mary acted as a Mediatrix between Jesus and mankind, there was another reason why her cult should become popular. Primitive religious thought among the Hebrews was wholly opposed to the existence of a female Deity, and when, as was inevitable, attempts had been made to introduce the worship of pagan goddesses (e.g. 1 Kings xi. 5) the orthodox Jews were, with more or less difficulty, eventually able to stamp out the innovation. But pagan converts to Christianity were for the most part accustomed to the worship of Isis, of Maia or of some similar goddess; and the lack in Christian theology of any cult of a female deity no doubt impressed such converts unfavourably. So theologians, consciously or otherwise, gradually began to provide what their disciples looked for. Thus, for example, St. Cyril of Alexandria, in a sermon preached in 431, referred to Mary as she

> through whom the Trinity is glorified and worshipped, ... through whom heaven triumphs, the angels are made glad, devils driven forth, the tempter overcome and the fallen creature raised up even to heaven.

And in course of time certain legends, similar to those which had accumulated round the earthly mission of Jesus, came to be adapted to the life and death of Mary. The most noticeable of such adaptations is to the effect that after her death her body, after having been laid in the tomb, was miraculously taken up to heaven. St. Gregory of Tours (*c.* 590) is the first writer of repute to give this story the weight of his authority. The Roman Church has instituted an important feast, the Assumption of the Blessed Virgin Mary, in commemoration of the event. There does not seem to be any authoritative pronouncement as to exactly what should be understood by the expression "Assumption," and consequently it is considered that Roman Catholics enjoy a certain latitude as regards their belief. But the Offertory for the day (August 15th) is: "Mary is taken up (*assumpta*) into heaven, the army of Angels rejoice and bless the Lord with praises."

The question is sometimes asked whether Roman Catholics worship the Blessed Virgin. Before attempting to answer this question it is well to point out that the word "worship" may be correctly used in English to imply a degree of respect far short of that which we owe to the Deity. A Mayor of an English town is addressed as "Your Worship," and in the marriage service of the English Church the bridegroom states, perhaps not always truthfully, that he worships the bride. So our question should rather be: Do Roman Catholics give to the Blessed Virgin that worship which Protestants believe to be due to God alone? The Roman theologians reply emphatically in the negative. They distinguish between *latria*, *hyperdulia* and *dulia*, understanding by *latria* that adoration which is due to God alone: *hyperdulia* is that extreme homage which is due to the Blessed Virgin alone among the saints, while *dulia* is that veneration which is due to the apostles, martyrs and others of God's chosen.

An example of *hyperdulia* is to be found in the "Litany of the Blessed Virgin" in the Roman office book. There the Mother of Jesus is addressed as:

> Amiable Mother, Admirable Mother, Mother of Good Counsel, Mother of the Creator, Mother of the Saviour, Most Prudent Virgin, Venerable Virgin, Praiseworthy Virgin, Potent Virgin, Clement Virgin, Faithful Virgin, Mirror of Justice, Seat of Wisdom, Cause of our Joy, Spiritual Vessel, Honourable Vessel, Eminent Vessel of Devotion, Mystic Rose, Tower of David, Tower of Ivory, Golden House, Ark of Alliance, Gateway of Heaven, Morning Star, Safety of the Infirm, Refuge of Sinners, Consoler of the Afflicted, Help of Christians, Queen of Angels.

The function, as popularly understood, of the Blessed Virgin as an intercessor is well illustrated by the celebrated masterpiece by Rubens, now in the Beaux Arts at Brussels, painted about 1633 for the Franciscans at Gand. Jesus is represented as being on the point of hurling thunderbolts against a guilty world, but being restrained by the joint intercession of St. Mary and St. Francis. This may be taken as a typical instance of the substitution, in popular theology, of Jesus, considered as an Advocate, by Mary.

It is moreover interesting to note the extent to which the Blessed Virgin has tended to become a local object of veneration. The most striking example of this tendency is perhaps to be found in the cult of Our Lady of Loreto, concerning which a few words of explanation are desirable.

In the fifteenth century mention first seems to be made of the Holy House (Santa Casa) of Loreto, and in 1518 a bull of Leo X gave formal recognition to the complete legend. This legend is to the effect that in 1291, that is to say when Acre was taken by Sultan Khalil and means of communication with Nazareth were definitely cut off, the house formerly occupied by the Blessed Virgin, and where the Annunciation took place, was miraculously carried to Tersatto near Fiume; and further in 1294 was similarly removed to a laurel grove (*laurentum*, probably hence Loreto) near Recanati in Italy.

Perhaps the most charitable observation which can be made with respect to this so-called miracle is that it was probably not a deliberate invention, because, had it so been, the propagators of the legend would have been careful to choose a house in Italy bearing some resemblance to an Oriental residence. The "Santa Casa" of Loreto is built of the dark stone common in the neighbourhood, and quite unlike the grey limestone found in the vicinity of Nazareth. The inherent improbability of the legend, however, did not prevent the cult of Our Lady of Loreto attaining immense popularity. Dean Stanley, writing in the middle of the last century, describes the church, built over the Santa Casa, as "undoubtedly the most frequented sanctuary of Christendom." He goes on to tell us that two soldiers, sword in hand, protected the Holy House during the daytime, while throughout the night, when the church was closed to pilgrims, Franciscan friars kept watch on their knees. One hundred and twenty masses were said daily at the various altars of the church.

But in 1860, in the near vicinity of the Holy House, the papal troops suffered a total defeat by the Italians; the shock to Roman Catholic sentiment was enormous and the popularity of Our Lady of Loreto began to wane. Two years previously the Blessed Virgin was said to have appeared at Lourdes in a series of visions to a peasant girl named Soubirous. From that time onwards numerous miracles were alleged to have taken place on the site of the visions, and the cult of Our Lady of Lourdes rapidly took the place of that of Our Lady of Loreto. The immense popularity of Our Lady of Lourdes very naturally caused a falling off in devotion at the other French shrines. Anatole France, who early in the present century visited Liesse, near Laon, refers to the local Virgin as "formerly so frequented and now fallen into neglect." He goes on to say:

> Our Lady of Lourdes has done great harm to the Lady of Liesse, as indeed to all the holy Virgins of old France. That beautiful Lady of Lourdes, with her blue scarf, attracts all the pilgrims to her watering-place, and there is no talk of any one but her.
>
> The Virgin of Liesse does not know how to arrange her affairs so well. She has become forgotten, a fact which is noticed immediately one enters the sleepy little town. People say that next month the town will wake up, on the occasion of the important pilgrimages, but I see only too clearly that, although formerly visited by kings, she now attracts, even on her festival

days, no more than a few worthy ladies from Rheims, Laon and S. Quentin.

She has had her days of splendour. Everything passes, and Our Lady of Lourdes will pass like her. This is a reflexion which may console Our Lady of Liesse in her irremediable decline.

(ANATOLE FRANCE, *Pierre Nozière*.)

The above facts have been adduced as illustrative of the cult of the Blessed Virgin Mary as a local object of veneration. But the word "local" demands a certain modification. Our Lady of Loreto is not regarded as a subject of veneration at Loreto only. On the contrary, at Rome we find that amongst the eighty churches erected in honour of the Blessed Virgin, there is in the Piazza del Foro Trajano a handsome sixteenth-century building dedicated to St. Mary of Loreto, notwithstanding the fact that Rome also venerates a local St. Mary (of the Snow), in whose honour an even more magnificent edifice (S. Maria Maggiore) has been constructed. Similarly at Paris we find in the Rue Châteaudun an important church erected in honour of Our Lady of Loreto, notwithstanding the fact that the cathedral itself is dedicated to Our Lady of Paris.

What has actually taken place therefore is somewhat analogous to the development of the doctrine of the Blessed Trinity. Christians commenced by insisting on the unity of the Godhead, but nevertheless the worshipper eventually came to distinguish between three different Persons. The Blessed Virgin came to be venerated under many different aspects and associated with many different localities; and the result is that the faithful, while never abandoning the belief that there is but one Blessed Virgin Mary, nevertheless address their devotions to her almost as if she were a great number of different saints.

Early Christian records other than literary

In former sections of this book frequent mention has been made of the early Christian writings, the most important of which we generally class together under the style of "the New Testament." It is now desirable to say something about such Christian records as consist of pictures, frescoes, inscriptions on tombs, monuments, etc.

In view of the prominence given to the crucifix both in medieval and in modern Roman Catholicism, it is natural that we should enquire exactly how the early Christians represented the death of Jesus, and we are not a little surprised to find that there is no conclusive evidence of such death having been depicted by Christians at all until about the fifth century. It is commonly said that the earliest known representation of the crucifixion is scratched on a piece of wall-plaster now in the Museo Kircheriano at Rome. This plaster was found on the site of the Pædagogium (or school for the imperial slaves) on the Palatine Hill, and the design represents a man with an ass's head, attached to a cross, with another man praying at the side. The inscription (in Greek) may be translated "Alexamenos worshipping his god." This scratching is believed to date from about the third century, but it is clear that either the crucified figure does not represent Jesus (in which case Seth is probably intended) or else the drawing is a mere anti-Christian caricature. The earliest genuine representation of the crucifixion is possibly one of the panels of the principal doors of St. Sabina on the Aventine Hill. These doors are believed to date from the fifth century.

The natural inference to be drawn from the foregoing is that in the eyes of the very early Christians the manner of the death of Jesus was a matter of less importance than it became in the opinion of later generations. This of course harmonises with the conclusions come to in other parts of this treatise.

As is of course well known, the burial places of the Roman Christians form a most important mine of information as regards the early Church. It would appear that the earliest of such burial-places was chosen at the site where the Church of St. Sebastian now stands, along the Appian Way, a little to the south of Rome. A series of vaults was there constructed, and hence the district came to be called *catacumba* (from Greek words meaning "hollow underneath"). In course of time further series of vaults, connected by subterranean passages, were built in other localities, and this went on until in all perhaps some six hundred miles of subterranean passages had been excavated. The name "catacumba," originally applied to one locality, became common to all the sets of vaults and passages. The catacombs seem to have formed a convenient hiding-place for Christians in times of persecution, on which occasions, as doubtless at other times, the vaults were used as places of worship. Their decoration sheds remarkable light on early Christian beliefs.

In the first place we are reminded of the fact that when

the catacombs were decorated, Christianity was still absorbing its symbolism from alien cults. So we are not surprised to find Christ represented as the Good Shepherd, in a manner reminiscent of the older pictures of Hermes the Good Shepherd. Again we find Christ as Orpheus, playing his harp and surrounded with beasts and plants listening to his music. This picture recalls the words of Eusebius of Cæsarea:

> Orpheus made wild beasts tame by playing the lyre; and by the magic of his song he even induced oak-trees to follow him. Still more sublime was the deed of God's all-wise Word. In order to heal the corruption of men he took on him the nature of man, that instrument fashioned by his own wisdom, and he played on this instrument a magical music that calmed the customs of Greeks and Barbarians in that he healed the will and animal instincts of their spirits with the medicine of divine teaching.

Moreover we find Christ represented as the Sun God, seated in his chariot in the same manner as the Greeks represented Helios. Here we need not accuse early Christians of sun worship, but should rather see in their symbolism a recognition of the fact that, as St. Ambrose puts it: "What the sun is for the universe, that is Christ for the spiritual structure of the world. Christ is the spiritual Sun."

Jesus is generally represented as beardless, and gives the impression of being twenty to twenty-five years old. His general attitude is one of command and dignity, and he is frequently seen bearing in his hand the magic wand of the Hierophant.

A point which has given rise to much discussion is the frequency of the fish symbol in the decoration of the catacombs. It has often been observed, in explanation of the presence of the fish, that the initial letters of the phrase, in Greek, "Jesus Christ, God's Son, Saviour" form the word Ἰχθυς, meaning "a fish." This fact in itself however is clearly insufficient to account for the popularity of the symbol. It would appear that the early Christians were impressed by the analogy between a fish, which is born in the water, and Jesus and his disciples, who are re-born in the waters of baptism. Thus Tertullian:

> We little fishes (*pisciculi*), after the example of our great fish Jesus Christ our Lord, are born (*gignimur*) in the water, nor are we in a state of salvation except by abiding in the water.

It will be readily understood therefore why the fish-symbol

tended to drop out of use after Christians ceased to teach the re-birth of Jesus in baptism.

A circumstance which may be connected with the frequent reproduction of the fish as a form of decoration is the following. The early artists, when depicting a sacramental repast, do not seem to have usually had in mind any one of the specific incidents detailed in the Gospels, but rather appear to have formed mentally a kind of composite picture made up of (*a*) the Last Supper, (*b*) the miraculous feeding of the multitude with loaves and fishes (Luke ix. 13), and (*c*) the meal of fish and bread offered by Jesus to seven disciples after the resurrection (John xxi. 9).

In a mosaic, believed to date from the sixth century, in the Church of St. Apolinare Nuovo at Ravenna, we see Jesus and twelve apostles seated round a table. On the table are six objects presumably meant to be loaves of bread, but our attention is specially called to two large fishes placed in a very conspicuous position. If the Last Supper be really represented we naturally ask: whence the absence of wine and the prominence given to the fish? In general however we find that in the very early representations seven persons only are depicted as partaking of the mystic banquet. Thus in the Greek chapel in the Priscilla Catacomb we get seven persons sitting round a table and seven baskets of food. In a similar picture in the Callixtus Catacomb we also get seven persons, but with eight baskets of food. In another picture in the same catacomb we again get seven figures, with seven baskets of food and with two large fishes on the table. In the Lucina vault of the same catacomb we find a representation of a fish bearing on its back a basket with six loaves of bread.

So while we have to admit that the exact meaning of these symbols is not wholly clear, it would seem that we are justified in drawing the conclusion that the Last Supper (i.e. the Passover partaken of by Jesus and twelve disciples as described in Matt. xxvi. 26, etc.) did not have quite the same significance to the Roman Christians of the first few centuries of our era as it did to the medieval Church.

Unquestionably the most instructive of the catacomb paintings are those representing typical instances of spiritual transformation or initiation—Noah, Jonah and Lazarus.

The representations of Noah, or to be more exact the pictures and sculptures which are generally said to represent Noah,

FORMATION OF TRADITIONAL CHRISTIANITY 145

give us special food for thought. Noah is represented as being alone in the ark, which is merely a cubical chest, sometimes showing an open lid. This chest never appears very seaworthy, and indeed in one instance, in the Peter and Marcellinus Catacomb, it has four legs, suggesting that the artist possibly did not contemplate its having to float on the water at all. [It is interesting to note that in this fresco Noah appears to be much too young a man to have three married sons.] In all cases Noah is identified by the presence of the dove bearing the olive branch; he generally holds out his arms as if in blessing, and on one occasion, in the Domitilla Catacomb, we actually find him with a pair of wings as if he were about to fly out of the ark.

It may be suggested that some at least of these so-called representations of Noah have really nothing to do with the patriarch, but that the artist may have been merely trying to indicate the attainment of initiation by one of the blessed. It seems possible that in some of the esoteric sects of Gnostic Christians the neophyte may, during the period of unconsciousness referred to on pages 61 and 62, have been kept in a chest in the catacombs, and that the pictures now under consideration may represent him coming out of the chest on attaining initiation.[1] The approaching dove would of course on this hypothesis represent the Holy Spirit descending on the initiate in the same way as the Gospels tell us the Holy Spirit descended on Jesus at his baptism.

The fact that at the present day Roman Catholic nuns are, during the ceremony of taking the veil, instructed to lie down for a time in a coffin, may possibly be a relic of some ceremony of initiation in early Christian times.

The story of Jonah was a favourite one among the early Christians. An excellent example of their treatment of this

---

[1] M. Edouard Schuré (*L'Evolution Divine*) gives his readers some interesting information on the subject of Egyptian initiation. Unfortunately he does not give the authorities for the statements made by him: "In Egypt the initiate after lengthy tests was thrown by the hierophant into a deep sleep and passed three days in a sarcophagus placed in the temple. During this time the physical body became icy cold and had all the appearance of death. . . . When he awoke from this cataleptic sleep induced by the hierophant, the man who stepped from the sarcophagus was no longer the same. He had become a true initiate, a member of the magical chain associated, according to an old inscription, 'with the army of the higher Gods.'"

subject is found on a sarcophagus now in the Lateran Museum at Rome. We here get firstly Jonah being thrown from the ship, secondly his liberation from the whale, and thirdly his repose under the gourd. In each case the figure is nude, and the attitude of dignified ease assumed in the last panel confirms our conclusion that the subject is treated as an allegory, and intended to illustrate firstly the descent of the human soul into the material universe, secondly its liberation therefrom on attaining initiation and thirdly its happy condition after initiation.

A somewhat similar sarcophagus from the Church of S. Maria Antica in the Roman Forum gives us one scene only from the life of Jonah: he has been liberated from the whale and is resting under the gourd, and it is noteworthy that his attitude, which suggests an awakening or re-birth, is strongly reminiscent of that in Michael Angelo's "Creation of Adam" in the Sistine Chapel. The choice of this particular scene from Jonah's life supports the presumption that the sculptor desired to treat the subject as something symbolical. If he had merely desired to represent a striking incident from the Book of Jonah, he would presumably have selected either the prophet being thrown overboard, or his being swallowed by or ejected from the whale. But on the contrary, the sculptor seems to have desired to indicate the less spectacular subject of Jonah after his re-birth to a new life.

Special interest attaches to the manner in which the Raising of Lazarus is treated. We notice on the part of Jesus none of the human weakness suggested in John xi. 33, 35 and 38. On the contrary Christ is represented as a Hierophant pointing in a dignified and commanding manner towards the grave. Lazarus is an upright figure, standing at the entrance to the tomb, and indeed in some representations (notably on a sarcophagus in the Lateran Museum) the tomb itself resembles the chest which we find in the so-called Noah representations, and which, as already suggested, may have been that used in the early Church by candidates for initiation. Lazarus is generally represented as swathed like a mummy, and in some representations even suggests a chrysalis about to become a butterfly.

A very important feature of the various Lazarus representations is the fact that the tomb is always placed at the top of a short flight of steps. This lends weight to the theory, already enunciated, that we are not dealing with physical death and resurrection, but rather with the death unto sin and new birth unto righteousness experienced by the initiate. The steps, which would be out of place if we were dealing with a material tomb, are presumably represented in order to remind us that such death and new birth are not the lot of a mere novice, but that it is only after passing through many preliminary stages and after having gradually raised ourselves to the higher life, that we can be "buried with Christ in baptism," and be also "risen with him through the faith of the operation of God, who hath raised him from the dead" (Col. ii. 12).

CHAPTER VII

CHRISTIANITY AS AN INSTITUTION

In the foregoing pages an attempt has been made to set forth Christianity primarily as the doctrine of the entry into the individual human soul of the Christ Spirit, or, as the Fourth Gospel puts it, of the true light which lighteth every man which cometh into the world. But from the very earliest times Christians have formed a visible community, and the relationship of the individual to the community has been very properly looked on as a matter of great importance. By the end of the second century the increasing claims of the community on the individual had indeed brought about a certain reaction, of which Tertullian (c. 150–c. 230) was a notable exponent. In order to understand these claims we must bear in mind the fact that Christianity as an institution possesses two visible foci, a book and a ministry, and a little consideration of each of these is desirable.

The Book

It would doubtless be more accurate to speak of the Christian Books rather than of the Christian Book, because the early Church used the plural form (τα βιβλια) and if we speak of the Bible as one book, we run the risk of disappointing enquirers, who on investigation fail to find in the compilation that homogeneity which the title suggests.

What we to-day term "the Bible" may be regarded as consisting primarily of five parts, four of which were taken over from the Jews, and only one of which is distinctively Christian. A few words will be said concerning each of these parts.

Part. I. *The Thorah or Pentateuch*

This compilation consists, as indeed the second of the above titles implies, of five books—Genesis, Exodus, Leviticus, Numbers and Deuteronomy. The work is regarded by the Jews as an unique object of their special veneration. No historical account of its compilation exists. (The account given in 4 Esdras xiv. can hardly be accepted as historical.) One can only say that it is believed that the Pentateuch was completed, and accepted as authoritative, not long after 445 B.C.

Part II. The Prophets

This compilation consists of eight books, being four of "Former Prophets"—Joshua, Judges, Samuel, Kings—and four of "Latter Prophets"—Isaiah, Jeremiah, Ezekiel, together with a book containing the work of twelve less important prophetic writers. This compilation was probably completed, and considered as possessing considerable authority about 250 B.C.

Part III. The Sacred Writings or Hagiographa

This compilation consists of three groups:

(a) The poetical books—Psalms, Proverbs, Job.
(b) The "rolls"—Song of Songs, Ruth, Lamentations, Ecclesiastes, Esther (to x. 3).
(c) Three supplementary books: Daniel (i-xii, not including the Song of Azarias given in the Vulgate in chap. iii. 24-90), Ezra and Nehemiah (one book) and Chronicles (or Paralipomena).

The Hagiographa were probably completed between 150 and 100 B.C., but discussion as to exactly what books should be included was still going on in the Jewish schools early in the second century after Christ.

The above three groups form the Jewish canon, and are presumably what was referred to by Jesus as "the law of Moses and the prophets and the psalms" (Luke xxiv. 44). The Jewish manner of grouping the books has not however been followed by Christians.

Part IV. The Apocrypha

The term "Apocrypha" is a somewhat unfortunate one, and has given rise to considerable misunderstanding. The word originally means something hidden or stored away. Hence when we speak of Apocryphal Literature there are three conceivable meanings which we may have in mind: (a) esoteric works of great value, but suitable only for a privileged few, and to be carefully hidden from the ignorant; (b) supplementary works, useful to scholars but not necessary for general use; and (c) works which merit but little respect and credence.

Considerable confusion has arisen from the fact that among early authors examples may be found of the word being used in all three of the above senses. But when a historian speaks of the "Apocryphal Books," he customarily uses the word in the second sense, that is to say that he does not necessarily imply any opinion as to the theological value of the works referred to.

The books customarily referred to by Christians as "the Apocrypha" are: Esdras Books III and IV (Ezra and Nehemiah being reckoned as Esdras Books I and II), Tobit, Judith, Esther x. 4 to xvi. 24 (as given in the Vulgate), Wisdom, Jesus Son of Sirach, Baruch, Daniel iii. 24–90 and xiii–xiv (as given in the Vulgate), Prayer of Manasses, Maccabees Books I and II. All of these works are of Jewish origin but they do not form part of the Jewish canon, and for this reason much discussion took place in the early Church as to whether they should be considered authoritative. It may be said that in general such Christian theologians as were familiar with the Hebrew language were inclined to reject the books in question, while those whose knowledge of the Jewish scriptures was based on the Septuagint gave to the Apocrypha the same respect as was afforded to the Hebrew canon. Augustine accepted the authority of the disputed books. Jerome on the other hand, while attaching a high value to them, denied that they possessed canonical authority. This difference of opinion continued until 1546 when the Council of Trent recognised as sacred and canonical all the apocryphal books above enumerated, with the exception of Esdras III and IV and the Prayer of Manasses.

The tendency of the Protestant Churches has been to attach but little theological importance to the Apocrypha.

Part V. The New Testament

The earliest list of Christian canonical writings (as distinguished from writings accepted by both Christians and Jews) is found in a fragment associated with the name of Muratori, who published it in 1740. The "Muratorian Fragment" is believed to date from the end of the second century, and recognises: Four Gospels, Acts, Thirteen Epistles of Paul, Two Epistles of John, Jude, Apocalypse of John, Apocalypse of Peter. (As regards this last named work, only a few fragments are extant. It contains a description of the dwelling-place and blessings of the righteous, and also of the punishment of the wicked.)

We note the omission from the Muratorian Fragment of the Epistle to the Hebrews, of 3 John, of James and of both the Epistles attributed to Peter.

In the third century we find that nearly all the Churches

accepted 1 Peter, and that the Eastern Churches in general accepted both Hebrews and James. Early in the fourth century Eusebius, when summing up the situation, gives as undoubtedly canonical: Four Gospels, Acts, Pauline Epistles, 1 Peter, 1 John. He thinks that the Apocalypse of John may also be included in this list. He gives as works which are somewhat doubtful, but which are generally accepted: James, Jude, 2 Peter, 2 and 3 John.

The canon of the New Testament as we now have it seems to have been compiled by Athanasius. In 382 a Synod held at Rome under Pope Damasus I accepted the tradition of Athanasius, and the Council "in Trullo" of 692 formally ratified it. From 692 onwards therefore the canon of the New Testament may be regarded as definitely recognised both in the East and West.

The question of the attitude of Protestantism towards the New Testament canon will be touched on when dealing with the Reformation. In this place, however, it may be remarked that Luther rejected as uncanonical Hebrews, James, Jude and the Apocalypse, and placed these books together at the end of his translation of the Bible. On the other hand, Protestants have in general accepted all the books recognised by the Council of 692.

The attitude of the Roman Church with respect to the authority of the canonical scriptures is ably set forth in the Encyclical of Leo XIII on "The Study of Sacred Scripture" (1893). The following extracts are specially noteworthy:

> All the books which the Church receives as sacred and canonical are written wholly and entirely with all their parts, at the dictation of the Holy Spirit; and so far is it from being possible that any error can co-exist with inspiration, that inspiration not only is essentially incompatible with error, but excludes and rejects it as absolutely and necessarily as it is impossible that God himself, the supreme Truth, can utter that which is not true. This is the ancient and unchanging faith of the Church. . . .
>
> Because the Holy Spirit employed men as his instruments, we cannot therefore say that it was these inspired instruments who perchance have fallen into error, and not the primary Author. For by supernatural power he so moved and impelled them to write—he was so present to them—that the things which he ordered, and those only, they first rightly understood, then willed faithfully to write down, and finally expressed in apt

words and with infallible truth. Otherwise it could not be said that he was the Author of the entire Scripture. . . .

It follows that those who maintain that an error is possible in any genuine passage of the sacred writings either pervert the Catholic notion of inspiration, or make God the author of such error. . . .

All the Fathers and Doctors agreed that the Divine writings . . . in their entirety and in all their parts were equally from the afflatus of Almighty God, and that God, speaking by the sacred writers could not set down anything but what was true.

The foregoing sets forth the formal attitude of the Roman Church, although many liberal-minded Roman Catholics adopt, more or less privately, considerable reserve with respect to the papal dicta on the matter. The views adopted by Protestant bodies will be referred to in the section dealing with the Reformation. It is sufficient in this place to say that Protestants would certainly not endorse the words of Leo XIII in so far as they are applicable to the Apocrypha; but with respect to the remainder of the writings which the Roman Church regards as canonical, the old-fashioned orthodox Protestant view harmonises in general with that taken in the papal Encyclical. But on the other hand during the last few decades Protestant thought has become profoundly modified in this respect, and to-day a relatively small number of people, outside the Roman Church, defend what is called the "doctrine of the verbal inspiration of the Scriptures."

It will be observed therefore that the Roman Church has not only strictly defined what books are to be regarded as canonical, but has declared that every part of each of these books was written "at the dictation of the Holy Spirit." Consequently that Church has, here as elsewhere, gradually modified its standpoint, and has ended by defining what early Christians regarded as an open question. As regards the canon of the New Testament the Roman Church to-day enjoins its adherents to accept much which the Church of the first two centuries regarded as highly doubtful. And as regards the degree of respect due to the letter of scripture, we observe the difference in the attitude taken by the Roman Church from that adopted for example by Jesus in Matt. v. 21–48. The dominant note throughout this long passage is "Ye have heard that it was said by them of old time . . . But I say unto you . . .," implying always that while the so-called Mosaic Code may merit our respect as having been useful in its day, a loftier standard was necessary for those who sought union with God through Christ. How different is this position from that taken by the Council of Trent, when it declared that it "receives and venerates with an equal feeling of piety and reverence all the books of the Old and New Testament."

The evils which have resulted from insistence on the doctrine of the verbal inspiration of scripture are patent. Some of them are touched on below:

Firstly, even leaving aside the much vexed question of those incidents (e.g. that of Jonah and the "great fish") which so many readers regard as frankly incredible, it frequently happens that the canonical scriptures deal with wholly unimportant matters, and in these cases an undue burden is laid on the conscience of the reader if he is asked to believe that the text is necessarily free from error. Thus for example when Paul writes to Timothy and mentions having left a cloak with Carpus at Troas (2 Tim. iv. 13), one hesitates to believe that God in this respect specially protected the writer against some trifling lapse of memory.

Secondly, the Roman Church has found itself forced to discourage its laity from a free examination of the scriptures, seeing that such free examination would in a very large number of cases enlighten the reader as to the real nature of the documents in question. A very able Roman Catholic writer, Henri Lasserre, in a work published, with the imprimatur of the Archbishop of Paris, towards the end of last century, rather naïvely laments the practical result of this discouragement. He tells us that the Gospel:

> is very rarely read even by those who profess to be fervent Catholics; never at all by the multitude of the faithful. In fact ask your neighbours and your friends, all who make up your circle, ask yourself my dear reader, and you will not hesitate to affirm, not perhaps without profound astonishment, that for a hundred persons who practise the sacraments, there is often not a single one who has ever opened the Gospels, except at hazard, and to go through or to meditate here and there upon a few isolated verses.

On the other hand Cardinal Manning expresses no such regret:

> Catholics readily admit that they do not go to the text of Scripture for their devotion, as others do who are out of the

unity of the Church. . . . The Church puts into the hands of its people books of devotion which represent the whole order and completeness of revelation, and not the partial and un-ordered aspect of Scripture (*Temporal Mission of the Holy Ghost*).

Thirdly, the belief that every individual sentence in the whole Bible is "equally from the afflatus of Almighty God" has fostered the most unintelligent application of scriptural phrases. It must be admitted however that this is shared by the Jews, and is not an exclusively Christian failing. The New Testament writers were not wholly exempt from this weakness. The Fourth Gospel supplies us with a striking example. Psa. xxxiv. 19, 20 runs: "Many are the afflictions of the righteous, but the Lord delivereth him out of them all: he keepeth all his bones; not one of them is broken." The Fourth Gospel (xix. 36) describing the death of Jesus, and noting that the soldiers did not follow the usual custom by breaking his legs, says: "These things were done that the scripture should be fulfilled, *A bone of him shall not be broken.*" The inappropriateness of the quotation is manifest.

Let us take an example of the use of scripture by the Church at the present time. We read in Genesis (xli. 55) that Pharaoh appointed Joseph, son of Jacob, to be a public official, and when people made application for bread Pharaoh answered "Go to Joseph, what he saith to you, do." And if we to-day enter a Roman Catholic church, we very probably see in a prominent position a statue of Joseph, husband of Mary, with the inscription: *Ite ad Joseph* (Go to Joseph), the text being thus wrested from its context, made to apply to a wholly different individual and to appear to mean: "Apply to Joseph for spiritual consolation."

These examples of the misuse of scripture may seem harmless enough. But what has proved of vital importance in the progress of humanity is the fact that scripture has been quoted, with emphasis and conviction, in support of *inter alia* the Divine Right of Kings, the exemption of all ecclesiastical persons from lay jurisdiction, the burning of witches, slavery, the persecution of heretics and wars of aggression.

Fourthly, the doctrine of the verbal inspiration of Holy Scripture has had a most deplorable effect, partly in repelling potential believers who, unwilling to profess to believe the incredible, have declined to call themselves Christians at all, and partly in forcing vast numbers of professing Christians into an attitude of lukewarm hypocrisy. This is the cause of

CHRISTIANITY AS AN INSTITUTION

the paradoxical attitude taken by Matthew Arnold when he says (*Literature and Dogma*, chap. v):

> One of the very best helps to prepare the way for valuing the Bible and believing in Jesus Christ, is to convince oneself of the liability to mistake in the Bible writers.

And in the preface to the same work he ably says:

> To understand that the language of the Bible is fluid, passing and literary, not rigid, fixed and scientific, is the first step towards a right understanding of the Bible. But to take this very first step, some experience of how men have thought and expressed themselves, and some flexibility of spirit are necessary; and this is culture. After all the Bible is not a talisman to be taken and used literally; neither is any existing Church a talisman, whatever pretensions of the sort it may make, for giving the right interpretation of the Bible. But only true culture can give us this interpretation.

A very reasonable outlook on the question of the inspiration of scripture is indicated in the Prayer Book (as proposed in 1928) of the Church of England. A deacon on being ordained is to be asked:

> Do you unfeignedly believe all the Canonical Scriptures of the Old and New Testament, as given of God to convey to us in many parts and in divers manners the revelation of himself which is fulfilled in our Lord Jesus Christ?

A better formula would be hard to find.

The Christian Ministry

Attention has already been called to the fact that Jesus specially selected twelve of his disciples, and to each of these we customarily give the title of "Apostle," meaning "One sent forth.' The same title was given to Jesus himself by the writer of the Epistle to the Hebrews (iii. 1), and was moreover claimed with some insistence by Paul.

We further read that in the very early days of the Church the disciples, at the suggestion of the Apostles, chose certain men "of honest report, full of the Holy Spirit and wisdom," to attend to such matters as the distribution of alms. On these men the Apostles, after prayer, laid their hands by way of consecration. Hence the foundation of an inferior order of ministers, shortly afterwards called "deacons," a word believed to mean "messengers."

156 INTRODUCTION TO THE STUDY OF CHRISTIANITY

Some little time later we read that Paul and Barnabas when on their journeys "ordained elders in every church." The word "elder" is sometimes substituted by "presbyter," which is the English form of the Greek word, but this word "presbyter" is commonly contracted into "priest." The early Presbyters were also called "Overseers" (ἐπισκοποι, or Bishops). [By comparing Acts xx. verse 17 with verse 28, it is clearly seen that "Bishops" (ἐπισκοπους) and "Elders" (πρεσβυτερους) are synonymous terms.] In later years, after death had removed the original members of the Apostolic band, the Bishops and Priests (or Overseers and Elders) came to be considered as two different orders. The Ministry remained threefold, but instead of consisting of Apostles, Bishops (or Priests) and Deacons, it was made up of Bishops, Priests and Deacons.

The functions of the Bishops and Priests consisted of teaching and exhorting the faithful, baptising converts and infants, and generally conducting the public offices of the Church, including of course presiding at the sacred rite of breaking of the bread, or Lord's Supper. When the two orders came to be regarded as separate, the title Bishop was given to the chief minister in a town or district, and no minister other than he could lawfully appoint new priests or deacons. Hence there arose the doctrine of what came to be called the Apostolical Succession, it being taught that Jesus laid his hands on his personal disciples, that they in turn laid their hands on others, and so the grace of the Holy Spirit has been handed down in an unbroken succession, from Bishop to Bishop, until our own day. Hence the existence of the duly consecrated Bishop is understood to form a kind of outward sign of the presence of the true Church. This idea can be traced back to very early times. Thus Irenaeus:

> The true knowledge (i.e. *the Christian religion*) is the doctrine of the Apostles, and the ancient system of the Church in all the world, and the character of the body of Christ, according to the succession of the Bishops, to whom they (i.e. *the Apostles*) delivered the Church in each separate place.

And again Ignatius in his Epistle to the Church at Smyrna says: "Where the bishop appears, there let the people be; as where is Christ Jesus, there is the Catholic Church."

It is obvious that numerous advantages accrued to Christianity from the institution of a formal ministry. And in order to appreciate the magnitude of these advantages it is not necessary to tie ourselves down to the traditional view that a minister, from the moment that the Bishop lays his hands on him, receives a special gift of the Holy Spirit enabling him to discharge adequately his duties. Even leaving out of the discussion the question of the spiritual efficacy of the laying-on of hands, it is clear that it is of great practical advantage that in each congregation one man should be able to say "I am the minister (or chief minister) of this congregation," with the same assurance as that with which the captain of a vessel claims the right to command the crew. It is difficult to see how, during its many centuries of struggle, Christianity could have survived at all had it not possessed a regularly constituted ministry.

But at the same time we are compelled to admit that the practical disadvantages have also proved to be very great. Members of the sacred ministry soon came to consider themselves as a distinct caste, having the right to live at the people's expense, but on the other hand they not infrequently failed to recognise their corresponding duties towards those who should have formed their flocks. And very many members of the priestly caste came to regard as their primary duty the acquisition of wealth and power for their order, to the almost complete neglect of their apostolic mission.

On this subject we are reminded how Milton writes of—

> . . . such as for their bellies' sake
> Creep and intrude, and climb into the fold.
> Of other care they little reck'ning make
> Than how to scramble at the shearers' feast,
> And shove away the worthy bidden guest.
> Blind mouthes! that scarce themselves know how to hold
> A Sheep-hook, or have learn'd aught els the least
> That to the faithfull Herdman's art belongs.
>   (*Lycidas.*)

So the Christian priesthood came in time to present a certain analogy with the Jewish. We find that Hebrew prophets arose, both within and without the sacerdotal order, to condemn the priestly abuses of their day. Jeremiah, himself a priest, stood at the gate of the Temple and cried "Is this house which is called by my name become a den of robbers?" (vii. 2 and 11). Zephaniah complained that the priests had polluted the sanctuary and done violence to the law (iii. 4). Malachi said "And now O ye priests . . . ye are departed out of the way; ye have caused many to stumble at the law; ye have corrupted the covenant . . . therefore have I also made you contemptible and base" (ii. 1, 8, 9). In much the same way did Savonarola and Latimer lift up their voices against the abuses current among the priesthood in their respective generations, and both suffered at the stake the penalty of their courage.

We must be prepared therefore for the fact that if we study the history of Christianity we shall find two opposing tendencies, one of which lies in the direction of order, tradition, discipline, authority, orthodoxy and obedience: this is the priestly tendency. On the other hand there are many who lift up their voices like the Hebrew prophets of old, and are consumed with righteous indignation at the abuses brought about by the sacerdotal system. Such men feel working in themselves that Spirit which Jesus compared to the wind which bloweth where it listeth, and they cannot see the need for divine truths being rigidly defined by professed theologians, neither can they contemplate things of the Spirit being bought and sold. In their reluctance however to admit human authority in spiritual matters, they have in the past unhappily destroyed much that was worthy of being preserved. If the Church had been made up wholly of men influenced by the former tendency, it would have become as crystallised as Brahmanism. If it had been made up wholly of men influenced by the latter, it would have had no visible permanent organisation and must, we may fairly infer, in a few centuries have ceased to exist.

In the history of the struggle between these tendencies the prominent part on the side of tradition was from quite early days taken by the See of Rome, and it is therefore desirable to devote a section to this subject.

The See of Rome

We have already seen that Christianity was a religion founded by Galileans, who presumably spoke Aramaic. Owing to certain circumstances however, Jerusalem, the place of the death of the founder, came to be regarded as the headquarters of the new body and, as has already been described, it was at Jerusalem that the first General Council was held. But after the sack of Jerusalem in 70 Rome, the metropolis of the world, gradually assumed that preponderating position formerly possessed by the former city.

Now the Church of Rome is first known to us as a kind of Greek-speaking colony in the great Latin metropolis. The

CHRISTIANITY AS AN INSTITUTION 159

theology of the Church was Greek, and the offices were said in Greek. Relics of these Greek-speaking days are still to be found in the current prayer books of the Roman Church, where we get Greek sentences, looking very strange in their Roman characters, in the middle of the Latin offices. Thus in the service for Good Friday we get the following versicles and responses:

> *Deacon.* Agios ischyros.
> *Sub-Deacon.* Sanctus Fortis.
> *Deacon.* Agios athanatos, eleison imas.
> *Sub-Deacon.* Sanctus immortalis, miserere nobis.

It naturally happens that, seeing that in the majority of cases Latin and Greek, when sung or spoken, are equally unintelligible to the bulk of the congregation, but little practical inconvenience results from the mixing of the two languages.

Exactly why and when the Roman Church adopted the Latin language we do not know, but the event seems to have taken place before the middle of the third century. And we also find, as indeed might have been expected, that the Roman Church came to be permeated with Latin ideals, and consequently while taking but little interest in those philosophical and theological subtleties which delighted the Greek fathers, eventually came to be the great exponent of the principles of law, order, discipline and obedience.

The prominent position enjoyed by the Church of Rome was of course primarily the result of political and geographical considerations, seeing that Rome formed a meeting-place for men of all nations. Thus we see for example that Irenaeus (iii. 3), when finding it necessary for his argument to select as an illustration a typical Western Church, chooses Rome

> for to this church on account of her superior pre-eminence it must need be that every church should come together (or *be brought in contact?*) that is the faithful from all sides; and in this Church the tradition from the Apostles has always been preserved (*not as elsewhere by a merely local body but*) by men from all parts.

The origin of the primacy of the Roman See is further indicated with clearness in Canon xxviii of the Ecumenical Council of Chalcedon (451) which runs:

> The fathers have properly allowed the precedency to the throne of Old Rome, because it was the imperial city, and the

150 Bishops (*at Constantinople*) being moved with the same intention, assigned the equal precedency to the most holy throne of New Rome (i.e. *Constantinople*) judging with reason that the city which was honoured with the sovereignty and senate and enjoyed equal precedency with the elder imperial Rome, should also be magnified like her in ecclesiastical matters, being the second after her.

But the foregoing, although embodied in a formal Canon of an Ecumenical Council, by no means harmonised with the contention of the Bishops of Rome and their partisans. They put forward the claim that the primacy of the See of Rome has nothing to do with the political condition of the city, but results from a divine command and forms an integral part of the Christian religion. This claim eventually came to rest on the three following propositions:

(i) Jesus Christ made Peter the vice-regent of the Church, having unlimited powers in matters of administration, and being also the infallible exponent of divine truth with respect to both faith and morals.
(ii) The office conferred on Peter is not merely personal, but passes in an orderly manner from successor to successor. So he who denies allegiance to the holder of Peter's office cuts himself off from membership in the Church of Christ.
(iii) Peter was the first Bishop of Rome, and the occupants of the See of Rome are the successors of Peter in the sense of Proposition (ii).

The above form what are known as the "Petrine Claims" and the following section is devoted to their discussion.

The Petrine Claims

Few visitors to Rome can fail to be impressed by the colossal inscription, in blue mosaic letters six feet high, surrounding the dome of the Basilica of S. Pietro in Vaticano: TU ES PETRUS ET SUPER HANC PETRAM ÆDIFICABO ECCLESIAM MEAM ET TIBI DABO CLAVES REGNI CŒLORUM. (Thou art Peter and on this rock I will build my church and I will give thee the keys of the kingdom of the heavens.) The extraordinary prominence given to this inscription reminds us forcibly of the immense importance attached to the words by Roman controversialists; so our examination of the Petrine Claims may conveniently

CHRISTIANITY AS AN INSTITUTION

commence with an enquiry as to the extent to which this importance is justified.

Before attempting a direct reply it is of interest to point out that there is a distinct discrepancy between the evangelists as regards the ostensible attitude of Jesus with respect to his Messiahship. The Fourth Gospel represents Andrew, immediately after his first meeting with Jesus, as referring to the Master, apparently without any suggestion of secrecy, as "the Messias, which is being interpreted, the Christ." And we similarly read in the same Gospel that Jesus, towards the commencement of his ministry, at a chance meeting with a Samaritan woman, declared to her unequivocally that he was in fact the Christ. This seems to dispose definitely of any possibility of the writer of the Gospel believing that Jesus had attempted to keep secret the fact of his Messianic mission.

But on the other hand the synoptic evangelists represent Jesus as preserving considerable reticence on this point. All three (Matt. xvi. 13–20, Mark viii. 27–30, Luke ix. 18–21) tell us that on a certain occasion he asked his disciples what their opinion was of him, and that Peter replied recognising him as the Christ. All three agree in adding that Jesus commanded his disciples to preserve secrecy as to this fact, but Matthew tells us a good deal further, for he represents Jesus as saying:

> Blessed art thou Simon Bar Jona for flesh and blood hath not revealed it unto thee, but my Father which is in heaven. And I say also unto thee that THOU ART PETER AND UPON THIS ROCK I WILL BUILD MY CHURCH AND THE GATES OF HELL SHALL NOT PREVAIL AGAINST IT. And I will give unto thee the keys of the kingdom of heaven; and whatsoever thou shalt bind on earth shall be bound in heaven; and whatsoever thou shalt loose on earth shall be loosed in heaven.

We are struck by a certain analogy between the discrepancies in the above accounts and those existing in the different accounts of the crucifixion (*vide* pp. 20–21). It will be remembered that the Fourth Gospel gives us the simplest and most natural of the four narratives of the death of Jesus, that Mark and Luke put in a detail which inspires somewhat less confidence, and that Matthew adds matter which many people feel inclined to regard as frankly incredible. Similarly as regards the teaching of Jesus with respect to his mission: the account of the Fourth Gospel appeals to us as being wholly credible: those of Mark and Luke as perhaps a little less so, while as regards the additional matter introduced by Matthew, readers frequently feel a certain inclination to be sceptical.

Leaving aside however the question of the reliability of Matt. xvi. 17-19, and assuming the words in question to be really spoken by Jesus, we now come to investigate their meaning. It is clear that Jesus calls attention to the importance of the truth confessed by Peter, affirms that the truth was revealed to Peter by God himself, and promises Peter a high spiritual dignity as a reward.

It will be more convenient to deal at once with the sentence commencing: *And I will give unto thee, etc.* Here the situation seems fairly plain. Jesus, in the presence of the other Apostles, promises to Peter the powers of spiritually binding and loosing, and we find that, as already explained in a former chapter, Jesus after his resurrection actually conferred these powers on "the disciples," presumably including Peter.

Thus Theophylact (d. *c.* 1110) commenting on the above says very pertinently:

> Those who have obtained the grace of the Episcopate, as Peter had, have authority to remit and bind. For though the *I will give thee* was spoken to Peter alone, yet the gift has been given to all the Apostles. When? When he said *Whosesoever sins ye remit they are remitted.* For this *I will give* indicates a future time, the time that is after the resurrection (*in Matt.*, Hom. lxv).

We have now to consider the words:

> Blessed art thou Simon Bar Jona for flesh and blood hath not revealed it (i.e. the truth that I am the Christ) unto thee, but my Father which is in heaven. And I say unto thee that thou art Peter and upon this rock I will build my Church.

The key-note of the foregoing is apparently the word *it*: it is the truth that Jesus is the Christ which forms the rock on which the Church will be built. So the text quoted may be paraphrased as follows: Blessed art thou Simon, for the truth as to my Messiahship was revealed to thee not by man but by God. Thou art a Stone ($\Pi\epsilon\tau\rho\sigma$) and the truth thou hast just confessed is a Rock ($\Pi\epsilon\tau\rho\alpha$) and forms indeed the rock on which I will build my Church.

Thus John Chrysostom, commenting on this passage, says: "*On the rock,* that is on the faith of Peter's confession"; and, again a little farther on he speaks of Christ as having built "his Church on his (Peter's) confession" (Hom. lxxxii).

A second interpretation has been suggested, it being proposed to paraphrase the text in question as follows: *Thou art Peter, a stone, and it is this stone and stones like thee that form the rock on which I will build my Church.* Or to put the same idea into more colloquial English: *You are the sort of man that I choose for building up my Church.* This interpretation harmonises with the Book of Revelation (xxi. 14) which, when describing a vision of the Church triumphant, says that "the wall of the city had twelve foundations, and in them the names of the twelve apostles of the Lamb." We find that Origen seems to adopt this second interpretation. His words are:

> But if you think the whole church built upon Peter alone, what will you say of John, the son of thunder, or each one of the Apostles? Are we to dare to say that the gates of hell shall not prevail against Peter only, but that against the other Apostles, and those who are perfect, they shall prevail? Are not the quoted words *The gates of hell shall not prevail against it* and *Upon this rock I will build my Church* said of them all, and of each single one of them? Are the keys of the kingdom of heaven given to Peter only, and shall no other one of the blessed men receive them? And if the words *I will give to thee the keys of the kingdom of heaven* are common to the others, how are not all the words, said before and said after, said as they seem to be to Peter, also common to the others? For in this place the words *Whatsoever thou shalt bind on earth* seem as if they were spoken to Peter. But in the Gospel of John, the Saviour giving the Holy Spirit to the disciples by means of the breath says *Receive ye the Holy Spirit*, etc., etc. (*in Matt.*).

A third interpretation is: *Thy name Peter, suggests a rock, and thou formest the rock on which I will build my Church.* This is the interpretation adopted by Roman Catholic theologians, and it is the reason of the extraordinary prominence, already referred to, given to the words in question. But the same interpretation has been also adopted by writers who are by no means partisans of the papal claims. Thus St. Cyprian (d. 258) in his treatise *De Unitate*, while holding emphatically that "the other Apostles were what Peter was, endowed with an equal fellowship both of honour and power," and while affirming that "the Lord after his resurrection gives equal power to all the Apostles," nevertheless teaches that he built his Church upon one (i.e. Peter) to "make the unity of his Church plain."

And again Augustine in his earlier writings understands the

Rock to be Peter, though he subsequently modified this view in favour of the theory that the Rock is Christ as confessed by Peter. It is indeed clear that there are weighty difficulties in the way of accepting Cyprian's interpretation, irreconcilable as it is, as we have already seen, with the Book of Revelation, and, as we shall see shortly, with the Pauline Epistles. It is obvious that the maximum authority that Jesus could conceivably have given Peter would have been to have appointed him, and him only, as his (Jesus') successor, with the same divinely conferred powers as he (Jesus) himself had exercised when on earth. But in the disputed passage, Jesus, according to the Roman interpretation, compares his relationship to Peter with that of a builder with respect to a foundation. And clearly the relationship between the originator of a religion and his successor is radically different from that between a builder and a foundation. It is indeed quite incomprehensible that the originator of a religion could be said to build his Church on one disciple, however eminent. If an intelligent man, wholly ignorant of the history of Christianity, were told that Jesus had built his Church on Peter (alone), he would unquestionably understand that Peter was the earlier of the two teachers, that Jesus had borrowed the doctrines of Peter, probably making some modifications of his own, and had possibly attracted to himself a nucleus of followers drawn from Peter's disciples. So it would really be less misleading to say that Jesus founded his Church on John the Baptist than that he founded it on Peter.

The position of the Roman controversialists is that while admittedly Jesus personally founded the Church by conferring certain functions on firstly the twelve and secondly the seventy (Luke x), he nevertheless entrusted the government to Peter, just as the government of a vessel is entrusted to the captain. Now no unprejudiced reader can, from a study of the various books of the New Testament, fail to see that Peter did not act as if he had been so entrusted. But the immediate point that it is here desired to make is that if Jesus had intended to transmit this pre-eminent authority to Peter, he must have chosen other words in which to express himself, because there is nothing in the metaphor of a builder using a foundation to suggest the appointment of a (single) successor.

If we interpret the words "On this rock will I build my Church" as the Roman apologists desire us to interpret them, how clumsy and ill-chosen does the language of Jesus appear when compared with that of Paul (Eph. ii. 20), who uses the same metaphor. The Apostle to the Gentiles speaks of the Church as being built upon the foundation of the apostles and prophets, Jesus Christ himself being the chief corner-stone. About this language there is no ambiguity, neither can there be any question as to its perfect propriety. Paul makes it clear that the Church is built primarily upon Jesus himself, and secondarily upon the apostles and prophets collectively.

We consequently ask ourselves exactly what position Peter actually did occupy. In view of the controversy that this subject has raised, it will be convenient to examine both the words of Jesus other than those contained in Matt. xvi, and the testimony of other New Testament writers including Peter himself. Let us take these in order:

Emphasis is laid by Roman controversialists on the passage (Luke xxii. 32) in which Jesus says that he has prayed for Peter that his faith fail not, going on to enjoin him, when converted, to strengthen his brethren. This however hardly needs discussion. The passage is introductory to Jesus' prophecy of Peter's denial. It is reasonable to see in the words of Jesus an evidence of his affection for Peter, but impossible to conclude that the incident in any other way raised his status with respect to his fellow Apostles.

Further emphasis is laid on the threefold pastoral charge given to Peter (John. xxi. 15-17). Here however the purport of the words of Jesus is clearly to convey to Peter the fact that he has been forgiven for denying his master. The injunction to *Feed my sheep* conveys no increase in the full apostolic authority which, as we are told in the previous chapter, "the disciples" had already received (John xx. 21). To argue that the words *Feed my sheep* increase the authority conveyed in the words *As my Father hath sent me even so send I you* is as if we were to argue that Nelson's signal *England expects every man to do his duty* in some way implied an extension of the existing powers and functions of those to whom it was addressed. The Father had sent Jesus to give spiritual food to the human flock, and this commission Jesus formally transferred to "the disciples." To remind one erring disciple of his duty in no way detracted from the commission already entrusted to the others.

On this subject it is interesting to quote St. Cyril of Alexandria (d. 444):

> Through the thrice repeated confession of the blessed Peter, was annulled his sin in thrice denying: and through our Lord

saying *Feed my lambs* there is conceived to be a sort of restoration of the apostolate already given to him.

There is nothing in either of the two Epistles attributed to Peter to suggest that he claimed any authority which was not shared by the other Apostles. Moreover at the Council of Jerusalem, to which reference has already been made, it will be noted that Peter seems to have really taken a less prominent part than might have been expected in view of the fact that the Council was indirectly brought about on account of a vision granted to him. We find that he, although an important speaker, apparently neither opened nor closed the proceedings. The president was undoubtedly James, who pronounced the final decision with the phrase: "My sentence is." And the formal letters containing the decision of the Council were issued in the name of "The Apostles and elders and brethren" (Acts xv. 23), there being throughout no hint of any special authority belonging to Peter. Moreover in Acts viii. 14 we read that the Apostles which were at Jerusalem sent Peter and John to Samaria. This again is quite inconsistent with the contention that Peter possessed an authority not shared by his fellow Apostles.

It may be convenient to note that the Roman theologians have eventually felt themselves obliged to take up the position that to Peter alone was given the pastorate of souls, and that whatever authority the Apostles and other Christian ministers possess, they receive not directly from Christ but indirectly from Christ through Peter. This theory seems to have been first expressed by St. Leo (Pope 440–461):

> Great and wonderful is the fellowship in its own power which the divine condescension gave to this man. And if it willed the other rulers of the Church to have anything in common with him, it only gave through him whatever it did not withhold from the others (*Serm.* iv. 2).

And again:

> The mystery of this gift the Lord willed to belong to the office of all the Apostles in such sense that he made Blessed Peter, the chief of all the Apostles, the original depositary of it, and that he wills that from him as from a sort of Head, the gifts should flow down into the whole Body (*Ep.* x. 1).

In reply to the above it seems enough to say that not only is there a complete absence of any support in scripture for such

CHRISTIANITY AS AN INSTITUTION

a theory, but the language of Paul definitely opposes it. Paul recognised in Peter no authority in which he himself did not share, although it is true that he regarded the gospel of the circumcision as specially committed unto Peter, while that of the uncircumcision was committed unto himself (Gal. ii. 7). And he refers to "James and Cephas and John" as pillars of the Church (Gal. ii. 9). But both of these passages, while admitting that a very high degree of dignity is due to Peter, are wholly opposed to the Roman contention that the Church was built on Peter and on Peter alone.

Paul is emphatic in declaring that he is an apostle not of men neither by man, but by Jesus Christ and God the Father (Gal. i. 1), and that the gospel which was preached of him is not after man (Gal. i. 11). When indeed one considers the unique importance of Paul's work, and the many signs and wonders with which God is stated to have shown his appreciation of this work, one reflects that, had it suited the Roman argument, as good a case might perhaps have been made out for the primacy of Paul as for that of Peter. We can imagine the emphasis with which the ultramontane controversialists would, if it had suited their purpose, have stressed the message of the angel to Paul: "God hath given thee all them that sail with thee" (Acts xxvii. 24).

We are now able to sum up our conclusions as to the position of Peter among the Apostles. During the lifetime of Jesus, Peter's strong personality and the affection inspired by him made him generally, but not always, the chief and mouthpiece of the band. During the period immediately subsequent to the Resurrection, Peter fully maintained this position. At the Council of Jerusalem however he appears to have occupied no place of special pre-eminence, and in later years he seems as it were to drop out of the narrative, while Paul tends more and more to become the central figure. But when Peter was at the height of his powers he does not appear to have possessed any actual authority over his colleagues of the Apostolic college.

The foregoing portion of this section has been written by way of answer to Proposition (i) set forth on page 160. We now come to consider Proposition (ii) which is to the effect that Peter occupied an office, and as the existence of this office is necessary to the well-being of the Church, it is unreasonable to suppose that the office became extinct on the death of the office-bearer. To this it may be replied that Peter's position in the Church depended partly on his office and partly on his personal qualities. His eloquent tongue and striking personality gave him the informal, but unquestioned, leadership of the Apostolic band. But just as these personal qualities died with him, so died that special form of leadership which he had acquired. It would be as unreasonable to look for a successor of John the Baptist, or of either of the two Sons of Thunder, as for one of Peter.

We should naturally expect to find that, among the Bishops who have taken the place of the immediate followers of Jesus, there should be differences of rank and precedence. No group of human beings whose members are in close contact one with another, can long exist without someone becoming, formally or informally, its leader. But such precedence as any one Bishop may enjoy is not one which vitiates the fact that those who accept the principle of the Apostolic Succession ought logically to hold that each duly consecrated member of the episcopal body has received the full apostolic commission. In other words the doctrine of the Apostolic Succession seems to entail the principle that the spiritual rank of all Bishops is equal. Thus St. Jerome who was at one time papal secretary, and who was consistently a fervent supporter of the Roman see, nevertheless tells us (*Ep.* cxlvi):

> If it is a question of authority, the world is greater than the city. Wherever there is a bishop, at Rome, or at Gubbio, or at Constantinople, or at Reggio, or at Alexandria, or at Tanis, he has the same standing (*meritum*), the same priesthood. The power of wealth or the humility of poverty do not make a bishop higher or lower. They are all successors of the Apostles.

We now come to examine the third of the propositions set forth on page 160, i.e. that Peter became Bishop of Rome. Here we are dealing not with theological conjectures but with a question of alleged fact: there exists evidence to the effect that Peter founded the Christian Church at Rome, and we consequently enquire whether or no this evidence is conclusive.

Firstly, attention has been drawn to a passage in Peter's Epistle addressed to certain Asiatic Churches. The author (1 Pet. v. 13) gives his readers to understand that he is writing from Babylon, and it is alleged that the name "Babylon" was used by early Christians instead of "Rome" as a term of contempt and hatred. Consequently it is argued that we ought to understand that Peter really wrote not from Babylon but

CHRISTIANITY AS AN INSTITUTION

from Rome. This line of argument drew from Voltaire the remark:

> Acute and shrewd canonists have contended that by Babylon we ought to understand Rome; and upon the same principle if he had dated from Rome, we might have concluded that the letter had been written at Babylon. Men have long been in the habit of drawing such reasonable and judicious inferences as these, and it is in this manner that the world has been governed (*Dict. Philosophique*).

Indeed the very sane and well balanced tone in which Peter writes makes us indisposed to think that he is referring to Rome when he says Babylon. If hatred of the Roman government and Roman institutions had been a dominant thought in his mind, he would hardly have referred to civil rulers with the evident sympathy shown in a former portion of the Epistle in question (ii. 13 and 14). Moreover we should not forget that if Peter was actually at Babylon, it would be natural enough that he should address the Asiatic Churches. But if he was at Rome we know of no special reason why his first Epistle should not have been addressed to the Church generally, as was for example the second Epistle attributed to him.

The second allegation with respect to Peter's residence in Rome is the statement that he used to conduct divine service in the house of Pudens (*vide* 2 Tim. iv. 21). The present church of St. Pudenziana in the Via Urbana is by tradition the oldest in Rome, and is said to be built on the site of the house of Pudens, to be dedicated to his daughter, and to contain relics of a table on which Peter used to celebrate the Lord's Supper. This however can hardly be called evidence. If in point of fact Peter used to officiate at the house in question, why should the church, when eventually built, be dedicated to St. Pudenziana rather than to St. Peter? We do not hear of any church at Rome being dedicated to St. Peter in the very early days of Christianity. Constantine (Emp. 306–337) seems to have founded the Cathedral Church, first dedicated to St. Saviour and afterwards to St. John the Baptist. This church is styled the mother and head of all churches of the city and world (*omnium urbis et orbis ecclesiarum mater et caput*). The Church of S. Pietro in Vaticano is built on the site of Nero's Circus, where the Apostle is said to have suffered martyrdom, but there is no obvious reason for assigning a very early date to its foundation.

It appears that the first of the Fathers to mention the origin of the Roman Church is Irenaeus, who regarded Peter and Paul as the joint founders. This is undoubtedly weighty evidence, but hardly conclusive. Irenaeus probably came to Rome nearly a century after the death of Peter, and we do not know what means he possessed of verifying any current tradition as to the Apostle's martyrdom. (We have already seen that Irenaeus was probably mistaken in believing the Fourth Gospel to be the work of John.)

We have therefore investigated the "Petrine claims" and find that they rest on three propositions, each one of which is necessary for their justification. We have found the first two propositions to be unfounded and the third doubtful.

There is however a further argument which calls for attention as being commonly used in support of the Roman claims. Put with extreme brevity this argument is to the effect that Jesus founded one visible Church to serve as a fountain of divine truth, and that indeed it would be unreasonable to suppose that God, having done so much to reveal himself to mankind, would not continue his work by providing the human race with some supernal, but visible, guide. If this guide be a corporate body, it must have a visible head and mouthpiece, otherwise it cannot fulfil its mission of expressing divine truth. Such mouthpiece can, it is further argued, be none other than the Bishop of Rome.

Several considerations can be adduced against this contention:

(i) It is exceedingly dangerous to affirm *a priori* what God may be expected to do. If on the morning of All Saints' Day 1755 a pious inhabitant of Lisbon had been told, when on his way to church, that in a few hours some forty thousand of his fellow-townsmen would be killed, and the city itself would be a heap of ruins, he would very possibly have replied that it would be blasphemous to suppose that God would permit so awful a catastrophe. But "Who hath known the mind of the Lord?" asks Paul on two occasions (Rom. xi. 34, 1 Cor. ii. 16), on one of which he adds "But we have the mind of Christ." The Christ Spirit is our guide with respect to all such truth as is necessary for our salvation. But the ultimate purpose of Almighty God is hidden from our eyes, and we cannot predict the means whereby such purpose will be accomplished.

(ii) It will be observed that the early Christians regarded the various local Churches as forming collectively a witness to the truth once revealed, but orthodox believers by no means regarded either the Church as a whole or any individual Bishop as a fountain of new truth. For them the truth was once for all delivered (Jude 3) and Paul pushes emphasis to extreme limits when he reiterates his anathema on anyone who shall preach a new Gospel (Gal. i. 6–9). The early Fathers unquestionably support this attitude. Thus the *Commonitorium* of St. Vincent of Lérins (d. *c.* 450), a work enjoying very high authority, states: "To teach anything to Catholic Christians besides (*praeter*) what they have received, has never been allowed, is nowhere allowed, never will be allowed." And in another place: "The Church of Christ with respect to dogmas changes nothing, diminishes nothing, adds nothing." It will be observed that Vincent does not condemn merely what is contrary to the old faith, but what is additional thereto. And until the Vatican Council of 1870 the foregoing was the opinion of many (if not most) enlightened Roman Catholics. Thus Keenan's *Controversial Catechism* (1846) gives the following question and answer:

Can a General Council frame new matters or articles of faith?

No: a General Council can only explain what has already been revealed: it belongs to God only to reveal new articles of faith.

On the other hand Innocent I (Pope 402–417) and various of his successors took the view that God had committed to the see of Peter secret stores of divine truth to be utilised by the Pope for the good of the Church in times of necessity. To this pretension it may be replied (*a*) that it has no scriptural authority; (*b*) that it was unknown to the very early Fathers, and (*c*) that at no time of the Church's history was it universally admitted.

It is true that we read that Jesus said to his disciples:

The Holy Spirit shall teach you all things (John xiv. 26). The Spirit of truth shall testify of me (John xv. 26). The Spirit of truth will guide you into all truth (John. xvi. 13).

But in these passages there is no hint of the Holy Spirit operating by means of the Bishop of Rome or of any other specially authorised mouthpiece. It may be not out of place to remind ourselves that from Acts xv. 23 we learn that when the early Church decided to take formal corporate action, its decree was issued by "The Apostles and elders and brethren" collectively.

(iii) It may further be said that belief in the divine inspiration of papal utterances has actually opened up almost as many points of dispute as it has resolved. No school of theology makes such belief applicable to the Pope's everyday conversation. We have already remarked that believers in the verbal inspiration of the scriptures find themselves obliged to accept as divinely dictated Paul's statement that he left a cloak with Carpus at Troas, but no one holds that casual utterances of this nature are inspired when coming from the Pope's mouth. Where then is the line to be drawn? The Vatican Council of 1870 laid down the dogma that the Pope is infallible when

> in his character as Pastor and Doctor of all Christians, and in virtue of his supreme apostolic authority, he lays down that a certain doctrine concerning faith or morals is binding upon the universal Church.

Now many, probably most, Roman theologians argue that when the Pope, acting officially (or as it is generally expressed *ex cathedrâ*), publicly proclaims a certain doctrine as being true, it is not essential for him explicitly to add that belief therein "is binding upon the universal Church." Such theologians tend therefore to extol the papal authority and to extend the Pope's alleged infallibility to all his formal dicta concerning faith and morals. Thus Monseigneur de Ségur tells us: "The Pope is Jesus Christ on earth. He is relatively to Christ, as regards authority, what Christ is with respect to God his Father" (*Le Souverain Pontife*). Again Cardinal Patrizi claims that an Encyclical of Pius IX is "the very word of God, to be received on pain of forfeiting heaven."

But there exists a much more moderate school of Catholic theologians who restrict belief in papal infallibility to the precise terms of the Vatican Decree. Dr. Auguste Boudinhon, Professor of Canon Law at the Catholic University of Paris, in his article on "Infallibility" contributed to the *Encyclopædia Britannica*, states, with evident sympathy, that those who hold this moderate opinion:

> have been able to assert that since the Vatican Council no infallible definition had yet been formulated by the popes, while recognising the supreme authority of the encyclicals of Leo XIII.

It will be seen therefore how greatly weakened is the argument that the Papacy, as a fountain of divine truth, is a source of help and comfort to the faithful. On the very rare

CHRISTIANITY AS AN INSTITUTION

occasions when the Pope expressly imposes a new dogma on the Church (as was done in 1854, when the doctrine of the Immaculate Conception of the Blessed Virgin was promulgated), undoubtedly all Roman Catholics are obliged to accept the papal ruling, in the teeth of St. Paul, St. Vincent of Lérins and the early Fathers who held that the faith could not be added to. But with respect to other papal utterances, discussion is always liable to arise as to whether or no it is permissible to question their divine authority. The practical benefit to the Roman Church is therefore but slight.

(iv) We now come to consider the affirmation that the Church of Christ is one visible body, and that the test of membership of this body is allegiance to the See of Rome. This doctrine is carried to its logical conclusion in a dogma imposed on the Roman Church by Boniface VIII (Pope 1294–1303): "We declare, define and pronounce it to be absolutely necessary for salvation that every human being should submit himself to the Roman Pontiff." (*Porro subesse romani pontifici omnem humanam creaturam declaramos, definimus et pronunciamus omnino esse de necessitate salutis.*)

But if we reflect on the nature of the unity of the Church we shall very possibly form an opinion wholly opposed to that implied in the above dogma. In the first place it may be well to call attention to the distinction between the unity of a body and union among its individual members. For example, if a son quarrels with his father and leaves the paternal roof, the union of the family is impaired but its unity is not. The unity of a family is something essential, and results from consanguinity: consequently quarrels among the members, however lamentable they may be, do not impair this unity. It can reasonably be contended therefore that similarly the unity of the Church is something essential, and results from the fact that the Church is the Spirit-bearing body, or in other words the blessed company of all faithful people: he who is endued with the Holy Spirit is a member of Christ's Church.

To affirm the foregoing is not to deny the necessity for a visible Church served by a properly organised ministry. The great majority of anti-Roman writers argue that it is right and proper that the individual should submit himself for instruction to such Church, and should outwardly conform to its usages. Such writers admit that much harm has been done by the temerity with which zealous reformers have in the past broken with established usage, and brought about schism in the Church.

But nevertheless they maintain that the true Church of Christ consists of all those who have received, to a greater or less extent, the gift of the Holy Spirit, and the true Christian ministry consists of those to whom has been imparted the capacity for irradiating that gift among their fellow-beings. And the responsibility for schism will, it is argued, very frequently be seen to lie, not so much with those who have felt forced to separate themselves from their fellow Christians, as with those so-called ministers of the Church whom Milton describes as

> Blind mouthes, that scarce themselves know how to hold
> A sheephook or have learnt ought els the least
> That to the faithfull Herdman's art belongs.

The Progress of Institutional Christianity

In the preceding pages an attempt has been made to exhibit Christianity as manifesting two strongly opposed tendencies. Those who are decisively influenced by the one tendency may take as their motto the dogma, as decreed by Boniface VIII, that it is necessary for the salvation of every human creature that he submit himself to the Roman Pontiff. Those decisively influenced by the other are inclined to lay stress on the words of Jesus: "The wind bloweth where it listeth . . . so is every one that is born of the Spirit." The history of Christianity is that of a struggle between these two tendencies, and indeed becomes unintelligible if the above fact is lost sight of.

The first symptom of the development of the papal claims seems to have appeared in 196 when St. Victor I pronounced a sentence of excommunication against the Asiatic Churches who differed from their Western brethren as to the day on which the Easter festival should be kept. This excommunication fell flat because the other Western bishops, notably Irenaeus, refused to accompany the Pope in considering the Oriental Churches as heretical for adopting a different practice. The matter of the date of Easter thus remained an open question until the Council of Nicea, when the Occidental opinion finally prevailed. The dispute may therefore be said to have been finally decided in favour of the Papacy; while on the other hand on the question of exercise of authority the Pope was defeated, because his sentence of excommunication proved abortive.

Shortly after the incident above described, two African

CHRISTIANITY AS AN INSTITUTION

theologians, Tertullian and Origen, both of whom have already been quoted in these pages, commenced successively to exercise considerable influence on the Church. It is desirable to say something further about each of these writers.

QUINTUS FLORENS TERTULLIANUS was a Carthaginian, who seems to have migrated to Rome and there become a lawyer of some repute. He was probably converted to Christianity somewhat before 195, and shortly afterwards commenced his voluminous writings in defence of his new faith. Harnack states that he was

> the earliest and after Augustine the greatest of the ancient Church writers of the West. . . . He created Christian Latin literature: one might almost say that that literature sprang from him full-grown, alike in form and substance, as Athena from the head of Zeus.

The legal training of Tertullian profoundly influenced his style. He always seems to act as counsel for the prosecution: he sometimes attacks the Jews, sometimes the Gnostics, sometimes the heathen, and indeed frequently the Roman Church, whose increasing formalism and lack of spirituality he detested. Adopting always the attitude of prosecuting counsel, he took no pains to be consistent. That is to say, when he attacks one body he takes a standpoint different from that adopted when he attacks another. And like so many other theologians he failed to appreciate that mere animosity towards those who differ from us is a poor substitute for the profound truths enshrined in the teaching of Jesus and of Paul. Consequently he frequently gives us the impression that he whole-heartedly desires the death of a sinner, rather than that he should turn from his wickedness and live. The following extract from a treatise addressed to theatre-goers is adduced as an example of Tertullian's somewhat caustic style:

> You are fond of spectacles: expect the greatest of all spectacles: —the last and eternal judgment of the universe. How shall I admire, how laugh, how rejoice, how exult, when I behold so many proud monarchs and fancied gods groaning in the lowest abyss of darkness, so many magistrates who persecuted the name of the Lord liquifying in fires fiercer than they ever kindled against the Christians: and so many sage philosophers blushing in red-hot flames, with their deluded scholars.

ORIGENES ADAMANTIUS is termed by Harnack "the most dsitinguished and most influential of all the theologians of the ancient Church, with the possible exception of Augustine." He was born about 185 at Alexandria, a city where the early Church was noted for its tolerance in adapting the theories of the Greek philosophers to Christian thought. The so-called "catechetical school," which Origen attended in his youth, was for a long time the only institution where Greek philosophy and Greek natural science were taught side by side with Christian theology. In all three of these branches of knowledge Origen excelled.

Origen's principal apologetic work is called Κατα Κελσου and is a refutation of an attack made on Christianity by the philosopher Celsus.

In this work Origen tells us concerning the question of miracles:

> Though we should grant that it is difficult for us to determine precisely by what power our Saviour wrought his miracles, yet it is very plain that the Christians made no use of enchantments, unless indeed the name JESUS and some passages of the Holy Scriptures were a kind of sacred spell.

And in another place to the same effect:

> The power which the Christians had was not in the least owing to enchantments, but to their pronouncing the name JESUS and making mention of some remarkable occurrences of his life. Nay the name of JESUS has such power over demons that sometimes it has proved effectual, though pronounced by very wicked persons.

On the question of the miraculous birth of Jesus, Origen replies to Celsus:

> I have this to say further to the Greeks, who will not believe that our Saviour was born of a Virgin, that the Creator of the world if he pleases can make every animal bring forth its young in the same wonderful manner. As for example vultures, which propagate their young in this uncommon way, as the best writers of natural history do acquaint us. What absurdity is there then in supposing that the all-wise God, designing to bless mankind with an extraordinary and truly-divine teacher, should so order matters that our blessed Saviour should not be born in the ordinary way of human generation?

The above argument is not very convincing. We cannot of course blame Origen because his knowledge of ornithology was not in advance of his age; and we consequently offer no criticism on his statement as to the manner in which vultures bring forth their young. But the lack of logic is obvious. If it had been alleged that a certain human being had been born with wings, and had been able to fly a few weeks after birth, this allegation would be rendered none the more credible by the fact that vultures are customarily born with wings and fly a few weeks after birth. And in just the same way the statement that a certain human being was born of a virgin, would be rendered no more credible if it were a fact that vultures propagate their young without the intervention of the male bird.

But what is really admirable about the teaching of Origen is that he propounded theories which, while being genuinely Christian, were readily reconcilable with the best pagan philosophy and science of his day. He sincerely believed that the Christian faith embraced the highest ideals of all other religions; that God is immutable and is at one with all spiritual essences; that in consequence human souls have existed from all eternity and, notwithstanding the errors and sin which temporarily separate them from the Deity, will eventually return to their Divine source; that Holy Scripture, considered merely as a record of historical fact, is of comparatively little importance, and the real value of the Old Testament is only to be found in an allegorical interpretation; and finally that the Logos, who is coexistent with the Father from all eternity, accomplished union with a specially selected human soul, presented to mankind an esoteric doctrine of salvation, and experienced physical death.

The writings of Origen were, during his lifetime, very highly esteemed, though by no means unanimously so. After his death his detractors became more numerous, notwithstanding the fact that many distinguished theologians, including Athanasius and Eusebius of Cæsarea, were earnest admirers of his teaching. As Christian doctrine developed, current theology became more and more in disaccord with the views of Origen, who consequently fell into discredit, till finally the Council of Constantinople of 553 took the decisive step of anathematising his writings altogether.

It is of considerable importance to appreciate as clearly as possible the real divergence between doctrine regarded as tenable in the time of Origen and that eventually adopted by those who condemned him three centuries subsequently. The following observations may be found of interest:

Firstly: Origen believed in God as the Father of all mankind.

Herein he differed both from the Jews, whose belief in the Fatherhood of God was practically so restricted as to apply almost exclusively to their own race, and from the Christian Bishops forming the Council of 553, whose belief in the Fatherhood of God was practically so restricted as to apply only to those who accepted the Nicean Creed. And, as we have already seen, when Christian dogma became more rigidly crystallised, belief in the Fatherhood of God was, among the largest and most important body of Christians, even further restricted and was made to apply only to those who submitted themselves to the Roman Pontiff. Origen on the other hand held that the souls of all human beings are of divine origin, and must after a period of purification eventually return to God. Consequently he differed radically from those who excluded from God's family all those who feel themselves unable to accept certain dogmatic pronouncements.

Secondly: Origen taught that through contemplative isolation and self-knowledge the human soul can enter into communion with God. This communion is brought about through the Christ, or Logos, to whom the Christian should direct his thoughts and higher aspirations. So to Origen neither the formal rites of a highly organised Church, nor the gospel accounts of the life and death of Jesus, were of such paramount importance as they subsequently appeared to theologians of later generations.

Thirdly: Origen was a man of science. By this statement it is not meant to be inferred that his actual knowledge of science was extraordinarily in advance of his age; indeed his observations as to the breeding of vultures are in themselves enough to make us sceptical on this point. But to Origen there was no possible conflict between revealed religion and natural science. Hence he gave an allegorical interpretation to such passages of the Old Testament as are in patent disaccord with knowledge of the universe as acquired through the human senses. He agreed with Paul in thinking that the letter killeth but the Spirit giveth life. His detractors on the other hand regarded the first few chapters of Genesis as a divine revelation of the exact circumstances attending the creation of the world, and indeed sought to examine questions of natural science in general in the light of a literal interpretation of Holy Scripture. Augustine for example argued that the earth could not be a sphere, because Paul implies (Rom. x. 18) that in his day the gospel had already been carried unto the ends of the world, whence it follows that, as the gospel had never been carried to the Antipodes, clearly the Antipodes could not exist.

An equally good illustration is the case of Cosmas Indicopleustes, who was living at the time when Origen's works were anathematised and who was, unlike Augustine, a professed student of the natural sciences. He was a great traveller, and his observations, which are of very considerable value, bear the stamp of truth. When for example he describes a unicorn, he is careful to tell us that he himself had never seen one, a statement which the most sceptical of critics will be disposed to accept. Now this really competent scientist deduced from Heb. ix. 23, 24, that the Tabernacle constructed by Moses in the Wilderness was a model of the universe. He consequently went to some pains to prove that the heavens and earth have the shape of a rectangular two-storied box, with a vaulted roof. Fortified by the conviction that he had Holy Writ on his side, he consequently felt justified in denouncing:

> those who . . . scoff at all the divine writings as a collection of myths, slightingly calling Moses and the prophets, the Lord Christ and the apostles idle babblers, while . . . they present as a gift to the rest of mankind a spherical form and a circular motion for the heavens.

The foregoing rapid contrast between the theories of Origen and those of some of his opposers may enable the reader to appreciate the observation of Harnack:

> Orthodox theology has never in any of the confessions ventured beyond the circle which the mind of Origen first measured out. It has suspected and amended its author, it has expunged his heresies; but whether it has put anything better or more tenable in their place may be gravely questioned.

Relationships with the Civil Power

Until the latter part of the eighteenth century popular ideas in England with respect to the treatment of early Christians by the Roman authorities seem to have been somewhat crude. It was generally believed that it was only with the assistance of frequent miracles, whereby God directly intervened on behalf of the infant Church, that the divine work was carried on in the face of the bitterest and most violent opposition on the part of the civil power. It also seems to have been generally believed that as a partial protection against persecution, the Christians constructed the catacombs as hiding-places. The work of Gibbon (1737-1794) however did much to enable the public to see the facts in a clearer light, and to appreciate the unreliability of a good deal that is contained in the martyrologies that have come down to us. And with respect to the catacombs it seems sufficient to say that the fact that the Christians were able either to construct or to adapt to their own use several hundred miles of subterranean passages in the immediate vicinity of Rome, seems a proof of the tolerance with which they were in general regarded.

When we search the Acts of the Apostles for evidence as to the treatment experienced by the early saints, we find it necessary to bear in mind that, as already pointed out on page 50, the former part of the work was apparently written from hearsay many years after the events described, and is much less reliable than the latter part. In the former portion we get a description of such atrocious acts of barbarity as the murder of Stephen (vii. 59) and the attempt on the life of Paul (xiv. 19). But in the latter and more credible portion the author clearly desires us to feel that Paul, with whom he is now obviously in close touch, was treated harshly and unjustifiably, but not in general with that extreme wanton cruelty of which we hear so much in the Christian martyrologies; and indeed the narrative may almost be said to end on a note of hopefulness, telling us that Paul lived and preached two whole years in his own hired house at Rome, no man forbidding him.

It may be of interest for the purposes of comparison to consider a much later history, that of St. Ursula and her eleven thousand virgins. This story, which in its present form seems to date from about the eleventh century, is to the effect that Ursula, a British Christian princess, was to have been married to a pagan; that as the result of a dream she asked for a respite of three years; that she during this interval collected 11,000 virgins to accompany her on a journey; that the 11,001 travellers sailed from Britain up the Rhine to Basel, whence they walked to Rome to be blessed by the Pope; that they returned to Basel, took ship again and sailed as far as Cologne, where they were all slaughtered by the Huns, as the chronicler expresses it "in defence of their virginity."

This legend is an exceedingly popular one. In the Bollandist *Acta Sanctorum* no less than 230 pages are devoted to it. Carpaccio devoted five years to depicting it in the magnificent series painted for the Scuola di Sant' Orsola at Venice. And it so happens that although we cannot completely trace the origin of the story, a good deal of light has in point of fact been shed on it. A Cologne martyrology, dating it is thought from about the end of the ninth century gives under the date of October 21st: "XI virg. Ursule, Sencie, Gregorie, Pinose, Marthe, Saule, Britule, Satnine, Rabacie, Saturie, Paladie." It is comprehensible therefore that the name of Ursula began to be associated at Cologne with "eleven virgins," so two centuries later we get a *Passio XI. MM.SS. Virginum* (Passion of the XI Holy Virgin Martyrs). And it is easy to see how XI. MM. might be understood to mean XIM.M (11,000 Martyrs).

The above examples of narratives of persecution have been selected for an obvious reason. The account given by Luke in the second part of the Acts is worthy of very great respect: the account of the slaughter of the eleven thousand and one Virgins is probably almost wholly untrue. And if the student continues his studies in martyrology he will indeed be likely to form the following final conclusions: (*a*) The early Christian Church was the object of severe and repeated persecutions, the exact extent of which it is impossible to determine. (*b*) On the other hand, the nearer we can get to first-hand evidence of such persecutions, the less violent they are seen to be. We are indeed led to infer therefore that the persecutions were much less severe: (i) than subsequent generations of Christians have affirmed, or (ii) than those persecutions which, in subsequent centuries, certain bodies of Christians inflicted on rival bodies.

Having come to the conclusion that the antipathy shown by the Roman authorities to the Christians was less intense than the latter have sometimes represented, a question arises as to the cause of such antipathy as did in fact exist. In the first place it must not be forgotten that in the large cities of the Roman Empire Christianity began to make headway largely among the lowest classes. This point is strongly brought out by Celsus, a writer already referred to in this chapter, when criticising the readiness with which the early Christian apostles accepted criminals as converts. He says:

> When we are invited to the Mysteries the masters say: *Come to us ye who are of clean hands and pure speech, ye who are unstained by crime, who have a good conscience towards God, who have done justly and lived uprightly.* The Jews say: *Come to us ye who are sinners, ye who are fools or children, ye who are miserable, and ye shall enter into the kingdom of Heaven.* The rogue, the thief, the burglar, the

prisoner, the spoiler of temples and tombs, these are their proselytes. *Jesus* they say *was sent to save sinners*: was he not sent to help those who have kept themselves free from sin? They pretend that God will save the unjust man if he repents and humbles himself. The just man who has held himself steady from the cradle in the ways of virtue he will not look upon.

Now it is not unreasonable to suppose that in the second and third centuries of our era when victims were wanted for the amphitheatre, the police laid their hands on a suitable number of undesirables, and so fulfilled the double purpose of eliminating troublesome characters and diverting the public. And if among these undesirables there were any Christian converts, it would be reasonable to suppose that their co-religionists would be disposed to represent them as having died on account of their faith rather than because the authorities regarded them as being of criminal tendencies. Hence it is not improbable that the martyr's crown may have been attributed to many victims on very slight grounds indeed.

It has frequently been stated that as divine honours were awarded to Roman Emperors, both reigning and deceased, and as the Christians refused to take part in offering such honours, their persecution was an inevitable result. There is no doubt a good deal of truth in this statement, but it is far from explaining all the known facts. The Jews, whose religious system seems to have been incomparably more rigid than that of the Christians in the first three centuries of our era, were, we read, similarly unwilling to worship the Emperors; and we do not understand that the Jews suffered on this account so severely as did the Christians. Why then were the Christians specially singled out? One suggestion is that it would appear that the followers of Jesus made themselves very unpopular by what may be called "otherworldliness." They believed that the end of all things was at hand, and it seems likely that many of them refused to recognise that they had duties as citizens, and hence they did their best to live a life wholly separate from the outside world. Hence Celsus calls them disloyal, and states that their gatherings are illicit. He says of them: "If all were to follow your example and abstain from politics, the affairs of the world would fall into the hands of wild and lawless barbarians." He consequently appeals to their loyalty, and summons them to give their material and moral support to the government of the Empire.

CHRISTIANITY AS AN INSTITUTION

Until comparatively recent times, writers who discussed the question of the early struggle of Christianity dealt with this struggle as one waged against the traditional Roman religion —the cult of Jupiter and Mars, Venus and Mercury. But towards the end of the nineteenth century the important researches of Franz Cumont (*Textes et monuments relatifs aux mystères de Mithra*) led to the conclusion that it was Mithraism that had been the principal rival of Christianity. The cult of Mithra was introduced into the Roman Empire in the first century B.C., but it gained no strong foothold at Rome until perhaps two centuries later. In the middle of the third century of our era Mithraism seems humanly speaking to have had a good prospect of becoming the universal religion. It unfortunately happens that, notwithstanding the investigations of M. Cumont, there is very much about Mithraism concerning which we are still in ignorance, but it seems certain that in a great number of points of detail it was extraordinarily like Christianity; and this resemblance, instead of forming a common ground on which the two religions could together combat immorality and materialism, was made to become a matter of mutual dislike and recrimination. The cult of Mithra was especially developed in the army: Commodus (Emperor 180–192) was an adept, and in general one may say that Mithraism lent strong support to the throne and to the established social order. Christianity on the other hand, as has already been remarked, made itself unpopular on account of its indifference, if not actual hostility, towards all social or political organisations as then existing. It is easy to see therefore that the influence of Mithraism would very naturally be exerted to make matters unpleasant for its principal rival. It seems likely that it is here that lies at least to some extent the key to the problem as to exactly why Christianity was persecuted.

In 272 we get a kind of side-light on the relationships of Christianity with the State, and are led to infer that such relationships were at the time fairly amicable. As described on page 125, the Emperor Aurelian thought it worth while to intervene in the dispute between Paul, Patriarch of Antioch, and the members of the synod which deposed him. The Emperor seems to have looked on Christianity, if continuing united, as being an important force capable of giving cohesion to the different provinces of the Empire. Hence he was anxious that the theological system taught at Antioch should be the same as that taught at Rome.

184   INTRODUCTION TO THE STUDY OF CHRISTIANITY

In 312 the Emperor Constantine (who appears to have been impressed with the misfortunes which overtook some of the chief opponents of Christianity), before engaging battle near Rome with the forces of Maxentius, adopted as his device the monogram ☧ (the first two letters of the name *ΧΡΙΣΤΟΣ*, Christ). In the following year by his command the Christian religion was officially tolerated throughout the Empire. In 325 the Emperor presided at the Council held at Nicea as the result of the difficulties which had arisen with respect to the doctrines held by Arius. When these difficulties came to the knowledge of Constantine, he wrote a very sensible letter in which he showed every desire that the dispute should be quietly dropped. In view, however, of the wide interest already aroused in the controversy, Constantine finally consented to convene a Council, as he doubtless thought that his presence as President would strengthen the loyalty of those who attended. He was at the time still a pagan, and was indeed only baptised shortly before his death.

Five years after the Council of Nicea there occurred another event of great importance in the history of Christianity. Constantine transferred the capital of the Empire to Byzantium, for many centuries subsequently to be called Constantinople. It would be reasonable to have supposed that the result of this change would be a decline in the importance of the Latin Church and of its chief Bishop. Reference has already been made to the facts that it was indeed decreed, in consequence of the change, that "the most holy throne" of the Patriarch of Constantinople should have equal precedency with that of the Bishop of Rome, and that this decree was opposed by the Pope and his partisans.

It has however more than once happened that events which at first glance appear to be likely to constitute a staggering blow to the papal pretensions have eventually actually given the Popes even greater power. The adherents of the Roman system very naturally attribute this fact to the beneficent overruling of Almighty God. This argument clearly demands thoughtful consideration, though at first glance it reminds us somewhat of the reasoning of the immortal Pangloss, who based his system of philosophy on the assumption that *dans ce meilleur des mondes possibles tout est nécessairement pour la meilleure fin*. On the other hand the opponents of the Roman system attribute the lack of success of true Christianity very largely

CHRISTIANITY AS AN INSTITUTION

to the skill and energy with which successive Popes have sought and achieved the aggrandisement of their office rather than the application of the simple precepts of the Founder of their religion. But however this may be, the fact remains that the Popes first acquired prestige on account of the preponderating importance of the city of Rome, and subsequently acquired further prestige when, the government of the city having become greatly enfeebled after the departure of the imperial court, the population tended to look to their Bishop rather than to their civil rulers for leadership.

The extent to which the papal claims increased subsequently to 330 may be gathered from the terms of a forgery which it was eventually considered expedient to execute in their support. The forgery in question is called the *Donation of Constantine*, and purports to be a grant by the Emperor to Pope Sylvester and his successors for ever, not only of spiritual supremacy over the other great patriarchates, but also of temporal sovereignty over Italy. It is remarkable that the forger should have thought it worth while to make the Emperor invest the Pope with spiritual as well as temporal dignities.

This document, it is now thought, dates from the eighth century, but there is considerable difference of opinion as to exactly what were the special circumstances which caused the forgery to be executed. Gregory V (Pope 996–999) seems to have been the first Bishop of Rome who is known to have made use of it. Thenceforward it became the chief documentary support of the papal claims to temporal dominion. Dante, in ignorance as to its true nature, reproaches Constantine for having executed it (*Inferno* xix. 115).

> *Ahi, Constantin, di questo mal fu matre*
> *Non la tua conversion, ma quella dote*
> *Che da te prese il primo ricco patre!*

The genuineness of the *Donation* was first attacked in 1440, and since the end of the eighteenth century no serious attempt has been made to defend its authenticity.

In the latter part of the fourth, and the first part of the fifth centuries, two ecclesiastics, Jerome and Augustine, exercised considerable influence over the progress of the Western Church.

Eusebius Sophronius Hieronymus, better known to us as ST. JEROME (c. 340–420), was a Dalmatian, a man of immense learning, who became specially valuable to the See of Rome on account of his advocacy of the general principle that whenever divergencies arose, the doctrines and customs current at that city ought to prevail. But after having been papal secretary for a short time, Jerome left the West and travelled in Palestine and in Egypt, eventually settling down at Bethlehem, where up to the time of his death he was engaged on his vast literary work, including his translation of the Scriptures, such translation being the basis of the current *Vulgate* (i.e. edition in vulgar use). The religious terminology of the languages of Western Europe has been very largely influenced by Jerome's work.

AURELIUS AUGUSTINUS (354–430) is generally regarded by Roman Catholics as the greatest of the Doctors of the Church, while at the same time he is perhaps the one early Father whose authority is genuinely respected by practically all Protestant writers. While on the one hand it has been asserted that the doctrines of Calvin were those of Augustine carried to their logical conclusion, on the other Augustine's popularity in Roman Catholic Spain is so great that the saying has become proverbial: "No stew (*olla*) without garlic; no sermon without St. Augustine."

It so happens that we possess exceptionally full information as to the Saint's religious development. In his childhood he was impressed by the earnest Christian teaching of his mother, Monica, but as he grew up he became careless about religion. He was subsequently attracted by Manichæism, a system which may be said to be in a sense a successor of Mithraism. Manes attempted to blend the doctrines of Christianity with Persian Magism, the result being a system of dualism, the universe being regarded as divided into two opposing kingdoms —of light and darkness—with the former kingdom being associated God, virtue and happiness, and with the latter Satan, vice and misery.

Augustine was a disciple (*auditor*) of Manichæism for nine years, after which he became dissatisfied with dualism, which served, as he very justly thought, to shelve difficulties rather than to solve them. He subsequently fell under the influence of Neo-Platonism, of which school of thought Plotinus is the best known exponent. This truly great writer held that the One Original Being begets what he called the *Novs*, which is a perfect image of the One, and the archetype of all existing things. The individual human soul is to the *Novs* in the same relationship as the *Novs* itself is to the One, and it is the aim

CHRISTIANITY AS AN INSTITUTION

of the soul to regain union with the *Νovς*. It will be seen therefore that what Plotinus called the *Νovς* is really what Origen and his followers called the Christ. (It may be observed that Plotinus and Origen were pupils of the same master, Ammonius Saccas.)

Few subjects of reflection can be more profitable than an enquiry into the differences between Neo-Platonism and Christianity. Wherein lie the weakness of the former and the strength of the latter? Why did Augustine finally abandon the one to become so great an advocate of the other? An answer to these questions is contained in the article on Neo-Platonism, contributed jointly to the *Encyclopædia Britannica* by Dr. Harnack and Mr. J. M. Mitchell:

> Why was Neo-Platonism defeated by Christianity? Three essentials of a permanent religious foundation were wanting in Neo-Platonism; they are admirably indicated in Augustine's *Confessions* (vii. 18–21). First and chiefly, it lacked a religious founder; second, it could not tell how the state of inward peace and blessedness could become permanent; third, it had no means to win those who were not endowed with the speculative faculty. The philosophical discipline which it recommended for the attainment of the highest good was beyond the reach of the masses. . . . Thus it remained a school for 'the wise and prudent.'

The above merits our very careful attention. Taking the second item first, we are reminded of the fact that people of such widely different opinions as Plotinus, Mahomet and St. Thereza of Avila all had their experiences of intense religious ecstasy, but in none of the three was the state permanent, nor could it apparently be induced at will; so it is not easy to see why in this respect Christianity necessarily had any advantage over Neo-Platonism.

The first and third items seem to be closely allied, that is to say people not endowed with the speculative faculty require to look up to some leader or teacher, either living or historical, as their religious enthusiasm cannot be otherwise aroused. The truly spiritually-minded man cries out "O God, early will I seek thee: my soul thirsteth for thee: my flesh longeth for thee" (Ps. lxiii. 1), but those whose religious thought is on a lower level affirm: "We have Abraham for our father," or "We are the sons of the Prophet," or whatever the current phrase may happen to be.

We ask ourselves therefore why so spiritually-minded a man

as Augustine should need to look up to a personal religious leader. He tells us that he was converted to Christianity at the moment of reading the words of Paul to the Romans (xiii. 13, 14):

> Not in rioting and drunkenness, not in chambering and wantonness, not in strife and envying. But put ye on the Lord Jesus Christ, and make not provision for the flesh to fulfil the lusts thereof.

He adds: "I had neither desire nor need to read further."

Now if we examine the passage which produced so extraordinary an effect on the life of Augustine, we see that the greater part consists of moral precepts which might quite conceivably have been spoken by Socrates, or written by one of the Hebrew prophets. The only distinctively Christian phrase is *Put ye on the Lord Jesus Christ*, and it is consequently of special interest to try to determine exactly the meaning of these words. The phrase in question is clearly on a par with such expressions as: *As many of you as have been baptised into Christ have put on Christ* (Gal. iii. 27). Paul seems to be dealing with purely spiritual experiences. He is not telling his readers to hold certain beliefs as to the nature of Jesus, nor is he asking them to study the earthly life of Jesus with a view to following that great example. He tells them to *put on the Lord Jesus Christ*, and we are reminded of such phrases as *Little children of whom I travail in birth again until Christ be formed in you* (Gal. iv. 19), and it would appear that in each case he is urging his readers to strive to bring about the union of the individual soul with the Divine Christ Spirit.

The situation may possibly be rendered more clear if we study the language of the Third Gospel. We find that the Holy Spirit descended upon Jesus (iii. 22), that Jesus being full of the Holy Spirit then returned from Jordan (iv. 1) and subsequently returned in the power of the Spirit into Galilee (iv. 14). Now in the light of these passages we may again ask ourselves the meaning of the phrase *Put on the Lord Jesus Christ*: are we to understand that it should be our aim to attain spiritual communion with the man Jesus who became "full of the Holy Spirit," or with that same Holy Spirit which inspired him?

Herein lies the crucial point. Augustine was attracted by the idea of a personal historical Saviour, and hundreds of millions of Christians have followed his example, and as a result have eventually adopted the dogma that "it is necessary to everlasting salvation that (they) believe rightly the Incarnation of our Lord Jesus Christ." But the difficulties of Christianity when brought in contact with modern thought lie increasingly in the fact that so many thinking men and women find it hard to believe that a right comprehension of the nature of a historical character can be a vital part of religion. Religion is to many something which would remain unimpaired even if all history were blotted out. Consequently a certain type of evangelical preaching is received in a markedly different manner by the two classes of hearers. The familiar invitation to "Come to Jesus" and to "Accept Jesus as your Saviour" has proved itself attractive to millions of disciples, and immense benefit has unquestionably resulted. But there is another class of hearer to whom the so-called gospel message, as expressed in the above form, is practically meaningless. To members of this class the invitation to accept as Saviour a man, albeit divinely inspired, who lived nineteen centuries ago is quite unattractive. And many such people have most unfortunately been spiritually starved because traditional Christianity, while focussing attention on the earthly career of Jesus, has kept in the background its vital truths as to the indwelling of Christ in the individual human soul.

When about thirty-three years old Augustine was baptised, and some eight years subsequently was made co-adjutor to the bishop of Hippo Regius, a town near the site of the modern port of Bône. He subsequently became himself bishop of the see, making himself famous for his controversial treatises, directed firstly against his former friends the Manichæans, and secondly against the Donatists, a schismatical body of Christians who aimed at a more rigid discipline than that common among the orthodox party. More famous than these writings however were those directed against Pelagianism. It appears that Coelestius, a pupil of Pelagius, had been excommunicated for teaching that the sin of Adam, being a purely personal act, prejudiced no one but himself, and consequently children who die without having committed actual sin are saved, even though unbaptised. Augustine undertook the refutation of these heterodox opinions in a treatise in which, though as a theologian he rises to the full height of his powers, he shows himself emphatically at variance with twentieth-century ideas of justice.

From 413 to 426 Augustine was engaged with *The City of*

God, a work in which, as an attempt to meet the situation caused by the patent weakness of the Roman Empire, he advocated a social order based on the religion of Christ. To some extent the medieval Papacy may be said to be founded on the ideas first put forward in detail by Augustine. Roman Catholic controversialists have with perfect justice urged, against those Christian bodies which lie outside the pale of the Latin Church, that Augustine clearly never contemplated the permanent schisms which have existed ever since the separation of East and West in 1054. One answer seems to be that Augustine, who was a theologian and not a prophet, seems equally to have been unable to contemplate the permanent adoption of an alien creed by the inhabitants of any district once converted to Christianity. So if he had been told that his own diocese of Hippo would cease to be Christian two centuries after his death, and would continue to be non-Christian for at least another thirteen centuries, he would doubtless have been inexpressibly shocked. So would he have been if he had been told that war among Christian nations would at times become even more common than among the heathen. He indeed regards it as a proof of the divinity of Christ that nations converted to Christianity, however savage may have been their antecedents, thereafter cease to engage in war.

While Augustine was occupied in putting forward a philosophy based on the doctrine of the Blessed Trinity, the old Greek philosophy was falling more and more into disrepute. The celebrated school at Alexandria seems to have lost all real importance after the murder of Hypatia, a pagan teacher who in 415 was put to death by a Christian mob, instigated it is believed by St. Cyril the Patriarch of the city. The school at Athens, notwithstanding the excellent work done by Proclus (410–485), was definitely closed by order of Justinian in 529, and Gibbon was eventually able to write that he had described the triumph of barbarism and religion.

It has been said above that Augustine in *The City of God* outlined a society based on what he believed to be the principles of Christianity. Ten years after his death the See of Rome was occupied by Leo the Great, a man whose vigorous personality enabled him to go far towards putting the theories of Augustine into practice.

ST. LEO I (Pope 440–461). It is a testimony to the exceptional personality of this Pontiff that he was unanimously elected to

CHRISTIANITY AS AN INSTITUTION

the papal throne at a time when he was actually absent in Gaul, and when he was apparently only in deacon's orders. Some three years after assuming office he began to take measures against the Manichæans, then very numerous at Rome. Some little time subsequently we find him able to assert that of these heretics some had been converted to Catholicism, and a large number had been condemned to perpetual banishment, while he asks the help of the provincial clergy in seeking out those who had fled.

Shortly afterwards took place an important controversy between St. Leo and St. Hilary, Bishop of Arles. Into the details of this controversy it is unnecessary to go, but it is important to record the fact that Leo was able to secure an edict from the Emperor Valentinian III whereby the papal claims over the bishops of the Gallican Church were sanctioned by imperial law. In the history of the great struggle between the Popes and what afterwards came to be termed Gallicanism, this edict is of considerable importance.

The closing years of the reign of Leo were full of political troubles. In 452 Attila, King of the Huns, invaded Italy and seemed likely to advance on Rome. Leo thereupon met the King near the banks of the Po. Exactly what passed at the interview is not known, but the fact remains that Attila discontinued his southward march. It has been suggested that his disinclination to penetrate farther into the peninsula was due to his lack of sea-power. Three years afterwards the Vandal chief Genseric, who commanded a powerful fleet, was able to sack Rome, but he did so in a relatively humane manner, without murder or incendiarism. The mildness of Genseric's methods, as compared to what has frequently taken place when other cities have been plundered by hostile troops, is again attributed to the influence of Leo.

The intervention of Leo with Attila has given rise to one of those only too numerous distortions of history for which the student must be prepared. By order of Pope Julius II, Raphael painted (1512-1514) in the Stanza d'Eliodoro in the Vatican, his well-known fresco representing "the repulse of Attila." Leo I is depicted as seated on a white palfrey, in an attitude of blessing. Above him in the heavens are SS. Peter and Paul, who with swords in their hands strike terror into the hearts of Attila and his Huns. Now it is a little difficult to believe that SS. Peter and Paul really accomplished a miracle in 452 but made no attempt to prevent the sack of Rome in 455. Consequently, while great prominence has been given by ecclesiastical historians to the events of 452, it has been thought expedient to keep those of 455 in the background. So it has finally come about that even standard works of reference, which cannot be accused of partiality, when writing of Leo mention his success in prevailing on Attila to spare Rome but frequently say nothing at all about Genseric. The consequence is that for every moderately well-educated reader who has any knowledge of the sack of Rome during Leo's reign, there are probably a hundred who have read that this Pontiff was able, either miraculously or otherwise, to deter Attila from attacking the city.

The character of Leo merits study because in him we have the prototype of the series of great Popes who were subsequently called upon to play so prominent a part in European history. It seems fair to say of Leo and of his successors that they attempted to carry on the work of Jesus, but adopted widely different methods. They associated themselves wholly with their office, and regarded the aggrandisement of such office, by whatever means attained, as the aggrandisement of the Church. Bishop Gore (*Roman Catholic Claims*) sums up very ably the difficulties which beset them, and their manner of meeting these difficulties:

> The untamed, undisciplined races which formed the material of our modern nations were subjected to the yoke of the Church (mostly at the will of kings or chiefs) as to an external law, which was to train, mould, restrain them. The one need of such an age was authoritative discipline, and the Church became largely "a schoolmaster to bring men to Christ." She had in fact to deal with children in mind, with children whose one religious faculty, which was in full exercise, was faith in the form of a great readiness to accept revelations of the unseen world and to respect their ministers—the sort of faith which asks for nothing but a sufficiently firm voice of authority. Christianity thus became, by a one-sided development, a great imperialist and hierarchical system. The peremptory needs of government tended to overshadow earlier conceptions of the Church's function even in relation to the truth. Compare the Roman Leo's view of the truth with that of the Alexandrian Didymus or Athanasius, and the contrast is marked. Both Easterns and Westerns insist on the importance of the Church's dogma, but to the Easterns it is the guide in the knowledge of God, to the Westerns it is the instrument to subdue and discipline the souls of men. Thus the authoritativeness of tone

CHRISTIANITY AS AN INSTITUTION

which becomes characteristic of the Western Church makes her impatient of the slow and complex methods of arriving at the truth on disputed points which belonged to the earlier idea of 'the rule of faith.' The comparison of traditions, the elaborate appeal to Scripture, these methods are too slow and too indecisive: something more rapid and imperious is wanted. It is no longer enough to conceive of the Church as the catholic witness to a faith once for all delivered. She must be the living voice of God, the oracle of the Divine Will. And just as the strength and security of witness lies in the comparison and consent of independent testimonies, so the strength of authoritative oracular utterance lies in unimpeded, unqualified centrality, and Christendom needs a central chair of truth, where Divine Authority speaks and rules. Such has been broadly the Roman development of the Christian religion.

Somewhat more than a century after the death of Leo, the papal throne was occupied by another great Pontiff, GREGORY I (Pope 590–604). To the English-speaking world Gregory is chiefly known owing to the fact that he, apparently in the mistaken belief that the ancient British Church was wholly extinct, commissioned Augustine (subsequently called Augustine of Canterbury) to commence the conversion of England. Gregory is one of the occupants of the papal chair whose truly Christ-like character has been justly appreciated by thoughtful opponents of the Roman system.

A quarter of a century after the death of Gregory, the birth and rapid success of a rival religion inflicted on Christianity a series of blows, the effect of which is still being acutely felt. The following section is devoted to this subject.

Mahometanism

On June 20, 622, one of the prominent citizens of Mecca found himself forced hurriedly to leave the city for the oasis of Yathrib, about ten days' journey to the north. He had rendered himself unpopular among his fellow-townsmen owing to his attacks on the idolatrous nature of their worship, and also owing to his claims to be a prophet and to receive direct inspiration from the Deity. His name was something like Muhammad, but the form Mahomet, though probably not such a close approximation to the Arabic original, is more familiar to the English-speaking world.

If on the date in question an inhabitant of Mecca had been told that in consequence of Mahomet's flight Yathrib would cease to be given a name, but would be considered sufficiently important to be called simply "The Town" (*Al Medina*), the statement would probably have been received with incredulity. And if such inhabitant had been further told that his own descendants and hundreds of millions of other believers would for many centuries consider June 20, 622, as the commencement of their era, this incredulity would doubtless have been intensified.

In fact the rise and progress of the religion founded by Mahomet constitute a series of events of capital importance in the history of mankind, and these events have had so direct an influence on the progress of Christianity that it is necessary that a few remarks thereon be made in this treatise. It may be well to state as a preliminary that Christianity and Mahometanism have found themselves in direct conflict more especially during three epochs:

(i) The time of the early conquests in Asia, North Africa, Spain and the south of France. This phase commenced shortly after 622 and may be regarded as coming to an end with the defeat inflicted by Charles the Hammer on the Mahometans between Tours and Poitiers in 732.

(ii) The Crusades, which were a series of unsuccessful attempts on the part of Christians to regain permanent possession of Palestine. Their epoch may be regarded as commencing with an expedition led in part by Peter the Hermit in 1096, and ending with the fall of Acre in 1291.

(iii) The irruption of the Turks into Eastern Europe in the fourteenth and two following centuries. The most outstanding item of this series of events is the fall of Constantinople in 1453.

The events referred to under headings (ii) and (iii) will be touched upon in later sections of this chapter. In this place a few observations are offered concerning heading (i).

Mahomet, having settled down with his followers at Yathrib (Medina), soon acquired, possibly not wholly unjustly, the reputation of being a robber of passing caravans. Hence his ex-fellow-townsmen at Mecca sent out an expedition to crush him, and the repulse of this expedition forms the commencement of the extraordinary series of combined military and missionary operations which in less than a century carried the new religion from Arabia, across Northern Africa and the Iberian Peninsula to Provence. We are the more impressed with the magnitude of the Moslem achievement when we remember how comparatively small was the progress made by Christianity within the first hundred years after Jesus commenced his public teaching.

The early Mahometan successes are ably summed up in picturesque language by the brothers Tharaud, from one of whose books the following is taken:

> In the name of the all-powerful and merciful God, Amron, Welid, Yezid, Khaled, all the great chieftains of the new-born Islam, opened for themselves a sanguinary route through the neighbouring tribes, inflicting on them chastisement of such kinds as seemed appropriate, and taking as slaves all those whom they did not massacre. After which, throughout the desert, from the Hedjaz to the plateau of Nedj, from the Yemen to Irak, from the Yamama to the Hadramaout, the whole population appreciated the fact that the religion of the Prophet, concerning which executioners and victims alike understood practically nothing, was unquestionably the true one.
>
> This operation finished, the bands which had become accustomed to pillage, and in which converters and converted were mixed up indiscriminately, took on their own initiative the route to Syria, which has always seemed to the half-starved Bedouin, an eater of lizards and jumping-mice (*gerboises*), to be the land of plenty. Consequently one fine day people at Byzantium learnt that on the shore of the Dead Sea some frontier guards had been roughly handled. But at the moment the court of Heraclius was occupied only with the quarrel which divided the Syrian Church into orthodox and jacobites, the one party recognising a dual nature in Jesus and the other the divine nature only. The matter of the frontier guards passed unnoticed. Such was nevertheless the commencement of the extraordinary adventure which in less than three years placed Damascus, Jerusalem, Palestine, and the whole of Syria in Arab hands. Then came the turn of Egypt which has never resisted any conqueror whatsoever. The Empire of the Persians itself soon collapsed before these Bedouins whom the hope of plunder had at first enlisted, but who were now rendered fanatical by a success which they interpreted as a most evident proof of the genuineness of the Prophet.
>
> (J. and J. THARAUD, *Les Cavaliers d'Allah*.)

It may well be asked what was the secret which enabled a series of Moslem commanders, constantly engaged as they were in quarrelling among themselves and constantly suffering as they did from the intrigues of their followers, to be so marvellously successful when combating the infidel. This success seems to have been largely caused by the same combination of factors as that which in later years aroused in Christian countries such enthusiasm for the Crusades. Warriors saw every prospect of unlimited plunder if they were victorious: if defeated there was held before their eyes the sure and certain hope of a blessed immortality. In this respect, as in so many others, there is much in common between the histories of the two rival creeds. It may therefore be of interest to say something about the Mahometan tenets, with a view to noting points both of similarity to and of difference from Christianity.

In the first place we observe that Mahometan theology is, like the Jewish, vastly simpler than the teaching of the Christian creeds. The Jews indeed in their best days gave but little attention to theological speculation, to philosophy and to science. But they had a profound conviction of the unity, the wisdom and the presence of God. In these respects the outlook of Mahomet was far more Jewish than Christian. He indeed at the outset of his career confidently expected the Jews to recognise him as one who continued the work of their own prophets, and he was much disappointed when he found that stiff-necked people unwilling to modify its faith accordingly. On the other hand, he had no sympathy whatever with that development of Christian doctrine which, starting from Paul's tenet that *there is one God and one mediator between God and men, the man Christ Jesus*, had already adopted as its principal dogma the affirmation of the Godhead of Jesus, and was in further process of developing the cult of his mother as a semi-divine being. Moreover Mahomet shared with the Jews an intense horror of the veneration of any picture or image of the Deity, in which respect he again differed from established Christian usage.

For a convert to adopt the new creed was an exceedingly simple matter. If a man made his "confession of faith" saying: *There is no God but God, and Mahomet is the Prophet of God*, he was, in virtue of that confession alone, said to be "ennobled with Islam," and was reckoned among the true believers. It is true that this extreme simplicity was found to be not without certain practical disadvantages. Whenever the incursion of a powerful band of Moslem raiders suddenly convinced some peaceful tribe of the profound spiritual verity of the teaching of the Prophet, there was always the risk that twelve months subsequently the whole incident might have come to occupy only a secondary place in the memories of the new converts. To guard against this contingency the conquering Moslem generals

CHRISTIANITY AS AN INSTITUTION

sometimes adopted the simple precaution of cutting off either an ear or a finger of such tribal chiefs as they were successful in converting, so that the new believers might always keep before them a permanent symbol of the incalculable benefits accruing through their adoption of the true faith.

But while the Moslem theology is incomparably simpler than the Christian, the former religion is considerably more rigid in its demands on the individual worshipper. Mahometans believe that the Prophet received a revelation from God enjoining the recitation of prayers by the faithful no less than fifty times a day. Mahomet however, on descending from the highest heaven where he had received the Divine command, passed through that part of the celestial kingdom which is ruled over by Moses, whose long experience as a law-giver prompted him to advise Mahomet to re-approach the Deity with a view to obtaining some modification of this ordinance. As the result of successive applications at the throne of grace, God was eventually persuaded to reduce the number of daily prayers to five, and this command is still strictly followed. Moreover fasting among the Mahometans is a far more serious matter than among the Christian laity. During the month of Ramadan, the believer is not permitted to eat, drink, or smoke between sunrise and sunset. While of course this precept is not invariably strictly observed, such observance is in fact even to-day very much more conscientious than an uninformed person would deem probable. The result is of course very severe privation, especially when the month of Ramadan falls during the summer, and it then follows that towards the end of the fast a very unfavourable effect is shown on the physical health and mental balance of the population of Mahometan cities.

The Mahometans took over from the Jews both the practice of circumcision and the abstinence from certain foods, notably pork. A prohibition laid down by Mahomet with respect to the use of fermented beverages is probably to be accounted for by the Prophet's personal distaste for wine. Among Christians the consumption of wine, albeit on an exceedingly small scale, forms an essential part of the most sacred religious rite; so it is a little illogical for a Christian, however abstemious he may be personally, to adopt the tenet that the drinking of wine is in itself displeasing to God.

As regards sanitation and personal cleanliness Moslem nations were undoubtedly, up to comparatively modern times, far in advance of the Christians. The ultimate origin of the importance given by the Mahometans in this respect may have been the abnormally keen sense of smell possessed by the Prophet. On the other hand the early Christians belonged very largely to the poorer classes of the great cities of the Roman Empire, and in their own houses there were presumably but small facilities for cleanliness, the public baths supplying what private residences lacked. Unfortunately these public baths came to be the scenes certainly of immodesty and probably of immorality. Consequently the baths were in principle avoided by the Christians, who very properly thought that cleanliness of the soul was more important than that of the skin. So it unfortunately happened that the ideas of sanctity and dirt came to be, more or less subconsciously, associated in the minds of many Christians; and notwithstanding the immense world-wide progress in sanitation made during the past hundred years, this idea is not wholly extinct.

On the general subject of the conflict between science and religion it may be said that Mahometan and Christian teachers are both open to criticism, because both have appealed to a literal interpretation of their sacred writings in order to rebut the findings of physical science. But until the dawn of the Renaissance, the record of Mahometanism seems to have been in this respect somewhat better than was that of Christianity. In the twentieth century the so-called Christian nations are materially so much in advance of the Mahometans that we have difficulty in realising how relatively backward were the former during the dark ages. Medicine and mathematics especially were held in much higher esteem, from the seventh century to the fifteenth, in Moslem than in Christian countries. Hence it happens that our numerals in common use come to us from the Arabs (though their ultimate origin is said to be Indian). We also give the Arabic name to formal mathematics, which science the Arabs recovered from the early Greek writers and termed "the science of redintegration and equation" *ilm al-jabr wal muqabalah*, or more shortly *al-jabr* or *algebra*.

Mahometans have in general shown themselves vastly more tolerant than have the Christians both towards the Jews and towards their own co-religionists who differ from them on questions of detail. On the other hand, as regards the mutual relationships of Mahometans and Christians, no very marked degree of charity has been customarily shown on either side.

CHRISTIANITY AS AN INSTITUTION

Probably the most striking difference between Christian and Mahometan institutions relates to the relationship between the sexes. It must be remembered that Mahometanism was first propagated by nomadic peoples of a warlike disposition. For them the population problem was exactly the reverse of that which to-day confronts such overcrowded countries as England and Belgium. The desert tribes were continually seeing their numbers depleted in battle, and it was necessary for their very existence that a constant supply of young men should be growing up to take the place of the fallen. So Mahomet assumed that every young woman has the duty of producing children, and he consequently held that she should be permitted neither to remain a virgin nor to lead an immoral life. Polygamy was of course a logical outcome of these principles. Mahomet held that it was meritorious for a man to have but one wife, though four were permitted to the faithful in general, while he himself, as the result of a special Divine revelation, was allowed to have fifteen. He however in actual fact never seems to have had more than eleven at the same time.

The laws regulating the number of wives were in practice modified by the system of treating prisoners captured in war. The Mahometans, to some considerable extent at least, followed the general lines indicated in the Jewish Pentateuch (Num. xxxi. 17, 18): female captives no longer virgins were put to death; if still virgins they became the slaves of their captors, so that they might rear children to swell the numbers of the true believers.

The point has frequently been stressed that polygamy is frankly recognised in the Old Testament and is nowhere very clearly denounced in the New. The answer seems to be that Christianity aims at assisting the individual soul to attain union with God, and when this union is achieved, albeit incompletely, the Holy Spirit serves as a guide enabling the believer to order his conduct in harmony with the Divine Will. In other words, the true Christian escapes the bondage of the law and enters into the true liberty of the gospel (Gal. v. 1). Hence the New Testament does not profess to lay down any detailed and inflexible code of conduct: he who is in Christ and who has consequently become a new creature (2 Cor. v. 17) submits questions to his conscience in the belief that he will be guided aright by the Holy Spirit.

Now the uniform sentiment of Christianity has been that polygamy is inconsistent with the higher spiritual life, and for this reason should be eschewed. Mahomet, when recommending his followers to have but one wife, seems to have recognised the same general principle. But it would be an over-statement to affirm that the polygamous system in the form established by Mahomet had no advantages. Attention has already been called to the effect of multiplicity of wives on the birth-rate. And it must not be overlooked that under the Christian system of monogamy it has come about that it is frequently the women of exceptional talent and individuality who remain celibate, and who consequently are unable to pass on their gifts to their offspring. Mahomet would have had no great respect for a system which permitted women of such extraordinary abilities as St. Hilda of Whitby, St. Theresa of Avila, Elizabeth of England and Florence Nightingale to die without an effort to bequeath to their progeny some of their unusual talents.

It must moreover not be forgotten that Mahomet and his successors proved themselves more successful than Christian legislators in solving the problem of the professionally immoral woman. Again, under Moslem rule married women retain a control, quite unknown in Christian countries until recent years, over their own estates, including whatever presents their husbands may give them. It must therefore have been with a certain naïve surprise that Christian readers first studied the "Thousand and One Nights," with their humorous stories of how a rich wife, as a result of some domestic friction, would sometimes cause her servants to give her husband a beating and to turn him out of doors.

Reference has already been made to the fact that on more than one occasion circumstances have arisen which have had the unexpected effect of increasing the prestige of the Bishops of Rome as compared with that of the other Bishops. The rise of Mahometanism forms a case in point. The disaster to Christianity was incalculable. The religion of Jesus was stamped out of the country of his birth. In vast regions of Asia, in the greater part of North Africa, in parts of Spain, Christianity was either exterminated altogether or became the religion of a few politically unimportant bodies, resigned to suffer chronic oppression at the hands of their Moslem conquerors. But what was a disaster for Christianity as a whole, indirectly brought about the triumph of the Papacy, because this disaster caused the centre of gravity of Christendom definitely to move westwards. The rise of Mahometanism injured the Latin Churches to a very serious extent, but the blow to the Greek Churches was so incalculably more severe that the hegemony of Christendom was definitely left with the former. After the Moslem conquests the Eastern Bishops could still deny that the Pope was *de jure* the Primate of Christendom, but no one could deny his pre-eminence *de facto*.

Growth of the Papal Power

Mention has already been made of Charles the Hammer, "Mayor of the Palace" of Austrasia, or Eastern Gaul, and subsequently ruler of the whole Frankish kingdom. Some years after the death of Charles, his son Pippin the Short assumed the title of King of the Franks, and afterwards at the Pope's invitation invaded northern Italy. On this occasion, with that open-handed generosity which is sometimes observed in conquerors who find themselves in occupation of territory which they have no obvious means of governing, Pippin transferred to the Roman Pontiff dominion over Ravenna, Ferrara and five lesser Italian cities styled jointly " the Pentapolis." In this way were constituted the "States of the Church."

On Christmas Day 800 the son of Pippin, Charles the Great (Carolus Magnus or Charlemagne), was crowned Emperor at Rome by Pope Leo III. It is doubtful whether or no Charlemagne had been previously consulted, and indeed the imperial title proved a source of embarrassment to him, as he had previously hoped, by marriage with the Empress Irene then reigning at Constantinople, to obtain peaceably dominion over the entire Christian world. The fact remains however that he received at Leo's hands the imperial crown, and in consequence we find an Emperor at Rome as well as an Empress at Constantinople, both claiming universal dominion as successors of Cæsar Augustus and of Constantine. It has been remarked: "Two halves confronted one another, each claiming to be the whole: two finite bodies touched and yet each claimed to be infinite."

Thus was formed what was afterwards called the "Holy Roman Empire," though, as the dominion of Charlemagne collapsed soon after his death, it is perhaps more proper to date the real commencement of the Empire from 962, when Otto I was crowned by Pope John XII. The adjective "Holy" seems to have been incorporated into the title about the middle of the twelfth century, owing to the fact that the Emperors had become desirous, in face of the papal attitude, of emphasising the sanctity of their own office. The claims of the Emperors to universal dominion were specially brought to the notice of the English nation when Richard I, after having been taken prisoner by Duke Leopold of Austria and having been surrendered to the Emperor Henry VI (1193), was compelled to do homage to the latter for the throne of England. But when in 1416 the Emperor Sigismund paid a visit to this country, and Henry V sent three hundred ships to escort him across the Channel, on the arrival of the fleet at Dover the King's brother rode into the water and with drawn sword demanded that the Emperor should formally declare that he had not come to claim Imperial rights.

Leaving aside however the question of the influence of the Empire on European politics, we are here concerned with its relationships with the Church. From quite early times jurists had in mind the principles enunciated by Augustine in *The City of God*, and they conceived of an essentially Christian state of society, governed by Pope and Emperor working in complete harmony one with another. The twin powers, the spiritual and the temporal, were compared to the two swords mentioned in Luke xxii. 38, and the supreme aim of both was assumed to be the extension of the kingdom of Christ on earth. The Papacy was a visible witness to the unity of the Church; the Empire similarly bore witness to the fundamental political unity of Christendom. The arrangement would of course have been an excellent one if there had been any means of ensuring the harmonious co-operation of the parties concerned. And it would indeed appear that for about two centuries the system really did work tolerably well. But during these two centuries events occurred which had the practical effect of consolidating the papal position at the expense both of the secular authority and of local Churches.

About 850 an unknown writer adopting the name of Isidore, Archbishop of Seville, put together a kind of compendium of ecclesiastical precedents and legislation, now known by the name of the "Decretals of pseudo-Isidore." This composition, designed as it is to give support to the papal system, is a clever mixture of authentic materials and forgeries. It commences with a series of seventy forged letters attributed to the Popes of the first three centuries. Then follows a résumé of the acts of the various Councils, and this résumé incorporates among much genuine matter certain earlier forgeries, of which the best known is the "Donation of Constantine," reference to which has already been made. A third part of the work consists

CHRISTIANITY AS AN INSTITUTION

of thirty forged letters, attributed to Popes from Silvester to Damasus; then follow the genuine papal decretals together with thirty-five apochryphal ones. In this way the highly-centralised ecclesiastical system which it was sought to impose on the Church in the ninth century was represented as having been in force almost from the Apostolic ages.

Until the fifteenth century the decretals were universally accepted as genuine; since the sixteenth they have been universally admitted to be false, any further discussion being limited to the question of the influence actually exercised by the forgeries on ecclesiastical policy. Professor Boudinhon, who has already been cited in these pages, puts the case for the Roman Church as follows:

> In the papal letters of the end of the ninth and the whole of the tenth century, only two or three insignificant citations of the pseudo-Isidore have been pointed out; the use of the pseudo-Isidorian forged documents did not become prevalent at Rome till about the middle of the eleventh century, in consequence of the circulation of the canonical collections in which they figured; but nobody then thought of casting any doubt on the authenticity of those documents (*Encyclopædia Britannica*).

The above is not very convincing. It is not denied that the forgeries were regarded as authoritative by the Popes of the ninth and tenth centuries; it is merely argued that no very considerable public use was made of the forgeries till the eleventh. But even admitting this to be true, the point is that the forged compendium was for six centuries accepted as authoritative by the Popes and by the Church generally. Its influence therefore in moulding papal and ecclesiastical thought and policy must have been enormous, even though it cannot be proved that the Popes, during the ninth and tenth centuries, actually quoted from the compendium to more than a small extent.

Professor Döllenger and his colleagues (writing under the pseudonym of "Janus": *Der Papst und das Concil*), tell us with respect to the forged decretals that St. Nicholas I (Pope 858–867) assured the Gallican bishops:

> that the Roman Church had long possessed these documents in its archives, and venerated them as forming part of its ancient records. He added that, although not forming an integral part of the collection of Dionysian canons, all and every papal pronouncement had of itself the full force of law

for the Church (*Mansi. Concil* xv). It was in accordance with this line of thought that at a synod held in Rome in 863 he anathematised anyone who failed to respect any doctrine or order expressed by the Pope (*Harduin-Concil* v). From the moment that the whole Church obeyed the pontifical decrees, and the popes had the right of condemning or approving, at their discretion, the Synodical decisions (as Nicholas, basing himself on the fiction of pseudo-Isidoro, claimed), only one step more was needed to arrive at the promulgation of personal infallibility. A long time elapsed however before this step was actually taken.

The next important event which it is advisable to mention is the rupture between the Eastern and Western Churches in 1054. Previously to this rupture certain divergencies between the two great branches of Christianity, the Latin and the Greek, had been manifest. The Latin branch, as we have already seen, tended to emphasise the necessity for centralisation, discipline and obedience. The Greek branch was subjected to the interference of the civil power in a manner which would have seemed intolerable in the West; but what is of even more importance is the fact that the Greeks may be said to have had the theological temperament, while the Latins had not. It has been remarked that "Eastern theology had its roots in Greek philosophy, while a great deal of Western theology was based on Roman law. The Greek Fathers succeeded the Sophists, the Latin theologians succeeded the Roman advocates." It came about therefore that the Greeks, continually involved as they were in disputes as to the ultimate nature of the Deity, found themselves obliged to admire the calm of the Western Church, where discussions as to fundamentals were discouraged. We not infrequently find therefore that Eastern bishops have freely acknowledged and made use of the unique position of the Roman Pontiffs. When however the Western Church has attempted to insist, not on such preeminence as the historical position of the See of Rome clearly justifies, but on that absolute authority which results from enforcing the Petrine claims in their entirety, then the Eastern Churches have consistently protested. The actual point of dispute which brought matters to a head was the insertion of the word *Filioque* in the Creed. As explained on page 130 it seems probable that this insertion was caused by a copyist's error, but however this may be, a deadlock had long been reached owing to the refusal of the Western Church to delete the word and the refusal of the Eastern Church to insert it. Consequently in 1054 Pope Leo IX excommunicated the whole of the Eastern Churches, thus creating the definite breach which continues to our own day. This breach was of course a logical result of insistence on the Petrine claims: the Pope desired to be the acknowledged ruler of the whole Christian Church, and consequently declared in effect that those who refused to recognise his supremacy did not form part thereof.

So the events of 1054 divided the Church into two main sections, commonly called "Catholic" and "Orthodox." The word "Orthodox" gives us comparatively little trouble: it means "correct," so the Greek Church, calling itself "Orthodox," claims to teach the correct faith in much the same way as every other Church claims to teach the correct faith. But the word "Catholic," which means "universal," presents a certain difficulty. It would appear that, as Milton (*True Religion*) reminds us, the word was originally applied to the Christian Church because it aimed at the inclusion of all men, in contradistinction from the Jewish religious system, which only aimed in general at the inclusion of all men of Jewish race. In this sense of course the Mahometan religion is as catholic as the Christian, because each aims at converting the whole of humanity. So we find the word "Catholic" used freely by people who attach no very great importance to the term. Thus the Greek Church calls itself *The Holy Orthodox, Catholic, Apostolic, Oriental Church*, and the expression *the Holy Catholic Church* occupies a prominent place in the formularies of the Church of England, although a member of the latter, if asked the question "Are you a Catholic?" would quite possibly reply: "No, I am a Protestant." On the other hand the term "Catholic" is restricted by the Roman Church to its own body, and it is difficult to see the propriety of such restriction. We can imagine a Roman Catholic apologist putting his case somewhat as follows:

> Both before and after 1054 the Holy Catholic Church consisted of those who rendered due and effective obedience to its earthly ruler, the Roman Pontiff. A change of creed having been made, and certain bodies of Christians having refused to accept such change, such bodies were anathematised by the Roman Pontiff and cast out of the Church, which nevertheless remained as before both Holy and Catholic.

Leaving aside altogether any question of historical error here involved, it would seem that the word "Catholic" can only be rightly applied to the Roman Church in the sense that its followers desire their religion to be universally dominant. But a pious Protestant would obviously be inspired by a corresponding wish, and could therefore equally claim to be Catholic.

It will be observed that the excommunication of the Oriental Christians had an effect somewhat analogous to that of the Mahometan conquests; that is to say, while the number of human souls regarded by Romanists as members of Christ's Church was decreased, the importance of the Papacy was increased. After the excommunication of 1054, Leo IX was in a position to claim that all true Christians acknowledged the papal supremacy. Such claim might or might not have been just, but it undoubtedly forms a logical deduction from St. Leo's premisses.

St. Leo throughout his pontificate had the benefit of the advice of an ecclesiastic of very exceptional ability, a Tuscan named Hildebrand, who was able to render valuable services to no less than five of the former's successors. The reign of one of these, Nicholas II, was distinguished by a measure, ascribed to the influence of Hildebrand, whereby it was enacted that future Popes should be elected, independently of lay interference, by a body composed of (*a*) certain bishops having sees in the vicinity of Rome; (*b*) the parish priests of Rome; and (*c*) the deacons entrusted with the administration of the finances of certain Roman churches. The members of this electoral body, or college, were called Cardinals, as their functions were regarded of such importance as to be hinge-like (Lat. *cardo*, a hinge). Although it is true that the dignity of Cardinal has been and is frequently awarded to non-Italians whose connection with their respective parishes or churches may often be of the slightest, nevertheless the fact remains that the practical effect of the decree of Nicholas II has been that: (*a*) lay influence in papal elections has been, if not eliminated, at all events greatly reduced; (*b*) a certain continuity in papal policy has been, if not ensured, at all events rendered more probable; and (*c*) it has eventually come about that in general both the Popes themselves and the majority of their councillors have been Italian.

In 1073 Hildebrand himself ascended the papal throne and took the title of GREGORY VII. To this Pontiff belongs the merit, or the demerit as some critics might suggest, of having pressed

CHRISTIANITY AS AN INSTITUTION

the papal claims to their full and logical extent. His ultimate aim was the entire subjection of the laity to the clergy, and of the clergy to the Pope. Now it has already been explained that the Empire and the Papacy were looked on by medieval jurists as twin powers, jointly exercised in bringing about the extension of the Kingdom of Christ on earth. But this theory presents one very obvious point of weakness. If Pope and Emperor were equally to be looked on as powers ordained of God, the former, who never commanded an army of his own sufficient to impose forcibly his will on any important European nation, was clearly at a disadvantage as compared with the latter. And if, on the other hand, the Pope was admitted to be the supreme authority in all matters of faith and morals, or in other words to be the final judge as to what course of action was the right one, the Emperor merely became a kind of executive officer, obliged to mould his policy according to the papal direction, and subject to deposition when he ceased to enjoy the papal favour. Cardinal Manning (*The Vatican Decrees in their bearing on civil allegiance*, 1875) puts this doctrine in its most attractive form when he says:

> If Christian Princes and their laws deviate from the law of God, the Church has authority from God to judge of that deviation, and by all its powers enforce the correction of that departure from justice. . . . No just prince can be deposed by any power on earth, but whether a prince is just or not is a matter for the Pope to judge of.

The claim that *the Pope is the ruler over crowned heads, and has power to release subjects from their oath of fidelity*, had been put forward by Gregory IV (Pope 827–844), but it was not till the time of Gregory VII that this claim was pressed to its logical conclusions:

> If the Holy See received from God the power to judge spiritual matters, why should it not also judge temporal matters? . . . When God said to S. Peter "Feed my sheep," did he make an exception in the case of kings? The episcopate is as much superior to the crown as gold is to lead. . . . God, conferring on S. Peter the supreme right of binding and loosing in heaven and on earth, excepted no one, and freed no one from his authority: he submitted to him all the principalities, all the powers of the globe. In this manner Christ, the King of Glory, constituted the chief of the apostles Lord over all the kingdoms of the earth. Heathen is he who refuses obedience to the

apostolic see, and those sovereigns who have the audacity to disobey the decrees of the Holy See lose their royal dignity (Greg. VII, *Epist.* iv. vii, viii).

In the light of these claims it is not difficult to understand the difficulties which inevitably beset both Pope and Emperor in their mutual dealings. The situation may be likened to that of a castle inhabited by two rulers, one of whom is elected by a group of German princes and the other by a committee of Italian ecclesiastics. We can imagine the former of the two rulers saying: "I and my colleague divide between us jurisdiction over this castle and its domain: certain matters fall within the scope of my authority and others within that of my colleague." It is quite clear that the situation so created would most probably cause considerable friction. But now let us further imagine that the second ruler affirms: "I am the supreme governor of the castle and domain. The man who calls himself my colleague and professes to rule jointly with me is merely my subordinate, and only exercises such limited authority as I permit, and is always liable to be removed from his office should I so decide." It is now clear that friction is not merely probable but inevitable.

It consequently follows that the history of the Holy Roman Empire is very largely a history of disputes between Pope and Emperor, and those between Gregory VII and the Emperor Henry IV are among the most important. Into the details it is unnecessary to go: it suffices to say that Henry was excommunicated by Gregory, and was declared to have forfeited his crown. Henry in consequence travelled to Italy and presented himself before Gregory at Canossa, near Reggio Emilia (1077), where he did penance and was eventually absolved. (It is impossible to say what truth there is in the well-known legends as to the extreme personal humiliation inflicted on Henry before absolution was granted.) Three years subsequently Gregory again excommunicated his rival, but on this occasion he found that unless backed by a certain degree of public opinion the sentences of even the greatest of the Popes fall somewhat flat. A Council was summoned at Brixen in the Tyrol, Gregory was declared deposed, and Guibert of Ravenna nominated in his stead. Guibert was consequently enthroned as Clement III, and Gregory eventually died in exile.

The various stages in the series of disputes between Popes and Emperors have been discussed in detail by historians:

frequently such historians write from a purely ultramontane point of view and seek to prove that in all respects the Pope was wholly in the right; sometimes on the other hand less partial writers have tried to apportion the blame according to the circumstances of each specific incident. But the details are really not of vast importance to the general reader, because it is clear that everything depends on the question of principle involved. The Popes made certain claims which were either justifiable or otherwise. In the first hypothesis the Emperors were wholly and consistently wrong in having resisted the Divine will as manifested by the voice of the Vicar of Christ: in the second hypothesis the responsibility lies wholly with the Popes who wantonly distorted the Christian religion and needlessly involved Europe in costly and sanguinary wars. A point however to be borne in mind in judging of these quarrels is that the Popes consistently aimed at the subjection of the Emperors, not their extinction. The Empire finally collapsed when Francis II abdicated in 1806. At the Congress of Vienna held after the fall of Napoleon a few years subsequently the Pope formally protested against the failure of the Powers to restore the Empire as a "centre of political unity" of Christian nations.

It has already been observed that Hildebrand aimed at the entire subjection of the laity to the clergy. In order that this ideal might be fully realised, it was clearly necessary that ecclesiastics should keep aloof from the ordinary social and domestic life of their lay neighbours. Hence much of Hildebrand's energy was directed to the enforcement of a rule, laid down as early as 385 by Pope Siricius, to the effect that the clergy should remain celibate. The action of Siricius was presumably taken in view of the considerations mentioned on page 79, but it is noteworthy that such action should have been taken in face of the apostolic warning (1 Tim. iv. 1-3) that in the latter times some should depart from the faith, forbidding to marry. Much discussion has taken place as to the extent to which the rule of celibacy had been actually observed before the time of Hildebrand, but it seems certain that with respect to the parish priests a great deal of toleration was generally shown, while even as regards the bishops marriage does not seem to have been very exceptional. The celebrated Saint Swithun, Bishop of Winchester (d. 862), was married, and we read that during 112 years (942-1054) the

See of Rouen was successively occupied by three bishops, two of whom were actually married, while the third had a family.

In 1051, presumably under the influence of Hildebrand, Leo IX, in his attempt to enforce the rule of celibacy, decreed that the partner of a guilty priest should be condemned to slavery. This is one of the many examples of the general practice of ecclesiastical law whereby it came about that, in the event of an equal degree of guilt, a lay person was more severely treated than a priest. An echo of this decree was heard in England at the trial of Archbishop Cranmer, when one of the judges reminded the accused that his children were "bondmen to the see of Canterbury."

It is interesting to notice that as a result of the enforcement of the papal decrees, married clergy were treated with far less consideration than those guilty of simple immorality. We find even so sincere a Christian as St. Thomas More (1478–1535) writing that the clerical marriage "defileth the priest more than double or treble whoredom." This point is of importance as being symptomatic of the fundamental change which had come over organised Christianity: spiritual matters had been allowed to fall into the background, while questions of legality and discipline had attained a maximum of importance. We might imagine that a sincere Christian would believe that if a priest feels certain very human sentiments towards a female member of his flock, it is better that he should marry her than seduce her. But the ecclesiastic says in effect:

> This is not so. If he seduces her he can, after confessing his sin with due penitence, be absolved. But he is unable validly to marry her, and if he go through an invalid ceremony of marriage, he not merely seduces his victim but he openly rebels against established Church order, and cannot be absolved until he not only expresses due penitence but unreservedly undertakes to treat his so-called marriage as null and void.

Insistence on the celibacy of the clergy has been the subject of a certain amount of criticism even on the part of the Roman Catholic laity, but it seems to be generally agreed that the influence of ecclesiastics has thereby been greatly augmented. This matter forms one of the points of difference from the Greek Church, wherein candidates for the priesthood customarily leave the seminary for a few months in order to choose a wife so that they can be ordained when already married. They do not marry after ordination.

A little over a century after the death of Gregory VII, the papal dignity was assumed by INNOCENT III, whose reign (1198-1216) nearly coincides with that of King John of England. It is noteworthy that, as in the case of Leo the Great, the electors' choice fell on a man who was not, at the time of his election, an ordained priest. The policy of Innocent, possibly the greatest of the Popes, was practically identical with that of Gregory, but whereas the latter had been only partially successful, the former carried the papal power, spiritual and temporal, to a height equalled neither before nor after. His attitude towards European politics will be appreciated from two answers given by him, one to the Emperor at Constantinople, who had quoted the injunction of Peter (1 Peter ii. 13) to submit to the King as supreme, and to whom Innocent replied that these words were addressed to the laity and not to the clergy. The other reply was given to the ambassadors of Philip Augustus, to whom he said:

> To princes power is given on earth, but to priests it is attributed also in heaven; to the former only over bodies, to the latter also over souls. Whence it follows that by so much as the soul is superior to the body, the priesthood is superior to the kingship.

Considerations of space prevent any detailed account of the extraordinary success of Innocent in enforcing his purpose on the various European rulers, but three points may be lightly touched on: (*a*) the Crusades; (*b*) dealings with England; and (*c*) the suppression of the Albigenses. As regards the first question, Innocent showed the utmost zeal in preaching a holy war against the Saracens. To this end immense preparations were made, but what actually took place in his reign was that the commanders of the principal expedition allowed themselves to be deflected from their original purpose, and instead of invading Palestine they waged war on the Eastern Empire, stormed Constantinople, and proclaimed Baldwin of Flanders Emperor of the East (1204). This change of plan was opposed to the wishes of Innocent, but he very justifiably took the best possible advantage of the new situation: he found himself in the unprecedented position of being able to nominate a Patriarch of Constantinople, and he expressed the hope that henceforth the Church would be "one fold under one shepherd."

In this way the papal authority was increased, although in after years memories of the terrible sack of Constantinople by the armies of Western Europe formed an additional obstacle in the way of a possible reunion of the Oriental Church with the Occidental.

We now come to consider the special relationships of Innocent with England. At the period of which we speak the Archbishops of Canterbury were customarily the chief advisers of the Crown, and it was therefore not unreasonable that the right of nomination should be exercised by the reigning sovereign. But at that time, as in our day, the Chapter of Canterbury claimed the right to elect its Archbishop. At the present time the difficulty is in practice surmounted by the Chapter going through the fiction of electing whomever may be appointed by the Crown; but in 1206, the see having fallen vacant, the monks of Canterbury showed themselves less complaisant, and a deadlock ensued. The King, the bishops of the province and a part of the Chapter favoured the translation of the Bishop of Norwich to the vacant see: other members of the Chapter, being apparently the younger of the monks, privately elected their own Sub-Prior. The Bishop of Norwich was then elected by such of the monks as were favourable to him. Both candidates appealed to Rome for confirmation, and the Pope, holding both elections null and void, ordered that a fresh election should take place in his own presence. Innocent then induced the representatives of the monks to elect one of the Cardinals, Stephen Langton, an Englishman, and indeed a very suitable man for the office had King John's consent been obtained. The King refused to recognise this election, and Innocent in consequence laid England under an interdict (1208). The great majority of the English clergy in obedience to the Pope's command closed their churches, although baptisms, marriages and the unction of the dying took place in private. In the winter of 1212–1213 Innocent declared John deposed, and called on Philip Augustus of France to invade England. John, however, thereupon made complete submission to the Pope, agreeing to hold his crown as a papal vassal and to pay an annual tribute. This submission left the King in an unsatisfactory position as regards the nobles, people and the more patriotic of the clergy: they had previously been disgusted by his crimes and now they became emboldened by his weakness. The nobles drew up (1215)—and in this they seem to have been assisted by Cardinal Langton

CHRISTIANITY AS AN INSTITUTION

himself—a document (*Magna Charta*) consisting of sixty-three very heterogeneous clauses to which they practically forced the King to pledge himself.

The sealing of this Charter is an event of great importance in English history, not so much on account of any strikingly new principle therein adopted, but rather because the insistence on its acceptance served to remind the King forcibly of his duties, and warned him that deposition might follow failure to carry them out. The clauses to which subsequent generations have attached special importance are Nos. 39 and 40, which stipulate that no one shall be imprisoned except by legal process and judgment of his peers, and further that justice shall not be denied, delayed or sold. The reference to judgment by the peers of the accused seems to imply the maintenance of different courts of criminal jurisprudence for different classes of offenders—ecclesiastics, lay nobles, lay commoners. But the remaining portion of the two clauses in question appears merely to aim at calling the King's attention to his remissness in the past. No ruler, however unscrupulous or lazy, could possibly claim that it was consistent with his duty to deny, to delay or to sell justice.

The clauses to which the framers of the document evidently attached greatest importance are those which tend to limit the power of the Crown by confirming the "liberties" (i.e. privileges) of the tenants-in-chief, and (No. 15) by extending some of these "liberties" to the tenants of the tenants-in-chief. It is further somewhat vaguely stipulated that the English Church shall be free (Nos. 1 and 63). Hence the general policy of the framers is the precise opposite of that of the great statesmen—Louis XI, Henri IV, Richelieu and Mazarin—whose combined efforts raised France from a condition resembling anarchy to its pinnacle of prosperity in the first half of the reign of Louis XIV. It is interesting to note that so little was the Charter regarded as what we should to-day call a democratic document, that it does not seem to have been translated into English before the sixteenth century.

Almost immediately after affixing his seal, John wrote to the Pope asking that the Charter be declared null and void. The sympathies of Innocent must have been with his friend and protégé Cardinal Langton rather than with John his ex-opponent; but, as will be shown in a later chapter (pp. 272 and 274), the attitude of the Roman Church has consistently been to discountenance resistance, on the part of subjects, to the measures of any lawful prince, unless of course such measures be condemned by the Pope himself as Vice-Regent of God on earth. So Innocent issued (August 15, 1215) a bull to the effect that, being unwilling to dissimulate the audacity of so much malignity (*tantæ malignitatis audaciam dissimulare nolentes*) to the grave peril of all concerns of the Crucified One (*grave periculum totius negotii crucifixi*), on behalf of the omnipotent God, Father, Son and Holy Ghost, and also with the authority of the Blessed Peter and Paul and of himself (*ac nostra*), he prohibited the King under threat of the papal anathema from presuming to observe the Charter (*prohibentes ne ea observare praesumat*) and the Barons and their allies (*complicibus*) from demanding its observance. The "troublers of the King and Kingdom" were afterwards declared excommunicate, and the Cardinal himself was eventually suspended from his functions for his remissness in giving effect to this sentence. It so happened that in the following year both Pope and King died, and it can hardly be said that the final victory rested with Innocent, as the Charter was eventually ratified on behalf of John's nine-year-old son (Henry III) who, after coming of age, reaffirmed his fidelity thereto.

It is probably true to say that the most notable and successful work of Innocent was the suppression of the Albigenses, a name given to certain heretics of the south of France in the twelfth and thirteenth centuries. Exactly what were the tenets of these unhappy people is not exactly known, as such knowledge as we possess is almost exclusively derived from their adversaries (*vide* Appendix C, p. 298). It seems probable however that the great bulk of their number had become dissatisfied with the formalism and legalism of the Roman Church and with the avarice and corrupt morals of its priesthood. Such people, while becoming anti-sacerdotal, fully retained their Christian beliefs. (The doctrines of their inner circle, *Cathari*, *perfecti* or *bonshommes*, are touched on in a later section of this chapter.) Innocent at first attempted to suppress the sect by pacific means, but found that not merely the nobles but the bishops themselves tended to sympathise with the heretics. It is not clear how far the bishops actually held the same beliefs as the Albigenses, and how far they resented certain monks being appointed by the Pope as his legates to perform work which doubtless in their opinion should have been carried on by themselves. However this may be, in 1204 Innocent suspended the authority of the bishops in the south of France, and a few years subsequently declared a holy war against the Albigenses. Thereupon the nobles of northern France, allying themselves with the monks, invaded the south and dispossessed the landowners of their property, with such frightful slaughter as to make this persecution one of the most sanguinary in history. The brilliant Provençal civilisation was utterly destroyed, but it is impossible to deny that the success from the papal point of view was complete. The massacre of the Albigenses is the most outstanding exercise of the Pope's authority when the Papacy itself was at the pinnacle of its power, and it is impossible to dissociate our judgment of this incident with our conviction as to the nature of the papal office. If we believe that Popes are appointed by God to repress by fire and sword any creed other than that which they are divinely inspired to teach, it follows that Innocent acted in a wholly laudable manner: in the contrary event we are forced to regard his conduct as frankly indefensible.

General Nature of Medieval Christianity

In a former chapter a few pages were devoted to a glance at the infant Church as existing shortly after the death of its founder: it is now convenient to examine cursorily the situation of the fully-organised body when at the plenitude of its power. A point which immediately claims our attention is that Christianity found itself confronted with a great rival, Mahometanism, and although the two systems differed very widely in their details, nevertheless in certain respects they were strikingly similar. Each body taught the existence of one God, and each believed itself to be the recipient of that God's special favour. Each body eagerly appealed to arms in defence of its faith: such appeals continued for centuries with indecisive results, each side calling upon God for assistance against the other, each side regarding victory as a divine answer to its own prayers and refusing to regard defeat as a divine answer to the prayers of its rival. Each body was anxious to convert the other to the true faith, and each was convinced that, although something might be done on a small scale by argument and persuasion, nevertheless wholesale bloodshed really constituted the true missionary effort. We find for example that that most eminent of Portuguese poets, Luiz de Camões, in his magnificent description of Vasco da Gama's great expedition to India, began by glorifying the memories of those kings who dilated the Faith and the Empire, and who devastated the vicious lands of Africa and Asia. (*As memorias gloriosas d'aquelles reis que foram dilatando a Fé, o imperio; e as terras viciosas de Africa e de Asia andaram devastando.* Lusiadas i. 2.) The idea of propagating the Faith among the Mahometans and other unbelievers without an accompanying devastation of their vicious lands, would have had but small attraction for the militant Christians whom Portugal sent forth on her great maritime expeditions (*vide* Appendix D, p. 300).

A second very notable point about medieval Christianity is the marked line of demarcation of the faithful into two classes, clerical and lay. Somewhat as the Jew looked on the Gentile as a being in whom God took far less interest than he did in the chosen race of Israel, so was the medieval layman looked on as one meriting and receiving a smaller share in the divine favour than did the ecclesiastic. Gregory VII argued that the Pope is to the Emperor as the sun is to the moon, and Innocent III similarly affirmed that the priest is as much above the king as the soul is above the body. The history of the Christian religion is largely a history of attempts to apply these theories to practice. It resulted logically from the position taken up by the Church that an ecclesiastic who commits some criminal offence ought to be tried by his hierarchical superiors and not by the secular courts. This claim led to much discussion and ill feeling. For example, when so late as 1850 the so-called *privilegium fori* was extinguished in Piedmont, the Archbishop of Turin prohibited his clergy from appearing before the secular tribunals or obeying their mandates, and the Archbishop's action was expressly confirmed by Pius IX. In England however the controversy was far less acute, and the law courts early came to a kind of working arrangement, tolerated by the Church, whereby the death penalty in respect of certain offences was mitigated when a cleric was the criminal. It was only in 1841 that the last relics of this practice, called "Benefit of Clergy," were abolished by statute.

Another feature which claims our attention is the size, magnificence and number of the medieval churches, when contrasted with the number of laymen who might reasonably be expected to worship therein. Such relatively small towns as Bourges and Chartres possess cathedrals which would have excited our unstinted admiration even if they had been the principal churches of such cities as London and Paris. It is needless to add that the work of construction of such ambitious buildings was frequently interrupted, so a considerable time often elapsed between the laying of the foundation-stone and final completion. Florence and Cologne Cathedrals were both commenced in the thirteenth century and finished in the nineteenth. Many cathedral churches, especially in the smaller cities, remain unfinished; but such buildings frequently bear witness to the boldness with which the ecclesiastical authorities planned works which we should have considered wholly disproportionate to the size of the respective towns. The vaulting of the cathedral of Beauvais, a town of some 20,000 inhabitants, is over 150 feet high, about the same as that of St. Peter's at Rome, the largest and most magnificent temple in Christendom. We are not surprised to find therefore that the nave of Beauvais remains, and seems likely to remain, still unbuilt. If the nave of Siena Cathedral had been completed the building would almost have rivalled St. Paul's, London, in size, as well as far surpassing it as regards beauty.

The cathedrals were the scenes of very elaborate ceremonies, of which the bulk of the laity presumably understood but little. The language used was unintelligible to the common people, and even if the vernacular had been employed the effect so far as regards the laity would have been the same, because the offices in general were either sung in such a way as to obscure the sense, or else said in a very low tone of voice. In consequence the modern traveller is not surprised to find that in many immense places of worship the floor-space from which the laity can get a view of what is going on is remarkably small. We find a certain area, called "the sanctuary," which may be regarded as the stage where the principal ceremonies are carried out; and in the immediate vicinity there is a choir where the bulk of the ecclesiastics and customarily the singers are accommodated; but in such churches as Seville and Toledo Cathedrals and Westminster Abbey we see that of the floor-space allocated to the use of the laity only quite a small portion commands a good view of the sanctuary.

It is noteworthy that with the increase of the power and wealth of the clergy, their function of leading their flocks in prayer and praise tended to drop into the background, and they were regarded more and more as bedesmen, praying on behalf of the laity rather than with them. As an illustration of this tendency may be cited the fact, already referred to, that every day in the Church of Our Lady at Loreto a series of one hundred and twenty masses commenced at daybreak.

Assuming that the latest of the series was said in accordance with the normal custom about noon, we infer that the masses commenced at intervals averaging about four minutes. It seems clear therefore that the saying of a mass was and is regarded as something in itself agreeable to God, independently of the question as to whether a congregation can be found to take part in the service. We therefore ask ourselves exactly what is understood by the term "mass."

We have already made reference to the institution by Jesus of the ceremonial custom of breaking bread, and theologians hold that this custom can be rightly regarded in two different aspects—sacramental and sacrificial. When speaking of the ceremony in its sacramental aspect, it is usual to use the word "eucharist," or perhaps more frequently "holy communion." When speaking of the ceremony in its sacrificial aspect, Roman Catholics customarily use the word "mass." With respect to the sacramental aspect we note the importance attached to a literal rather than a figurative acceptance of the words: "This is my body": "This is my blood." Hence the decree promulgated by the Council of Trent:

> If any one shall say that in the holy sacrament of the Eucharist there remains, together with the body and blood of our Lord Jesus Christ, the substance of the bread and wine, and shall deny the wonderful and singular conversion of the whole substance of the bread into body and of the wine into blood, the species only of the bread and wine remaining—which conversion the Catholic Church most fittingly calls Transubstantiation—let him be anathema.

Two noteworthy consequences result from the acceptance of the above doctrine of Transubstantiation. Firstly, when once the body and blood of Jesus exist under the "species" (or outward appearance) of bread and wine, it is not necessary that anyone who desires to receive the spiritual benefit of this mystery shall have been present at the moment of transsubstantiation. On the contrary, the consecrated elements can be retained for an undefined period and partaken of by the communicant according to circumstances. And further it is current doctrine that each particle of that transubstantiated element which has the species of bread becomes body, blood, soul and divinity of Jesus; so it is not necessary that the communicant receive more than one of the two elements. In point of fact in the Church of Rome the communicant, other than the officiating priest, receives one element only.

Secondly: that transubstantiated element which has the species of bread can rightly be placed in a suitable receptacle, called a "monstrance," and exhibited to the faithful, who are thus, independently of any question of actually partaking of the Lord's body, afforded an opportunity of worshipping him hidden under the appearance of bread.

We have hitherto spoken of the ceremony in its sacramental aspect: it is the rite in which is believed to be effected the miracle of transubstantiation. We now come to speak of the sacrificial aspect. Paul tells us (1 Cor. xi. 26) that by eating and drinking at the breaking of the bread we "show (Vulg. *annuntiabitis*) the Lord's death till he come." Theologians interpret the words *show* and *annuntiabitis* as implying a re-offering before God the Father of the sacrifice made by his Son on Calvary. This idea of a re-offering is especially associated with the name "mass." And as medieval doctrine further developed, the mass frequently came to be looked on not so much as a re-offering but rather as a re-enactment of the great sacrifice. As an example of how this doctrine is now presented in popular theology, an extract is subjoined from Canon Gilbert's *Love of Jesus*, published with the imprimatur of Cardinal Manning:

> "We hold that here" (i.e. at the Altar) "in a mystical manner thy body and blood are separated, and that thou art as it were again nailed to the cross, and presented to heaven as a holocaust, for the propitiation of the sins of the world. . . . Why was not one atonement, dearest Lord, one sacrifice, one Calvary sufficient? Thou knewest . . . that we should contemn thy first sacrifice, and so, dearest Lord, every day thou art sacrificed again."

The doctrine above indicated forms the explanation of a point which has often raised enquiry in the minds of people outside the Roman Church. When there are a number of priests together, why do we so frequently find that each says his own mass individually? Why does not one celebrate the holy mysteries while the others join him in an act of collective worship? For example, *L'Illustration* of August 3, 1935, gave its readers a photograph, accompanied by a descriptive article, of a young priest saying his first mass at Cambrai. Three of his brothers, all priests, were present; so three altars were placed in the choir in front of the high-altar, and the four priests said mass simultaneously, the photograph showing the elevation of the chalice by all four at the same moment. The intention was that by this means four separate sacrifices might be offered in the sight of God, instead of one as would have been the case if the elder priests had merely accompanied with their prayers the act of their younger brother.

It is not easy to over-estimate the influence exercised by belief in the efficacy of the mass over the mentality of the medieval Christian. In later centuries there arose a school of thought which unreservedly accepted (*e.g.*) the miracle of the raising of Tabitha by Peter, but which rejected the miracle of the mass as a blasphemous fable (*vide* Art. XXXI of the Church of England). But in the belief of the medieval Christian, throughout each morning of the year the marvel of transubstantiation was taking place every minute, and Christ was continually being offered as a sacrifice before God. The fact that we are unable to perceive any physical change in the elements after consecration was and is looked on as a result of the act of God, who permits our senses to be so imperfect that this change cannot be observed. Thus in St. Thomas Aquinas's well-known hymn forming part of the office for Maunday Thursday we find the following:

> Verbum caro, panem verum
> Verbo carnem efficit:
> Fitque sanguis Christi merum;
> Et si sensus deficit,
> Ad firmandum cor sincerum
> Sola fides sufficit.

(*The Word-Flesh makes, by his Word, true bread to be flesh, and wine is made to be the blood of Christ; and if sense fails, faith alone is sufficient to strengthen a sincere heart.*)

It was believed that on extremely rare occasions the deficiency of our senses was, as a result of a special divine favour, partially remedied. The best known example is that of the "Miracle of Bolsena." The history is to the effect that in 1263 a pious priest when saying mass at Bolsena was troubled with doubts as to the truth of the doctrine of transubstantiation, and that the consecrated host thereupon commenced to bleed to such an extent as to stain a napkin (*corporale*). It appears that it was on account of this miracle that in the following year Urban IV, formerly Archdeacon of Liège, made the observance of the festival of Corpus Christi (which had previously been kept, in honour of the mystery of transubstantiation, in the diocese of Liège almost exclusively) obligatory on the whole Church.

The Pope also gave directions for the building of the present Cathedral of Orvieto, about twelve miles from Bolsena, so that the bloodstained *corporale* might therein be suitably lodged. This miracle forms the subject of one of Raphael's frescoes executed by order of Julius II in the Vatican about 1512. The priest is represented in the act of consecration, and the Pope, with the features of Julius II, kneels opposite. From a technical point of view this is probably Raphael's most perfect fresco.

Everything which was best in the religious system of the Middle Ages was associated with the celebration of holy mass. The doctrine of transubstantiation, held even to-day by the great majority of Christians, was then almost universally accepted. To the medieval churchgoer this dogma was one not to be argued about, but to be received unreservedly with all due faith and humility. The worshipper who entered a church where the sacrifice of the mass was being offered, or where the consecrated wafer was exposed, was rarely troubled by doubts as to whether he was really in the presence of the living God, and whether One fairer than the children of men was verily manifesting himself as an object of the adoration of the faithful. So when the medieval saint lifted his thoughts towards Almighty God, he very specially associated his highest and holiest aspirations with the blessed sacrament of the altar. Modern sceptics argue that the bread and wine form at best a mere material aid to devotion. This point is now a matter of controversy, but was hardly a matter of controversy in the days of which we speak, when with practical unanimity all those who professed and called themselves Christians accepted unreservedly the doctrine set forth by the Catholic Church.

But it can hardly be doubted that an intense and earnest conviction of the miracle of transubstantiation, as effected in virtue of certain supernatural powers conferred on a priest at his ordination, inclined people to believe, usually on very slight grounds, that the Deity frequently intervened in human affairs in a manner contrary to the normal processes of nature. Or perhaps it would be more correct to say that the processes of nature appeared much less uniform to the medieval theologian than they do to the twentieth century scientist. For example, few visitors to the Long Gallery at the Louvre fail to admire Murillo's exquisite masterpiece entitled *La Cuisine de San Diego*: a monastery cook has interrupted his work in order to pray, and angels have consequently received a divine mission to prepare the food while the cook himself remains in ecstasy.

222 INTRODUCTION TO THE STUDY OF CHRISTIANITY

Now it seems likely that those very devout people who, believing the legend to be literally true, commissioned Murillo to paint this picture, based their belief on somewhat slight evidence. The idea of an angel preparing food while the cook himself is occupied in prayer appealed far more forcibly to the average Spaniard even as late as Murillo's day than it does to the present generation, accustomed as is the latter to think that the more abnormal an alleged event the greater the need for conclusive evidence before accepting it. So it will readily be inferred how unfavourable was medieval mentality to the progress of scientific observation. A man who believes that, provided he be sufficiently devout, he may very possibly find an angel to prepare his food for him, is unlikely to enter into a serious technical study of the real nature of cooking, and to enquire exactly in what way heat modifies foodstuffs and renders them more suitable for consumption. So we are not surprised to find that throughout the Middle Ages the natural sciences were relatively little esteemed, and it can hardly be doubted that progress in hygiene and medicine was greatly impeded by the widespread belief that illness is normally a punishment for sin rather than the direct result of physical causes. Hence terrible plagues resulted from the generally insanitary condition of the houses. It is estimated for example that the Black Death in the middle of the fourteenth century carried off a third of the population of England.

ROGER BACON (c. 1214–c. 1294), the greatest and most original thinker of his age, urged in vain that knowledge of the working of nature should be sought empirically by actual experiment. The first result of Bacon's efforts was that he was placed under supervision, and prevented for ten years from doing any writing for publication. Pope Clement IV who had heard of his misfortunes then very wisely intervened, and Bacon was permitted to commit his theories to writing, but with the unfortunate result that he was kept in prison for a further term of fourteen years.

The intellectual stagnation of the Middle Ages was probably intensified by the celibacy of the clergy. The wealth and power enjoyed by the higher ecclesiastics were such as to form a great attraction to young men of exceptional mental ability. Such men, however, when once vowed to the religious life, were unable to bring up legitimate children to have a chance of inheriting their fathers' talents. This seems to be one of the various reasons whereby it came about that during the Middle

Ages institutional Christianity, while attaining a maximum of secular power, simultaneously showed such obvious signs of moral and intellectual decadence. Those who dispute the fact of this decadence call attention to the magnificence of the ecclesiastical buildings which form so prominent a feature of the period. It is however easy to understand why such great importance should have been attached to sacred architecture among medieval Christians. Undoubtedly a genuine feeling of piety played a highly important share in the planning and construction of their places of worship, but it seems probable that a desire to impress the laity with the power, wealth and authority of the clergy also formed a prominent factor. (A confirmation of this inference may be found in the fact that, contrary to the custom of the Mahometans, in the very elaborate ceremonies which take place in Catholic places of worship, a considerable part of the ritual consists of expressions of respect, sometimes thought by outsiders to be a little exaggerated, paid to the principal officiant.) It seems moreover likely that rivalry between the regular clergy (monks and friars) and the secular (bishops and parish priests) was largely instrumental in bringing about the extraordinary magnificence of the churches of the Middle Ages. On the whole it was the bishops and their clergy who found themselves enabled to put up the more ambitious buildings, although there are several striking instances to the contrary. The Franciscan Church of the Frari at Venice is far more sumptuous than the former Cathedral of S. Pietro di Castello.[1] And similarly at Padua the Cathedral, which is unfinished, is completely outshone by the Franciscan Church dedicated to St. Anthony, just as in Rio de Janeiro the Cathedral is outshone by the Church of the Candelaria Brotherhood.

Philosophy

The medieval ecclesiastics not merely took considerable interest in philosophy, but some of their writers made very real advances in that science. Later generations arose to whom the terminology used by these writers was unfamiliar, and such generations found it easier to ridicule the so-called scholastic philosophy than to understand it. Thus it came about that the name of one of the most eminent of the thirteenth-century writers, Duns

---

[1] In 1807, on the initiative of Napoleon, the Patriarch's seat was removed from S. Pietro di Castello to the Church of S. Mark, which is now used as the Cathedral.

(surnamed Scotus) came eventually to mean "a backward pupil." But we in our own day may well feel admiration for the acuteness of intellect with which many of the schoolmen attempted to solve the fundamental problems which confront humanity. It was of course inevitable that freedom of thought and of discussion, whenever permitted, should produce occasional deviation from orthodoxy. PIERRE ABÉLARD (1079–1142) is particularly noteworthy as having had the courage to maintain that "a doctrine is believed, not because God has enunciated it, but because we are convinced by reason that it is true." We are not surprised to find therefore that Abélard's spirit of free enquiry led him to a view of the nature of the Blessed Trinity closely allied to that of Sabellius (*vide* p. 128), and Abélard was consequently condemned at the Councils of Soissons and Sens. So he fell into disrepute, and it has indeed come about that whereas in his early manhood his exceptional mental gifts received extraordinary appreciation, and he may be fairly said to have fixed more than any other teacher the scholastic manner of philosophising, later generations remember him almost entirely on account of a very unfortunate love affair. Of the thousands of people who yearly visit his tomb in the Père Lachaise Cemetery, probably not one in a hundred has ever read a line of his writings, excepting possibly in the popular hymn commencing *O quanta qualia sunt illa Sabbata* ("O what their joy and their glory must be, those endless Sabbaths the blessed ones see").

No other scholastic writer, of ability approaching to that of Abélard, permitted himself similar independence of thought, and some little time after Abélard's death orthodox philosophy received a powerful stimulus from an outside source. It happened that an Arab writer, Abul Walid of Cordoba, commonly referred to as AVERROES (1126–1198), did some excellent work in his *Commentaries on Aristotle*, and the Commentaries, in a Latin translation, practically introduced the system of the Stagirite to Christian scholars in the West.

Scholastic writers had all along seen, as Augustine had seen nine or ten centuries previously, the difficulty of reconciling the principles of Plato with those of traditional Christianity. Hence the teachings of a rival philosopher were eagerly welcomed, and Christian thought, among the more intellectual of the scholastic writers, came to be a blend of Aristotelian principles with Catholic dogma. Of these writers by far the most prominent is ST. THOMAS (*c*. 1226–1274), a Dominican friar, born near Aquino in Campania, whose *Summa* has consistently commanded great authority among Catholics.

The Dominican adopted the fundamental principle that human knowledge has two foundations, faith and reason; the former causes us to accept divine revelation, and the latter enables us both to acquire knowledge as to the visible universe and to judge of such theological points as revelation leaves undecided. St. Thomas held that faith and reason do not clash, but nevertheless that the truths we acquire as a result of revelation are more important than those which we acquire through reason.

In 1567 St. Thomas was formally ranked with the other four great Latin Doctors of the Church—Ambrose, Augustine, Jerome and Gregory, and he is specially designated as "Angelic." Leo XIII directed the clergy (August 4, 1879) to take the teachings of St. Thomas as the basis of their theological position. He was indeed a man of vast learning and of extraordinary power of synthesis; and even a hostile critic could hardly deny that he performed admirably his task of blending into a harmonious whole Aristotelian philosophy with Roman theology. But on the other hand it would appear that by insisting on the importance of revelation as compared with reason, he merely shelved difficulties without attempting to solve them; so he, like so many other theological writers, may be not unfairly accused of having based his works on a *petitio principii*.

On the matter of persecution of heretics St. Thomas enunciates principles (*Summa* ii. 9, 11) concerning which the most charitable thing that can be said is that the writer was in no way in advance of his age.

The name of St. Thomas has further become prominent in connection with the controversy anent the Immaculate Conception of the Blessed Virgin Mary. A doctrine was preached by the Franciscan friars, and especially by Duns Scotus, that the Mother of Jesus was born free of original sin. St. Thomas and the Dominicans in general however opposed this teaching on the ground that Paul tells us that Jesus gave himself as a ransom for all (1 Tim. ii. 6), including presumably the Blessed Virgin. They argued not unreasonably that if she had not inherited original sin she could not have been ransomed therefrom. This controversy was not settled till 1854 when Pius IX published a decree formally imposing on the faithful belief in the Franciscan teaching. So notwithstanding the extraordinary honour paid to the writings of the Angelic Doctor, the fact remains that they contain matter which if written since 1854 would have entailed their author in condemnation as a heretic.

An important matter on which medieval doctrine was at variance with modern practice is the lending of money at interest (or "usury," to adopt the old-fashioned term). We know that the Jews, while still a very primitive people, formed the conclusion that usury was immoral when the borrower was a fellow Jew, but not otherwise (Deut. xxiii. 19, 20). The reason of this prejudice is easy to understand. In a primitive community well-to-do people rarely borrow money as a commercial speculation, and applicants for loans are almost always impecunious and often insolvent. And it is evident that the habitual lending of money to needy borrowers without tangible security cannot be carried on without ultimate loss to the lender unless he secures himself by charging a rate of interest which is highly onerous on the borrowers. It was presumably in view of such considerations as the foregoing that the Church prohibited usury altogether, independently of the question whether the rate of interest was high or low. The Mahometans of our own day still refuse, in principle at all events, to permit the practice.

But as mercantile transactions came to be more extensively developed, and became better organised, an entirely different class of borrowing was found desirable. Merchants enjoying good credit were desirous of obtaining loans for their legitimate commercial speculations, and were able to offer rates of interest which, without being onerous on the borrowers, were attractive to lenders. To such transactions there could be no objection on moral grounds, and it was on that account that in course of time the Church's prohibition was modified, although the prejudice against usury is still strong in Roman Catholic countries. In France for example banking operations remain largely in the hands of Protestants and Jews, most but perhaps not all of whom carry on worthily the traditions of their honourable calling. It may also be not out of place to refer to the daily press of those not unnumerous Latin-American countries which are in default to their foreign creditors: the reader will notice how lofty a moral tone is taken by the native journalist when he extols on the one hand the dignified and patriotic attitude of his country's government in dishonouring

CHRISTIANITY AS AN INSTITUTION

its obligations, and condemns on the other the contemptible greed of the vulgar usurer who asks for payment of his bond.

It now seems desirable to say something about that extreme cruelty which appears to many people to be the most conspicuous feature of medieval ecclesiastical administration. In considering this question it seems right to point out as a preliminary that we have no real proof that this cruelty was so very exceptional. We read for example that on a certain day in 1245 two hundred heretics were burnt at Montségur. This fact is of course very shocking, but we ought to remember that while we possess information as to what was going on in Montségur in 1245, we do not know accurately what was being done in that year in Senegal or in Borneo or in many other parts of the world; and it is quite conceivable that other atrocities equally revolting but which had nothing to do with Christianity were in fact then committed. Leaving however this point aside, it is easy to see why and how institutional Christianity became closely associated with extreme cruelty. Like other governing classes the medieval ecclesiastics aimed at wealth and authority, and it was only to a relatively small extent that they were able to attain their ends by the direct use of military power. They were forced to rely on their hold on the minds of men, and they in consequence represented themselves as the possessors of a mysterious power which gave them the keys of heaven and hell, and which caused men who died on good terms with the Church to obtain in the next world a reward far exceeding all possible merit, while those who failed in this condition were doomed to an eternity of the most frightful suffering. In other words the ecclesiastics found it to be in their interest to represent the Deity himself as intensely cruel, and this doctrine inevitably reacted on their own mentality. If we accept the traditional teaching as to eternal punishment, it is reasonable to infer that it is a small matter to burn a few hundred heretics, because such chastisement is merely a comparatively insignificant preliminary to the eternity of torment which awaits them hereafter. So we find that under the influence of traditional Christianity men developed morally in two directions simultaneously. A certain standard of genuine Christian morality was customarily taught, and many individuals were in fact able by God's help to raise themselves to exalted spiritual levels. But at the same time the training which was universal in their day caused even the best of ecclesiastics

228 INTRODUCTION TO THE STUDY OF CHRISTIANITY

to subordinate the teaching of the Gospels to what was held to be the interest of the Church. In consequence the history of the development of Christianity is for many centuries the history of the opposition between two different standards of morality—that of Jesus and that of the Church. Centuries before the commencement of our era, Micah (vi. 8) had asked *What doth the Lord require of thee, but to do justly and to love mercy and to walk humbly with thy God?* And it was on the basis of the teaching implied in this question that Jesus founded his community. But the qualities of justice, mercy and humility could have but little place in a system which aimed primarily at the complete subjection of the laity to the clergy, and which, in pursuance of that aim, suppressed most ruthlessly all independent thought. So the student must be prepared to find that while the Christian virtues undoubtedly continued to exist, their exercise was unhappily subordinated to that terrible cruelty and injustice which form the key-notes of medieval Christianity. As an example of the opposition between the two standards of conduct, the following incident may be related:

> Early in this year (1569) . . . a poor Anabaptist, guilty of no crime but his fellowship with a persecuted sect, had been condemned to death. He had made his escape, closely pursued by an officer of justice, across a frozen lake. It was late in the winter and the ice had become unsound. It trembled and cracked beneath his footsteps, but he reached the shore in safety. The officer was not so fortunate. The ice gave way beneath him and he sank into the lake, uttering a cry for succour. There was none to hear him except the fugitive whom he had been hunting. Dirk Willemzoon, for so was the Anabaptist called, instinctively obeying the dictates of a generous nature, returned, crossed the quaking and dangerous ice at the peril of his life, extended his hand to his enemy, and saved him from certain death. Unfortunately for human nature, it cannot be added that the generosity of the action was met by a corresponding heroism. The officer was desirous, it is true, of avoiding the responsibility of sacrificing the preserver of his life, but the Burgomaster of Aspern sternly reminded him to remember his oath. He accordingly arrested the fugitive who, on the 16th of May following, was burned to death under the most lingering tortures.
>
> (Gerard Brandt, *Hist. der Reformatie*.)
> Quoted in Motley's *History of the Rise of the Dutch Republic*.

The foregoing forms an excellent illustration of the state of morality. We find that the officer of justice was by no means

CHRISTIANITY AS AN INSTITUTION

destitute of the Christian feelings of mercy and gratitude. But such feelings were strictly subordinated to what he believed to be his duty, which was of course to assist in putting down all divergence from traditional Christianity by any means however atrocious.

Something has now been said about the triumph of institutional Christianity under Innocent III and other Pontiffs. It is in consequence convenient to give attention to the various difficulties which the Holy See encountered in attaining its maximum of power, and which eventually caused this power to decline. These difficulties can be mentioned under the heads of (a) Mahometanism; (b) Decentralisation, and the tendency to demand independence, total or partial, for local churches; (c) Protestantism, although this name was only invented long after the death of Innocent; (d) Liberal theology, sometimes tending to scepticism; and (e) Mysticism.

(a) *Mahometanism*

The relationships between Christianity and Mahometanism in Western Europe and in North Africa can now be very rapidly indicated. It has already been stated that in 732 the Moslem troops suffered a serious reverse near Poitiers. The effect of this reverse on the progress of civilisation has, as might indeed have been expected, been diversely appreciated by adherents of different schools of thought. Dr. Arnold (*The Later Roman Commonwealth*) seems to give to the Battle of Poitiers the first place "amongst those signal deliverances which have affected for centuries the happiness of mankind." And Schlegel (*Philosophy of History*) speaks of how "the arms of Charles Martel saved and delivered the Christian nations of the West from the deadly grasp of all-destroying Islam." On the other hand Anatole France in one of his books of personal reminiscences (*La Vie en Fleur*) tells us of a friend who used to argue that 732 was the most disastrous (*funeste*) date in history, because at the battle of Poitiers "Arab science, art and civilisation were driven back before Frankish barbarity." But however this may be, it is clear that 732 must be looked on as the high-water mark of Arab expansion in Western Europe, though on the other hand the final expulsion of the invaders from Gaul only took place considerably later. When Charles Martel died, nine years after his great victory, he left the Arabs in possession of Septimania (South-Eastern Gaul) whence they were expelled by his son

Pippin. But about 884 they again came northwards and succeeded in firmly establishing themselves in Provence, where they maintained a footing for nearly a century, being finally dislodged only in 973.

South of the Pyrenees we find that the relationship between partisans of the rival creeds long remained one of almost constant hostility, the fortunes of war tending sometimes in one direction and sometimes in the other, the general advantage however lying with the Christians. We read of a cultured and pleasure-loving people, interested in science, philosophy and the liberal arts, seeking to maintain its hold on the most agreeable and fertile parts of the Iberian Peninsula, and being dislodged, province by province, by sterner, hardier and less refined warrior races. Moslem rule disappeared from Spain in 1492; and North Africa subsequently became the battlefield between the contending creeds. The year 1578 may be said to form a high-water mark of Christian expansion in Africa, because in that year a formidable Portuguese army, led by King Sebastião in person, took the field against the Arabs in Morocco, and was totally defeated at Alcacer Kebir, the King himself presumably being amongst the slain. After this great defeat we do not seem to hear of any military operations on a really first-class scale against the North African Mahometans until more than two centuries subsequently, when Napoleon obtained a temporary footing in Egypt. And genuine permanent conquest of considerable tracts of territory, leaving aside the holding of seaports such as Ceuta and Mazagan, was only begun in North Africa in 1830 when, during the last few weeks of the reign of Charles X, the French captured Algiers.

Relationships during the Middle Ages between Christians and Moslems in the East are of even greater importance to the historian. Charlemagne, after his coronation in 800, cultivated amicable relationships with the Sultan of Bhagdad, Haroun al Raschid, who showed himself fully as urbane a monarch as the *Thousand and One Nights* would lead us to expect. Haroun recognised Charlemagne as "Protector of Jerusalem," and the Frankish Emperor there founded a hospital and a library. But a quarter of a century afterwards we find the Arabs commencing the conquest of Sicily; and some years subsequently they attacked the mainland of Italy, and Pope Leo IV took the very significant and far-reaching step of promising (848) a sure and certain hope of salvation to those who died combating in defence of Christianity. Somewhat more than two centuries subsequently

Gregory VII assembled an expedition for the sake of capturing Asia Minor from the Mahometans and restoring this territory to the Eastern Emperors, in return for which benefits the Oriental Churches would, it was hoped, make their submission to the Roman See. This expedition came to nothing, but some twenty years afterwards (1095) Urban II journeyed to Clermont-Ferrand in Auvergne, where he convened a Council at which he urged primarily the need for the recovery of the holy places of Christianity, and secondly the advisability of helping the Eastern Empire in its struggle with the Moslem infidels. He called for a truce to all quarrels among the nations of Western Europe, and urged the equipment of an expedition which should set forth to Palestine with the promise that participation therein should be considered as full and complete penance for sin.

It is noteworthy that Urban should have gone to France to launch this appeal. Less than thirty years previously Pope Alexander II, presumably under the influence of Hildebrand, had given his blessing to a great piratical raid which had taken place from Normandy against England, and the success of this expedition had exceeded all expectations (1066). Hundreds of the adventurers who had followed Duke William to Pevensey had attained, at the cost of possibly a few hours' sea-sickness and of participation in a single pitched battle, wealth and prosperity ever since. The younger generation of those who listened to Urban's address at Clermont-Ferrand were probably therefore the sons of men who had either taken part in the conquest of England, or who had passed their lives regretting that they had not done so. And further, when we consider the motives underlying the actions of the French and Norman nobles, we should not forget the fact that the right of primogeniture, as adopted by French law, left the younger brothers of the feudal lords with practically no choice of a profession other than the military or the clerical. Hence their readiness to take part in any operation which offered a fair prospect of profitable fighting. So it will eventually be seen that, while we should not under-estimate either the genuine religious zeal of many of the Crusaders, nor the powerful assistance rendered by the Genoese and Venetian merchant-adventurers who were anxious to establish trading stations in the Levant, yet the military success of Urban's expedition was principally due to the French (and especially the Norman) adventurers who sailed to the Holy Land with the same efficient organisation as their fellow-countrymen possessed when they embarked on the conquests of England and of the two Sicilies.

In the summer of 1096 large but unorganised bands of men began to move eastwards. Some ten thousand Jews were massacred in the Rhine Valley, but no military result was attained. Less than half of those who set out reached Constantinople, and those who crossed the Bosphorus seem to have perished almost to a man. The most celebrated of the leaders of this expedition, Peter the Hermit, a priest from Amiens, was one of the few survivors.

On the other hand, what may be considered as the officially organised expedition, headed by Bishop Adhemar, the papal commissary, assembled at Constantinople in the spring of 1097, and set out thence for Palestine. Two years later the Holy City fell, after frightful slaughter, into the hands of the Crusaders, and the Kingdom of Jerusalem was established. This brilliant victory occasioned great rejoicing throughout Christendom, and the prestige of the Papacy was very naturally and justifiably enhanced. But unfortunately the qualities necessary to take a city by storm are widely different from those necessary to impose permanently an alien rule on a conquered people. And the difficulties of the new rulers of Jerusalem were added to by a stream of fresh adventurers who continued to arrive, attracted as they were by the glowing reports which reached Europe with respect to the wealth and luxury acquired by the victorious Crusaders. These newcomers were naturally hostile to any kind of truce with the infidel; like the Portuguese of a later age of whom Camões wrote, what they wanted was to "dilate the faith" and to "devastate the vicious lands" of the unbeliever. So amicable relationships with neighbouring chieftains were found impossible and a permanent state of hostility prevailed. Less than half a century after the founding of the new kingdom, Edessa (the modern Urfa) was re-taken by the Saracens, and Pope Eugenius III thought it necessary to proclaim a new Crusade, commissioning St. Bernard to preach on its behalf. Louis VII of France and Conrad III of Germany took the vow, but the expedition was a disastrous failure, and few people can have been surprised when in 1187 Jerusalem in its turn fell to the Moslem. In consequence of this severe blow, as it was deemed, to the Christian faith, we find the three chief temporal monarchs of Christendom—Richard of England, Philip Augustus of France and Frederick I of Germany—taking part in the next expedition (1189-1192). Though this effort resulted in by no means as complete a failure as the last, nevertheless its measure of success was but small. It is interesting to notice in this connection how the ideals of a Holy War were now assuming a secondary place. Richard gravely suggested to Saladin that the former's sister should marry the latter's brother.

In the reign of Innocent III, who was the Pope who most consistently preached the duty of reconquering Jerusalem, the actual crusading effort was, as has already been noticed, chiefly utilised in sacking Constantinople, though in Innocent's time there were some very painful incidents styled "Children's Crusades." In France and Germany tens of thousands of young boys, possessed with religious fervour but lacking proper equipment and provisions, set out to march to Palestine and perished miserably in various ways.

In 1228 the Emperor Frederick II conducted a Crusade of his own under somewhat singular circumstances. He had taken the vow more than ten years previously, but had for one reason or other postponed his departure. The Pope consequently excommunicated him, invaded his dominions and levied a tithe from Christian Churches to pay for the expenses of this operation. Frederick nevertheless sailed for the Holy Land, and by diplomatically taking advantage of disputes among the Mahometans was able to obtain, without any fighting, possession of Jerusalem, Nazareth and Bethlehem. So having crowned himself King of Jerusalem (as he could find no cleric to perform the ceremony) Frederick sailed back to Europe to reconquer his own possessions and to make peace with the Pope. Jerusalem was in Christian hands from 1229 till 1244, and in Moslem hands from 1244 until the Great War. Acre, the last Christian stronghold in Syria, fell to Sultan Khalil in 1291, and the Crusades, in the sense in which the word is generally used, came to an end.

The effect of the Crusades on Christianity in general, and especially on the prestige of the Papacy, has often been discussed. Certain benefits undoubtedly resulted to Western civilisation through its contact with the learning and the culture of the East. But these benefits are small when compared with the frightful sacrifice of human life and the economic waste entailed in these ill-fated expeditions. The papal power however was undoubtedly increased by the success of 1099. On the other hand it is reasonable to suppose that subsequent disasters, and the success of the excommunicated Emperor Frederick II, had a contrary effect.

The Turks, who in their turn became the attackers, were successful in crushing Serbia and Bulgaria towards the end of the fourteenth century. In 1453 they took Constantinople, a victory which had far-reaching results on Western culture, because Greek-speaking refugees carried Greek manuscripts into the various centres of Occidental learning, and consequently popularised the study of the Hellenic classical authors. In 1526 a great part of Hungary passed into Turkish possession, and by 1571 the Ottoman power had become such that it seemed as if all Europe was in danger. But a naval battle which took place in that year near the entrance to the Gulf of Lepanto proved a decisive check to the Oriental invaders' sea power. On land they continued to meet with a considerable measure of success, and we find that Samuel Pepys thought it worth while to note in his diary under date of December 31, 1663: "The Turk very far entered into Germany, and all that part of the world at a loss what to expect from his proceedings." But the Ottoman armies subsequently met with a series of defeats at the hands of King John Sobieski of Poland; and after the relief of Vienna (September 12, 1683) the Moslem power definitely declined.

A very rapid summary has now been given of the relationships between Mahometanism and Christianity. The great struggle which took place during so many years is represented in much Christian literature as being one between truth and falsehood, between good and evil, between light and darkness. Thus Camões in the great poem to which reference has already been made, stimulates the enthusiasm of the Portuguese reigning monarch Dom Sebastião by expressing his hope that the King will become the "yoke and bane of the ignoble Ishmaelitish cavalier" (*Vós que esperamos jugo e vituperio do torpe ismaelita cavalheiro. Lusiadas* i. 8). Now we know that it was the ignoble Ishmaelitish cavalier who finally proved himself to be the yoke and bane of Dom Sebastião, who, as we have already seen, lost his throne and presumably his life at Alcacer Kebir. And we cannot but lament the fact that so many millions of human beings, throughout so lengthy a period, should have consistently refused to recognise the common fatherhood of God, and should have expended so much energy and treasure in iniquitous and fruitless warfare. Where lay the greater share of the blame it is exceedingly difficult to say, as historians on both sides have adulterated facts to meet their purposes. But as regards material civilisation there seems no doubt that

CHRISTIANITY AS AN INSTITUTION

during what are called the dark ages the Moslems, in some countries at all events, were far ahead of the Christians. Mr. Joseph McCabe (*The Splendour of Moorish Spain*) tells us:

> In the tenth century there was not anywhere in Europe, outside Arab Spain and Sicily, and there would not be for at least two centuries, a single city with 30,000 people, with even the most rudimentary sewerage, with any paved or lamp-lit streets, with a communal supply of pure water, with an elementary regard for hygiene, with a single public bath (and few if any private baths) or school. . . . In the tenth century Cordova had a population of 1,000,000 souls, a lavish supply of pure water and miles of well-paved and lamp-lit streets. . . . It took 5,000 mills along the river to grind the corn for the workers of Cordova. Nine hundred public baths met their passion for cleanliness, and six hundred mosques (Ballesteros admits the larger number of 3,000), each with a school attached, served their devotion.

To the foregoing it may very plausibly be objected that whatever may have been the extent of the achievements of the Hispano-Moslems in other directions, their buildings as a whole seem to compare unfavourably with those produced a few centuries later by the great Christian ecclesiastical architects. The reply would appear to be that the Spaniards either destroyed or disfigured so much of the Moslem handiwork that any true comparison has become exceedingly difficult. However, there are two notable buildings which may not unfairly be contrasted one with another—the Minaret (now called *La Giralda*) of the Great Mosque at Seville and the Campanile at Pisa. The former was begun in 1184 and took twelve years to construct; the latter was commenced a little earlier (1174) and was only finished in 1350. Now even if we overlook the initial error of building the Pisa Campanile on insecure foundations, thereby giving it its well-known inclination, we still feel that the artistic sense of the architect was far behind that of his Moslem rival at Seville.

What was formerly the Great Mosque at Cordoba occupies a walled-in area approximately as great as that of St. Peter's at Rome, but this comparison is unfair to the latter building, seeing that about a third of the Mosque consists of an unroofed court-yard (*Patio de los Naranjos*). On the other hand, if we to-day walk through what remains of the aisles at Cordoba, we still find sufficient traces of former magnificence to lead to the conclusion that for genuine artistic feeling the architects

236 INTRODUCTION TO THE STUDY OF CHRISTIANITY

of the Mahometan building were by no means unworthy of comparison with those who some centuries later constructed and adorned the great Basilica on the Vatican Hill.

(b) *Decentralisation, and the Tendency to Form National Churches*
Non-Roman writers have not infrequently pointed out with perfect propriety the debt which Western civilisation in general, and Latin Christianity in particular, owes to the early medieval Papacy for having formed a bulwark against the general anarchy of its time. Thus Dean Milman, an eminent Church of England divine (1791–1868), tells us:

> The Papacy . . . was the only power which lay not entirely and absolutely prostrate before the disasters of the times. . . . It was this power which was most imperatively required to preserve all that was to survive out of the crumbling wreck of Roman civilisation. To Western Christianity was absolutely necessary a centre, standing alone, strong in traditionary reverence, and in acknowledged claims to supremacy. . . . On the rise of a power, both controlling and conservative, hung, humanly speaking, the life and death of Christianity—of Christianity as a permanent, aggressive, expansive and to a certain extent uniform system. There must be a counterbalance to barbaric force, to the unavoidable anarchy of Teutonism, with its tribal, or at the utmost national independence, forming a host of small, conflicting, antagonistic kingdoms (*History of Latin Christianity*).

Now it is evident that any institution exercising the authority above indicated must necessarily incur considerable unpopularity. The Papacy felt it to be both lawful and expedient to repress heresy ruthlessly, the word "heresy" being interpreted in an even more elastic manner than "treason" in the times of the Tudor sovereigns. And if we examine many of the papal measures taken in repression of heresy, we notice not merely that they seem severe, but that they are of a nature to excite considerable resentment among many of those whose opinions are wholly orthodox. Two of the best known papal bulls dealing with heresy are the *Cum ex apostolatus officio* and the *In cœna Domini*, concerning which a few details may be found interesting.

The former of these bulls was promulgated by Paul IV in 1558 and was expressly stated to be a piece of permanent legislation, effected "in the plenitude of the apostolic jurisdiction." The Pope, as vice-regent of God and of our Lord Jesus

CHRISTIANITY AS AN INSTITUTION

Christ (*qui Dei et Domini nostri Jesu Christi vices gerit in terris*), therein claimed absolute authority over all princes and peoples: he enacted that should any rulers of any kind, spiritual or temporal, become heretical or schismatical they should *ipso facto* be deposed and condemned to death, but in case of repentance they should be imprisoned for life: further, that any prince who should grant any shelter or assistance to any heretical or schismatical ruler should also be deposed: further that if any bishop held privately any heretical opinions which only became public subsequently, the bishop's acts during the time he held such opinions were null and void. The faithful were enjoined not to oppose the bull in question under penalty of incurring the indignation of Almighty God and of the Apostles St. Peter and St. Paul.

The bull *In cœna Domini* actually dates from 1568, but is a kind of codification of older decrees. For two centuries this bull was read publicly at Rome on Thursday in Holy Week, the custom being that the Pope, when the reading was finished, cast a lighted torch into the Piazza di San Pietro as a token of the anathema incurred by those who contravene its terms. The bull anathematises all heretics, and those princes and magistrates who permit heretics to live unmolested in their territory: also all those who read or possess heretical books: also all those who appeal from any papal decision to any future Council: also such lay judges, officers of the secular courts and executioners as may attempt to render ecclesiastics subject to lay jurisdiction. Such anathema when incurred can only be removed, except *in articulo mortis*, by the Pope himself.

Now it is quite clear that the provisions of these decrees must inevitably have caused considerable resentment among even the most orthodox of the faithful. In France in 1580 the *Parlement* ordered that any bishop who published the bull *In cœna Domini* should be considered guilty of high treason, and that his estate should be confiscated. The King of Spain and the Viceroy of Naples both refused to allow the bull to be published in their territories. The Emperor Rudolph II similarly protested against its publication in Germany. But it was in Venice that the controversy actually became most acute (1605–1607). The Republic had convicted and imprisoned two clerics for criminal offences, and moreover had asserted its right to impose taxes on ecclesiastical property. After admonition a bull of interdict and excommunication was issued by the Pope. But the secular clergy remained faithful to the

Republic: some of the regular clergy who advocated submission to the Holy See were expelled: the Spanish army on which the Pope had apparently been relying finally decided not to attack, and the interdict remained almost a dead letter. There seems no doubt that the Venetians had in general no thought of leaving the Roman Church to become Protestant. It would indeed appear that their principal technical adviser throughout this controversy, Friar Paolo Sarpi, had certain mild leanings towards Protestantism, but the great bulk of the Venetians were wholly loyal to Catholicism: what they wanted was that the Pope should be a constitutional, and not an absolute sovereign. Eventually both sides agreed to accept the services, as mediator, of Henri IV of France. The Venetians, without going back on their general principles, agreed to surrender, as an exceptional act, the two clerical criminals to the French ambassador; and the Pope gave it to be understood that the interdict, while not formally withdrawn, would be practically disregarded. The victory clearly rested with the Venetians, who continued to exercise jurisdiction over clerical offenders and to impose taxes on ecclesiastical property.

In treating of the Papacy as a great unifying and consolidating power, attention is naturally directed to canon law, which long formed a kind of code common to the Christian nations of the West. This code dealt not merely with purely ecclesiastical matters, but also with marriage and kindred subjects. Now the advantage of the existence of a uniform system of jurisprudence, current throughout Western Christendom, is very obvious. A single illustration will show the practical disadvantage of lack of uniformity. George IV of England went through a ceremony of marriage with both Mrs. Maria Fitzherbert and Princess Caroline of Brunswick. He cohabited firstly with the former, then with the latter, then again with the former. All parties agree that he lived with one of the two ladies in holy matrimony, and with the other in sin. But opinions differ as to which was which. Those who hold that English statute law is valid in English matrimonial cases regard the marriage with Princess Caroline as alone lawful: those who hold the supremacy of the (Roman) can on law take a contrary opinion. It is unnecessary in this place to say anything about the merits of this matter: the point which it is desired to make is merely that it is undesirable that such cases should be possible.

But appreciation of the advantages of a uniform code should

CHRISTIANITY AS AN INSTITUTION

not blind us to certain disadvantages which resulted from considering Rome as an ultimate court of appeal from the decisions of local authorities. One result seems to have been that the pecuniary advantages of the practice of ecclesiastical law were such that at Rome theology tended to be dropped into the background, while the more intelligent members of the clergy devoted their attention to jurisprudence. A certain discontent inevitably ensued in the less favoured countries, where litigants were obliged to pay in fees to Roman officials and legal practitioners sums of money which in their opinion might quite well have remained at home. Thus Voltaire (*Pot Pourri* XIII) makes the calculation that in his day in France every year about forty uncles were married to their respective nieces, and about two hundred pairs of cousins were also married. He assesses the fees payable at Rome as 80,000 livres in each of the former cases and 18,000 livres in each of the latter, making the important sum of 6,800,000 livres going yearly out of the country on this score alone. In England in 1353 the improper carrying of any legal process before a foreign court of justice (Rome was aimed at but not mentioned) was made punishable by loss of all civil rights and imprisonment. Subsequent legislation extended the scope of this statute. To understand the origin of the legislation above referred to, it is desirable to remember the events of the reign of John, which events cannot have failed to leave a profound sense of injury in the minds of the English people. It is of course quite possible for apologists to argue that the Pope was wholly in the right, but the point which it is here desired to make is that the English people must inevitably have resented the treatment they experienced; and hence they, without any desire towards schism, necessarily welcomed any affirmation of the principle that the Pope is a constitutional and not an absolute monarch. Proof of this is seen in such legislation as the statute of 1306 which prohibited the proceeds of any tax imposed by any religious person being sent out of the country, and the statute of 1350 which, after premising that the Pope had acted "as if he had been patron" of English benefices "as he was not of right by the laws of England," enacted that election to all dignities and benefices should be free, "as they were granted by the King's progenitors."

Matters came to a head in the first half of the sixteenth century. The English throne was at the time occupied by Henry VIII, a cruel, vicious and tyrannical monarch, but nevertheless a man of considerable intellectual ability and an earnest student of theology, so much so that Pope Leo X had granted him the title "Defender of the Faith." Henry's matrimonial affairs have proved themselves to be of such importance in English history, and have been the subject of so much discussion, that it is extraordinarily difficult to write thereon with impartiality. It seems however fair to say that when he was some thirty-five years of age he found that his health was bad; his wife had given him one daughter, Mary, and was unlikely to have further children; and he had a very earnest desire to have a male heir to whom he might leave his crown. There was at the time no precedent for a queen ruling in her own right over England[1] (or indeed over France), and Henry not unreasonably believed that the likelihood of Mary's claims being disputed was increased by the fact that his union was of an illegal nature (he had married under formal protest his brother's widow), such union being condemned in Lev. xviii. 16, and having been made possible only by a papal dispensation, the validity of which was questioned.

Henry, presumably taking advantage of a moment when relationships between Pope Clement VII and the Emperor Carlos V (the nephew of Henry's Queen, Catalina) were specially strained, applied to the former for a declaration of nullity of his marriage. Thereupon there commenced a controversy centering round the question whether the King's deceased brother had ever had actual marital relationships with his wife. The delicacy of proving such a matter is obvious. Those who upheld the cause of the Queen pointed out the tender years of her first husband, but Francis Bacon (*History of Henry VII*) replies: "The Prince was upon the point of sixteen years of age when he died, and forward, and able in body." The impression left in the mind of a reader who follows this controversy is likely to be that Henry had no moral right to claim, after many years of conjugal life, that his marriage was void. On the other hand the King's conduct is quite comprehensible in view of the facility with which the Roman ecclesiastical authorities customarily granted declarations of nullity (*vide* p. 252 *infra*). That is to say, that while such declarations are in general open to grave objection, the case

---

[1] The case of Mathilda, daughter of Henry I, hardly constitutes an exception to the above. Although it is true that she was crowned in 1141, her so-called reign is more properly regarded as a (finally) unsuccessful attempt to deprive Stephen of the throne.

CHRISTIANITY AS AN INSTITUTION

on behalf of Henry VIII was a particularly strong one. His critics have created a prejudice against him by representing him as so infatuated with Anne Boleyn that he desired to raise her to the throne at any cost. But the evidence points the other way. While no one would regard Henry as a moral man in the Victorian sense of the term, nevertheless in this particular instance what Henry seems to have wanted was a male heir.

It appears probable that Clement at the commencement of negotiations really favoured Henry's cause, but that he altered his attitude when subsequent events brought about a *rapprochement* with the Emperor. In any event it is clear that if the Pope did not wish to annul the marriage he had every reason to try to gain time, because if Henry defied him, as eventually turned out to be the case, his only recourse was to excommunicate Henry and to absolve his subjects from their allegiance. Now obviously the Pope cannot conceivably have desired to excommunicate the King unless he felt that he could rely on some Catholic power—the Empire being of course indicated by medieval tradition and by circumstances generally—to invade England in order to make the sentence effective. So negotiations were protracted till Henry lost patience and caused Parliament to enact the Statute of Appeals, strongly emphasising the conception of the Church of England as a national body, ruled over by the King, and not as merely the English branch of a body ruled over by the Pope.

About the same time Henry asked the Archbishop of Canterbury to declare in his archiepiscopal court the invalidity of the marriage with Catalina (1533). When this was done, the fact of Henry's recent marriage with Anne Boleyn was made public. The Pope was now led to believe that the Emperor Carlos would be prepared within four months to invade England and to depose Henry. Consequently definite judgment was given: the marriage with Catalina was declared valid, and Henry was enjoined to respect it under penalty of excommunication and forfeiture of the allegiance of his subjects (1534). But the Pope found European politics unfavourable to the deposition of Henry. The Emperor realised that the papal favour had veered in the direction of France—in 1533 Clement went to Marseilles to marry his kinswoman Catarina dei Medici to Prince Henri (afterwards Henri II), and suspicion of France rendered the Emperor reluctant to risk an attack on England. Clement died in 1534, and was succeeded by Paul III, who after his accession made strenuous efforts to enlist the help of

242 INTRODUCTION TO THE STUDY OF CHRISTIANITY

France. In a letter to the French King dated July 26, 1535, His Holiness, after declaring Henry deposed, appealed to François saying:

> We cast ourselves and our necessities on your piety; and we entreat you . . . to execute our sentence upon the said Henry, when by ourselves you shall be invited to take arms. . . . To your Majesty's protection we commend the dignity of the Apostolic See and the honour of Almighty God.

But just as the Emperor had refrained from overt action for fear of François, so François seems to have refrained from action for fear of the Emperor; so what actually happened was that jealousy between the two great Catholic powers saved England from certain invasion and probable defeat. In the summer of 1538, however, there took place a reconciliation between the Emperor and François, and His Holiness took advantage of this reconciliation to attempt to induce the monarchs to take joint action against this country. Both the French and the Flemish Ambassadors were in fact withdrawn, and the English looked on invasion as inevitable; but Henry had taken full advantage of his period of respite and had pushed forward his preparations for defence so energetically that his enemies were reluctant to commence hostilities. In April 1539 the French Government received a confidential report to the effect that—

> No landing at Dover could now be attempted with any chance of success. Boys of seventeen and eighteen have been called up without exemption of place or person. They are prepared on all sides to the very extent of their ability, and the great Lords are at their posts as if the enemy were already at their doors (*Marillac to the Connétable: 3 April* 1539).

So what actually happened was that the great expedition against England was delayed for half a century, and, undertaken by the son of the Emperor against the daughter of Henry, it finally proved a total failure (1588).

History as customarily written sometimes reminds us of the dramas of Racine, in which we hear a great deal about the intimate thoughts of emperors and princesses, but in which the minor characters merely appear in order to give the principals an excuse for orating. Volumes have been written about the exact attitude and real motives of Clement VII, Henry VIII, his three children who in turn succeeded him, and his son-in-law, Philip II. But it seems fitting that instead

CHRISTIANITY AS AN INSTITUTION

of paying undivided attention to these half-dozen individuals, the student should give some thought to the millions of Englishmen whose lives were profoundly affected by the events now under discussion.

About this time men naturally tended to divide into three parties: (i) those who upheld the ideas of Henry himself, that is to say who wished the Catholic faith to be maintained in its entirety, but with the proviso that the Pope be recognised only as chief Bishop of Christendom, having under normal circumstances no direct intervention in English affairs. Such people naturally reflected that apart from other evils the papal power had sanctioned the atrocious invasion of England in 1066, had tried to bring about a similar disaster in the time of John, and was actually inviting two foreign potentates to make a further attempt. Moreover no one could fail to be impressed by the fact that the papal rule had throughout the last five centuries caused an immense drain of national wealth in the direction of Rome, while any corresponding benefits to this country were by no means easy to discover even by the most orthodox of believers; (ii) those who had been influenced by Protestantism (a school of thought which will be discussed in the next section) and who welcomed a breach with Rome as a preliminary to the adoption of the new doctrines; and (iii) those who maintained a thoroughly conservative attitude, who continued their allegiance to the Pope, and who were forced to consider their fidelity to the King as extinguished by the papal excommunication. Such men were placed in a very cruel embarrassment. By the principles of the modern state, if a man perform loyally his civic duties, he may give what spiritual obeisance he likes to any religious leader resident in Rome or elsewhere. But the papal conception of society admitted of no divided allegiance. If Pope and King quarrelled, a man could not logically say: "I render to Cæsar the things that are Cæsar's, and to God the things that are God's, and therefore in questions of religion I am loyal to the Pope, but in secular matters I am loyal to the King." The papal attitude from the time of Gregory VII onwards had made this compromise logically impossible. No one can reasonably deny that the danger to Christian princes in bad odour with the Vatican was a very real one. The assassination by Catholic fanatics of Henri III and Henri IV of France and of William the Silent of Orange, are cases in point. And Guy Fawkes, when examined by James I in person, alleged as a reason why he had attempted to assassinate the

King the fact that the latter had been excommunicated by the Pope. So the individual was called upon to choose, and must have been guilty of disloyalty to either Pope or King. It is for this reason that the religious persecutions which took place in the reigns of Henry VIII and of his immediate successors were of widely different natures. Henry as a religious fanatic condemned to death Protestants for denying the truth of transubstantiation, while at the same time as a temporal ruler he punished as traitors men who were convinced that he had, in virtue of the papal sentence, forfeited his crown. His son Edward was under the influence of strongly Protestant advisers, and was able to impose a markedly Protestant character on the English Church. But Henry's daughter Mary, who had been made to suffer acutely by what was in effect a declaration of her illegitimacy, very naturally had a deeply rooted regard for the papal power which had sustained her position. Mary became in consequence a persecutrix from religious motives. Her sister Elizabeth was a stateswoman and by no means a fanatic, but the Pope's active hostility compelled her to regard with at least suspicion all those of her subjects who professed allegiance to the sovereign Pontiff. So it seems not unfair to say that while both Mary and Elizabeth persecuted, the former acted out of conviction and the latter because her hand was forced by her enemies.

The behaviour of Elizabeth towards her Catholic subjects has indeed been the cause of such acute controversy that some further detail seems desirable. On February 25, 1570, Pope Pius V issued a bull, cutting off Elizabeth from the communion of the faithful, releasing her subjects from their allegiance, and forbidding them, under pain of incurring the same sentence of excommunication as herself, to recognise her as their sovereign. The Queen's situation thus became critical in the extreme. Her predecessor, Mary, had considered her illegitimate, and a similar attitude was adopted by the heiress presumptive, Mary Queen of Scots, who was for many years the centre of a series of intrigues directed against Elizabeth. A large part of the English nation, including a very high proportion of the nobility, had remained attached to the ancient regime, and the consequent danger of overt rebellion was a pressing one. Felton, the papal agent who actually promulgated the bull by nailing it on the door of the Bishop of London, stated when on trial that in England 25 peers, 600 gentlemen, and 30,000 commoners were ready to die in the

CHRISTIANITY AS AN INSTITUTION

Pope's quarrel, and this statement seems to have been well founded. In the following year (1571) the Spanish Court received from an agent confidential information with a list of thirty-nine of the English peers who were stated to be prepared to take arms under the Duke of Norfolk, and it was affirmed that of the remainder fifteen at the most could be depended upon to be loyal to Elizabeth. In March of that year Norfolk wrote asking that the King of Spain and His Holiness should furnish 6,000 soldiers, together with 3,000 horses and a supply of arms, to assist in an attack on Elizabeth. It so happens that a despatch (April 7, 1571) of the Duke of Alva, who was then Governor-General of the Netherlands, enables us to understand accurately the attitude of Philip's government towards Norfolk's request. Alva wrote to the King:

> "I have written to Don Juan de Cuniga" (Spanish Ambassador to the Vatican) "to impress on His Holiness the necessity of caution. Should the Queen of England hear of what is going on, she will have a fair excuse to execute them both" (i.e. Norfolk and Mary Queen of Scots). . . . "His Holiness sent some one here a little time ago to press these English matters upon me. I said then that he ought not to believe that the matter was as easy as the English Catholics pretended. The difficulty was not so much in the enterprise itself as in the impossibility of any common understanding about it between your Majesty and the French. . . . It would never do simply to send our troops as these people propose, on the chance of what may follow. A large force will be required, many persons will have to be admitted into the secret, and a secret which is widely shared will infallibly be betrayed. . . . But there is another possibility. Suppose the Queen of England dead—dead by the hand of nature or by some other hand; or suppose the Catholics to have got possession of her person before Your Majesty has interfered; the case is then altered. . . . The enterprise will be as honourable to Your Majesty as it will then be easy to execute. So confident am I of this, that if I hear that either of these contingencies has taken place, I shall act at once without waiting for further instructions from Your Majesty."

The above extract makes the situation very clear to us. We know from other sources that Philip had from the commencement regarded the bull as ill-timed, and consequently the result of Alva's cautious advice was that the Spanish King sent instructions to the Duke to confine himself for the present to making due preparations for shipping an army from Flanders to England. Had Philip been bolder, it seems probable that the throne of the Tudors would have fallen; but what actually happened was that the English Government had time to obtain information as to the plan of campaign, and Norfolk went to the scaffold (1572).

But circumstances rendered it obviously necessary that the English Government should take urgent measures for the safety of the Queen's person and for the stability of the realm; and it was inevitable that there should be a tendency to regard every papal adherent as a potential rebel. It can hardly be doubted that much injustice consequently resulted. Emphasis has frequently been placed on the lamentable case of Father Edmund Campion, who was executed in 1581. Campion was a brilliant scholar and man of high moral character, who, after having taken deacon's orders in the English Church, was converted to Catholicism and entered the Order of Jesus at Rome. He was sent to England as a missionary, and about a year afterwards was arrested, and after repeated torture was charged with having conspired at Rome and elsewhere to raise sedition in the realm and to dethrone the Queen. He does not seem to have denied that he travelled from Rome with funds supplied by the Pope, and that he entered England in disguise. In view of the status created by the papal bull, it was possible to argue that these acts in themselves constituted treason, but there was no real evidence of any overt act of sedition. Campion was nevertheless convicted, and suffered the extreme penalty of the law. It is remarkable that when under examination he was asked if he acknowledged Elizabeth to be really Queen of England, and he not only replied in the affirmative but maintained this attitude even after it was plain that his death was inevitable whatever he might say. It is not easy to see how under the circumstances fidelity to both Queen and Pope was possible, and indeed it seems likely that Campion had in mind the hope that his protestations of loyalty might influence the attitude of the authorities towards his co-religionists.

Campion was doubtless treated with great injustice, and he fully deserves the title of martyr for his faith. But on the other hand it is not easy to see how Elizabeth's Government could with safety have avoided very severe measures towards papal agents. And the protestations of loyalty of Campion possibly did his cause as much harm as good, seeing that they tended to increase in the minds of the public doubts as to the complete ingenuousness of many statements made by Roman Catholic controversialists.

CHRISTIANITY AS AN INSTITUTION

The attitude of Philip throughout these events has been much discussed. There is no doubt that his reluctance to invade England was genuine, and was based on: (*a*) his failure to dominate the Netherlands; (*b*) the possibility of France either siding with England, or at least taking advantage in some way of hostilities between England and Spain; and (*c*) the fear that a permanent union between Scotland and England, under a ruler hostile to Spain, might result from the overthrow of Elizabeth. So there is no reasonable doubt that Philip was eventually influenced, against his better judgment, by religious motives. But on the other hand when he finally decided to accede to the injunctions of Pope Sixtus he was sufficiently guided by mundane considerations to ask that His Holiness should pay half the expenses of the expedition, and leave him (Philip) with a free hand as regards the political results. Eventually the Pope promised a million crowns, the first half to be payable on the arrival of the Armada in England, and it was on that understanding that the ill-fated fleet sailed from Lisbon (1588). The total failure of this expedition occasioned a considerable loss of papal prestige, and this loss was accentuated by the behaviour of the English Catholics, the great bulk of whom remained loyal to the Crown rather than to the Pope.

(*c*) PROTESTANTISM

About the middle of the eleventh century Berengarius, Archdeacon of Angers, acquired considerable notoriety by his heterodox views on the nature of the Lord's Supper. He taught that the body and blood of Jesus are therein indeed received by the faithful, but not materially and rather after a heavenly and spiritual manner. He was induced to recant (1059) and to sign a declaration that the body of Christ is "touched and broken by the hands of the priests, and ground by the teeth of the faithful, not merely in a sacramental but in a real manner." He however reverted to his former opinions, and continued to be a cause of grave scandal; but he seems on the whole to have been treated with considerable toleration by Gregory VII, and he was permitted to end his days in retirement. His case is noteworthy because he was a precursor of a school of thought which numbered a very large body of adherents from the sixteenth century onwards. Such men regarded themselves as orthodox Christians; they accepted the creeds and recognised the authority of Holy Scripture, but they exercised considerable reserve in submitting to ecclesiastical discipline. They showed a certain readiness to question the scriptural interpretations considered authoritative in their day, and to ask themselves if such interpretations rightly represented the meaning of the original writers. In other words they claimed to exercise what is called the "right of private judgment." This phrase is a common one, but is perhaps a little illogical, as all Christians necessarily exercise the right of private judgment. The difference lies in the fact that one man after the exercise of this right comes to the conclusion that the Roman Church is an infallible guide, and another forms a contrary opinion.

Such Christians of Western Europe as form this contrary opinion have from time to time been designated by various names to distinguish them from followers of the Roman Church. The best known of such names is "Protestant," which term was first applied to those who protested against the decisions of a Diet (or Assembly of the Empire) held at Speyer in 1529. As will have been already gathered, Protestantism coincides with traditional Christianity as regards a large number of essential doctrines, while as regards points of divergence the attitude of the former is generally negative rather than positive. Protestants are agreed that various tenets of the Roman Church are wrong, but they are not all agreed as to exactly what is right. All Protestants for example unhesitatingly reject the doctrine, as promulgated by Boniface VIII, that it is necessary for the salvation of every human creature that he submit himself to the Roman Pontiff. But Protestants do not by any means agree in answering the questions obviously raised by this rejection: (a) what living ecclesiastic has the greatest claim on our respect? and (b) what are the nature and extent of the respect due to such ecclesiastic? So it seems not unfair to compare Protestants to a group of individuals who criticise a piece of workmanship and who, while unanimously urging that some drastic alterations are necessary, nevertheless differ widely among themselves as to exactly what those alterations should be. It will be seen therefore that it is not correct to look on Protestantism as a system rivalling Catholicism in somewhat the same way as Mahometanism rivals Christianity. Roman Catholics sometimes compare their position with that of the Protestants somewhat as follows:

> Jesus Christ founded one Church, not many Churches. This one Church he entrusted to Blessed Peter, who

CHRISTIANITY AS AN INSTITUTION

centralised it at Rome, and who confided its government to his successors, the Bishops of Rome. The various so-called Churches to which our opponents belong were established by such men as Martin Luther, Jean Calvin, Henry VIII or the brothers Wesley, and the visible heads of such Churches are certain pastors who may or may not in themselves be worthy men, but who are wholly lacking in that divine commission which was imparted with the words "Feed my Sheep," spoken to the Rock on which the Church was built and applicable to the successors of that same Rock.

To the foregoing we can imagine a Protestant replying as follows:

From the Apostolic age Christians have been divided into local Churches, concerning the actual foundation of which we frequently possess no details; it is possible to regard all these Churches as offshoots, direct or indirect, of the Church of Jerusalem, but impossible to regard them in general as offshoots of the Church of Rome. Now it is highly desirable that all these Churches should work together in visible union, such union being important for their *bene esse*, though not however necessary for their *esse*. And the lack of union which in fact exists is not the fault of Protestants, because it has most paradoxically come about that it is the Bishops of Rome, in their unjustifiable desire to establish an absolute universal monarchy, who have destroyed that very union which is essential for the realisation of their ambition.

It will be seen therefore that the divergence between Catholics and Protestants as regards the unity of the Church resolves itself into the question of the Petrine claims, already discussed in this treatise. If we believe that the Popes are what they claim to be, we must believe that Almighty God ratifies and confirms the sentence which cast out of the unity of the Church the Oriental Orthodox Christians. We must further believe that Almighty God similarly ratifies and confirms that sentence which cast out of the Church those English who allege the validity of Magna Charta. But as all Protestants in point of fact reject the papal claims, it is logical that they should contend that it is not they but their opponents who are primarily responsible for the lack of union in the Church.

One result of the divergence above indicated is that the Protestant occupies his thoughts far less with the idea of a visible Church than does the Catholic. The former as a rule looks on the Church primarily as an invisible body—the blessed company of all faithful people—consisting of all those who are to a greater or less degree genuine followers of Christ. If the Protestant requires instruction on Christian doctrine he can gather it from the New Testament. If he desires to pray he is taught in the Gospels (Matt. vi. 6) how he should proceed. So he very explicably has a tendency to that process which in commercial parlance is called "cutting out the middleman." He does not ask either a priest to offer mass on his behalf or the Blessed Virgin Mary to intercede for him with Jesus, but rather does he direct his prayers to his Father which seeth in secret, in the hope that his Father which seeth in secret will reward him openly. While therefore the Protestant maintains a professional ministry, he does not usually conceive of Christian pastors as being endowed with supernatural powers, neither does he favour the idea of their holding themselves aloof from the social and domestic life of their flocks. Again, among Protestants public worship is less frequent than among Catholics; and Protestants use their churches for private devotion much less than do Catholics. Protestant churches are as a rule less ornate than those of their rivals, and are also less numerous in proportion to probable congregations. It seems unlikely that any Protestant town of corresponding size has as many churches as one sees for example in such Latin-American cities as Olinda and Bahia.

Discussions between Catholics and Protestants very largely turn on the question of priestly absolution from sin, concerning which a few remarks are desirable. In the chapter dealing with the Fourth Gospel attention was called to the words of Jesus: "Whose soever sins ye remit they are remitted," and a suggestion was offered as to the real meaning of this passage. The Roman Church with its genius for discipline has consistently enjoined on its members the necessity for privately confessing their sins to a priest, so that they may receive absolution in accordance with the powers understood to be conferred in virtue of the words above quoted. The influence of the Church on the private lives of its individual members has of course been incalculably increased by the above practice, and experience has shown that this influence is largely bound up with the celibacy of the clergy. It is patent that female penitents would

CHRISTIANITY AS AN INSTITUTION

frequently hesitate before disclosing their most intimate thoughts to a married priest, who it is feared might not inconceivably discuss with his wife the matters dealt with in the confessional. It is for this reason that the laity in Roman Catholic countries is more disposed to tolerate an occasional lapse from the moral code on the part of a celibate priest than to contemplate the idea of a married clergy. Agreeably with the same general principle there are indeed in several of the older canons instances of prohibitions of priests living in the same house as their mothers or sisters. While the whole subject is admittedly surrounded by difficulties, there are two conclusions which an impartial observer can hardly fail to draw: (a) In controversy concerning the benefits and dangers of auricular confession, enough attention is in general not given to human individuality. There are many people who prize very highly the privilege of being able to explain their troubles in detail to a sympathetic and experienced spiritual director. But on the other hand there are others, neither more nor less virtuous and spiritually minded, to whom such self-exposure is wholly repugnant; (b) So long as the practice of auricular confession is enjoined as a duty instead of being offered as a privilege, opposition thereto is likely to continue.

But coming back to the days of the outburst of Protestant feeling in the sixteenth century, there is one feature connected with priestly absolution that had a great influence in bringing about and intensifying this outburst. It had long been a general principle of the Church that the penitent sinner should undergo some punishment before being regarded as fully reconciled. Such punishment, or penance as it is called, was and is normally merely symbolical, the penitent being in general told to recite in private one or more prayers or psalms. But at one time it became not unusual to ask for money as the price of readmittance into the Church's privileges, and we accordingly find that, with that special genius for organisation and codification which has consistently characterised the Roman Church, the authorities nominated men called "pardoners" to travel about and to collect on behalf of the papal treasury monies paid as sin-offerings. Thus in *Piers Plowman* we read:

>Ther preched a pardoner as he a prest were,
>And broute forth a bulle with bishopis seles,
>And seide that hym-selue myghte asoilie hem alle
>Of falsnesse of fastings, of vows to-broke.

The system was in itself a bad one, and moreover the abuses to which it gave rise were atrocious, because the people who purchased pardons came to understand that the mere payment of the sum demanded absolved them from all guilt in God's sight, independently of any question of their own penitence and amendment of life. The indignation occasioned by this abuse constituted one of the principal causes of the Reformation. A secondary cause, of a very similar nature, was the following. The Roman Church holds that the faithful after death pass into an intermediary state called Purgatory, where they generally spend a considerable time in purification before they become fit to rise into the higher celestial regions. Such purification can, it is taught, be expedited by the prayers of the saints in heaven and of the friends left by the departed on earth. Masses on behalf of the deceased are regarded as especially acceptable to God. Consequently it came to be considered a meritorious act to pay for the maintenance of priests whose duty it was to offer masses for the holy souls of the departed, and eventually the abusive idea gained ground that the mere payment of money could obtain the deliverance of a soul from purgatory.

The question of the dissolubility or otherwise of the marriage tie is also one which has formed a fruitful cause of controversy between Protestants and their adversaries. Christians are agreed that the marriage bond should be entered into on the understanding that it is to be permanent; but Church history shows that when the parties so desire ways of obtaining release have in practice always been looked for. The teaching of the Roman Church is that the marriage tie cannot be undone, but that in many ostensible marriages nullities exist which enable the ecclesiastical courts to release the parties by declaring that the tie was never made. When it is said that canonists enumerate fourteen classes of impediments to marriage, it will be seen what extensive possibilities are opened up to the ecclesiastical lawyer. Thus Chief Justice Coke (1552–1634) mentions a case in which a marriage was annulled because the husband had stood godfather to his wife's cousin. A statute of Henry VIII calls attention to the uncertainty accruing through such decisions:

> "Marriages have been brought into such an uncertainty that no marriage could be so surely knit or bounden but that it should lie in either of the parties' power . . . to prove a pre-

contract, a kindred and alliance, or a carnal knowledge to defeat the same" (32 Hen. VIII, c. 38).

The disadvantages of an avoidance of the marriage tie, as compared with divorce, or loosening, are: (i) stigma is placed on the ostensible wife, often a wholly innocent party, on account of her having cohabited with a man not her lawful husband; (ii) children of the ostensible marriage become illegitimate; and (iii) legal processes are brought into contempt, because it is frequently patent that the plaintiff merely desires a dissolution of the tie, and the alleged ground of nullity is only a pretext. The well-known cases of the avoidance of the marriages between the French kings Louis XII and Henri IV and their respective first queens, may be cited as instances. Napoleon indeed informed the senate that in annulling his marriage with Josephine he was following the example of thirteen French sovereigns.

Protestantism on the other hand has tended to emphasise the teaching of Jesus in Matt. v. 32 and to admit divorce *a vinculo* as an exceptional remedy to be applied, as against the guilty party, in the event of adultery. This is a much-discussed question, on which the last word has yet to be spoken. It seems however fair to call attention to the fact that the attitude of the Roman Church results from its general tendency to formalism and legality. All parties start from the general principle that a marriage is a permanent union, but afterwards they differ: the Roman theologian is much more shocked at the idea of a valid union being formally and ostensibly dissolved than he is at the idea of ecclesiastical courts proclaiming, on very flimsy grounds indeed, that such union has never taken place.

It is now desirable to say something about the Protestant attitude towards the Bible. Reaction to Roman Catholic doctrine and practice led some of the earlier of the Protestants to a critical examination of the Biblical canon, and we find for example that Luther looked with considerable suspicion on four of the New Testament books (Hebrews, James, Jude, Apocalypse). But here a difficulty presented itself. The Catholic position was and is that the Christian should regard as authoritative the Church and the Bible, looking on the two as mutually supporting. If therefore Protestantism rejects entirely the authority of the Church and partially that of the Bible, what standard remains? It was apparently in view of the difficulty so created that Protestants went back on their early attitude, and came to base their position unreservedly on the Bible (accepting however the Old Testament in the manner advocated by Jerome, i.e. the Apocrypha being regarded as of only secondary value). Thus Chillingworth writing in 1637 claims that "the Bible, the Bible alone, is the religion of Protestants," and this phrase has met with considerable approval.

It has consequently come about that there is in practice a great difference between the use of the Bible among the Catholic and Protestant laity respectively. While the Roman Church has, as has already been pointed out, consistently affirmed the sacredness and canonicity of Holy Scripture, nevertheless it has forbidden in the severest terms the use of unauthorised translations (*vide* e.g. the Encyclical *Inter Praecipuas* of Gregory XVI, May 8, 1844), and has at the same time done but little to encourage the use by the laity of the authorised Latin translation, or Vulgate (*vide* p. 151). But Protestants customarily place freely in the hands of their adherents the whole of the Scriptures regarded by them as canonical. While many and various blessings have unquestionably resulted from this practice, it can hardly be denied that certain disadvantages have accrued. Many passages of the Scriptures are frankly unsuitable for general reading, and, leaving aside the question of propriety, a certain proportion of the Old Testament to-day hardly repays careful study. What interest can a modern reader take in the list of the fourteen sons of Heman (1 Chron. xxv. 4)? But the most unfortunate effect of the orthodox Protestant's attitude towards the Bible is seen in its influence on his conception of God's work in the universe. If an impartial student read the scriptural account of Jonah and the great fish, or of Balaam and his ass, his impressions are probably (*a*) that the respective writers imparted their meaning by fables, and did not profess to be relating actual events, and (*b*) even if this be not so, there is no obvious reason why one should believe an unsupported account of occurrences so remote from normal human experience. But Protestants have frequently felt that if they begin to cast doubt on the literal veracity of the Bible, no visible source of authority remains for them; and they consequently have often insisted with some emphasis that it is the bounden duty of the true Christian to believe certain affirmations which appear *prima facie* to be very highly improbable. Consequently we find that the orthodox Protestant of the old school, while turning a deaf ear to those numerous witnesses who testify in favour of such alleged phenomena as Cardinal Newman's "motion of the eyes of the pictures of the Madonna in the Roman States," will unhesitatingly accept the story of how Elijah twice called down fire from heaven to consume, on each occasion, a company of fifty soldiers, who were merely the wholly innocent agents of their commander (2 Kings i. 9).

Protestantism has also differed widely from Catholicism with respect to the observance of Sunday. From very early times Christians have kept the first day of the week as a holy day in remembrance of the Resurrection of Jesus. But Protestants have gone farther and have regarded certain very rigid ordinances, laid down in the Mosaic Law with respect to the Sabbath, as applicable to Christians, with the proviso however that such ordinances now refer to the first, and not the seventh day of the week. But to this their opponents may not unreasonably reply that the injunction to respect the Sabbath is found side by side with a similar injunction to allow land to lie fallow one year in seven "that the poor of thy people may eat" (Ex. xxiii. 11 and 12). If the former is still to be respected as a Divine command, why not the latter?

Identification of the Jewish Sabbath with the Christian Sunday has been carried to such an extent that in some Protestant countries it is quite usual to hear the first day of the week actually spoken of as "the Sabbath Day," whereas in Catholic Spain and Portugal Sunday is called "*Domingo*" (the Lord's Day), Saturday being called "*Sabado*" (the Sabbath). The French names "*Dimanche*" and "*Samedi*" have the same etymology.

Two characteristics of Protestantism are very commonly emphasised by its opponents: the first being its tendency to split up into a number of relatively small and mutually antagonistic bodies. This tendency, unfortunate as it is, seems to be the inevitable result (*a*) of a lack of any visible central authority and (*b*) of a disposition to read, mark, learn and inwardly digest the words of Holy Scripture. Secondly, it is objected against Protestantism that in its work among the less educated classes it has been inclined to over-emphasise the teaching of the Epistle to the Hebrews, and has consequently brought into great prominence "the blood of Jesus," rather than "the example of Jesus" or "the work performed by Jesus." Origen referred to the name of Jesus as "a kind of sacred spell," and it is to be feared that in many cases the less thoughtful of the Protestants have fallen into a similar error with respect to his blood. Thus for example William Cowper (1731–1800), better known to most readers as the author of *John Gilpin*, wrote a hymn commencing:

> There is a fountain filled with Blood
> Drawn from Emmanuel's veins,
> And sinners plunged beneath that flood
> Lose all their guilty stains.

The above lines have become very popular among uneducated congregations, but it is to be doubted if the effect is always edifying. Too many hearers are carried away by religious fervour, and believe that the blood of Jesus has cleansed them from their sins, only to discover after the excitement has died down that they unhappily fail to bring forth the fruit of the Spirit, which is all goodness and righteousness and truth (Eph. v. 9).

Politically the benefits derived from Protestantism are immense: it can indeed be said that it has prepared mankind for the idea of the modern state. Medieval society was based, in theory at all events, on the idea of the subjection of the heathen and the heretic to the Christian layman, of the Christian layman to the Christian clergy, and of the Christian clergy to the Pope. Hence justice, as the word is to-day understood, was not merely impossible but was considered undesirable. Now it cannot of course be claimed for the Protestant that as soon as he found himself freed from the medieval system, he at once set to work to constitute a society in which he should have exactly the same rights as his adversary who was still actively engaged in attempting to bring about a reversion to the *status quo ante*. Unhappily the Protestant, in those countries where he gained the upper hand, showed himself in many respects as intolerant as had been the Catholic. But an important distinction must be made. Open hostilities between Catholics and Protestants originally arose because the latter claimed a right to worship as they pleased, and the Catholics denied this right. So the Protestant states, when they finally came to feel themselves reasonably secure against attempts to disturb forcibly the exercise of the Protestant cult, were bound by their principles to extend toleration to Catholics, and did in point of fact sooner or later act on these principles. The Catholic states in so far as they have extended toleration to

Protestants, seem to have done so in opposition to the directions laid down by the Holy See. (*Vide* Appendix E, p. 301.)

Coming back however to the time of the Reformation, we find that reaction, on the part of the Catholics, against the spread of Protestantism very naturally took two different directions—active hostility against the Reformers themselves, and genuine reforms carried into effect within the Roman Church in order to place it in a position to combat its enemies more effectively. The question of active hostility to the Reformers is one of the most painful in the history of the human race, but it is not proposed in this place to go into any detail. It suffices here to say that the combined effect of the work of the Inquisition and of the great religious wars has been to leave a profound and lasting impression on European mentality, and to form to-day a grave impediment to the propagation of Christianity.

The subject of reform within the Church itself is a much more agreeable one. In commencing to deal with this matter it may be said that the Emperor Carlos V, notwithstanding the fact that his policy was frequently in direct conflict with papal interests, was wholly orthodox in his religious views, and ardently desired to see such genuine reforms within the Church as would enable it to combat successfully the growing tendency to Protestantism. With this end in view he pressed for the convocation of an Ecumenical Council. The University of Paris had advocated the same measure in 1518. Now the steps taken by the Ecumenical Councils of Constance (1414) and Basel (1431) had been exceedingly unfavourable to the papal prestige. Both Councils had acted formally on the principle that the authority of a Council is greater than that of a Pope. The Council of Constance deposed John XXIII, and that of Basel Eugenius IV, though in the latter case the final victory rested with the Pope rather than with the Council. So we are not surprised to find that in 1459 Pius II, notwithstanding the fact that in early life he had been a prominent opponent of Eugenius, published a bull affirming the supremacy of the Pope over Councils, and anathematising anyone who should appeal to the latter. It will be readily understood therefore that in the first half of the sixteenth century, when the doctrines of Protestantism were beginning to take a strong hold on men's minds, Pope Paul III should have regarded the occasion as unpropitious for convening a Council, even with a view to what may be called "conservative reforms," that is to say reforms which might be expected to increase the efficiency of the Church without modifying its doctrine. So a policy of procrastination was adopted. A Council was however eventually convened for 1537, and actually commenced to function, at Trent, in 1545. Arrangements were made whereby about two-thirds of the members of the Council should be Italian, and Cardinal Pallavicini (1607-1667) in his *History of the Council of Trent* tells us very frankly that the Italian bishops had no other aim than the support and the greatness of the Apostolic See (*non tendevano ad altro oggetto che al sostentamento ed alla grandezza della sede apostolica*). So we are not surprised to find that the Council performed its labours throughout under the assumption that it did not form an autonomous assembly, but merely acted under the commission and direction of the Pope. Such proposed changes as the optional marriage of the clergy, and the administration of Holy Communion to the laity under the species of both bread and wine, were rejected. But nevertheless the constructive work of the Council is of immense importance, and is ably summed up by Charles Seignobos in his *Histoire Sincère de la Nation Française*:

> The Council effected a reform by reestablishing discipline by measures which were, in part, imitations of the proceedings of its adversaries. It maintained obligatory celibacy for priests and religious orders; it ordered bishops to visit their dioceses in order to superintend their priests. It prescribed the foundation of seminaries to instruct young men destined to the priesthood. It ordered priests to reside in their parishes, regulated their costume, their habits and their manner of life, and also indicated severity of deportment. To reinforce the authority of the clergy over the faithful it ordered them to preach sermons on Sundays and to teach the catechism to children. . . . The Council . . . in condemning clerical abuses which were a cause of scandal, deprived its adversaries of one of its most popular arguments. The Church, reformed in a traditional sense, was thenceforth provided with means of making itself respected and obeyed by the laity.

(*d*) *Liberal Theology, sometimes tending to Scepticism*

Students of history have been impressed by the fact that among the influences hostile to the papal power at the time of the Reformation, so relatively unimportant a place is occupied by so-called liberal theology, or in other words theology regarded as unorthodox by Catholics and Protestants alike. It is true that we read that Miguel Serveto (1511-1553), a

Spanish physician, after publishing two very heterodox works unluckily happened to visit Geneva, then a Protestant city, where at the instance of Calvin he was tried for heresy and burnt, notwithstanding the fact that his offence, if offence it were, was committed outside the jurisdiction of the Swiss authorities. But this incident was an exceptional one, and if we study the activities of the Roman Church, although we learn a good deal about the persecution of Protestants and of such Jews as, after having submitted to baptism, were accused of having relapsed, we read relatively little about writers having the courage to propound such doctrines as a Protestant would regard as contrary to the fundamentals of the Christian religion. It is true that in the second half of the sixteenth century the Sozini (or Sozzini) family of Siena made itself remarkable for its heterodox views as to the person and mission of Jesus, and indeed the name Socinian is still used to indicate one who denies the divinity of the Founder of Christianity. But although Cornelio, one of the less-known members of the family, was at one time imprisoned in Rome, the Sozini seem to have suffered but little for their unusual opinions.

It seems therefore on the whole fair to say that until the second half of the nineteenth century Catholicism and orthodox Protestantism were troubled surprisingly little by what came to be known as liberal theology. In the eighteenth century a school of Deists acquired considerable influence among the so-called "intellectuals" in France and elsewhere, but this school, which was regarded with extreme aversion by Catholics and Protestants alike, opposed the claims of Christianity *in toto.*

In England the "Blasphemy Act" (1697–1698) penalises very severely anyone who, after having once professed or been educated in the Christian religion, denies the authority of Holy Scripture. But, at all events during the nineteenth century, this law only seems to have been put into full operation when an unreasonably violent attack on Christianity was made. It is true that Shelley's *Queen Mab* was held (1841) to be a blasphemous libel, but in this case the prosecutor was a man who had himself been indicted for a similar offence, and who seems to have instituted proceedings merely to test the opinion of the courts.

(e) *Mysticism*

Something has already been said about the mystic as one who, instead of looking forward to a time when he may come to enjoy God's presence in heaven, seeks rather here on earth to realise that actual union with the Deity which seems to be indicated in the prayer of Jesus: *That they all may be one, as thou Father art in me and I in thee, that they also may be one in us* (John xvii. 21). According to this conception of religion, man's duty is consciously to struggle to raise his being Godwards and to seek union with the Almighty. Now an objection at once presents itself: in accounts of religious experiences self-deception is not infrequently intermingled with what is genuine. An intimate conviction as to union with God might indeed be quite conceivably facilitated by such extraneous means as the use of drugs.[1] How then is the Christian to know that his inmost feelings with respect to the indwelling of the Spirit are not a mere subjective delusion? The most obvious answer is of course that we are known by our fruits. The fruit of the Spirit is love, joy, peace, longsuffering, gentleness, goodness, faith, meekness, temperance (Gal. v. 22). If a man bring forth this fruit surely it forms evidence of the Divine approval. But though the above argument is indubitably weighty it must be admitted that it by no means closes the question, because it may still be suggested that the mystic may have erroneous ideas about the relationships between the Deity and mankind, but nevertheless he may be a choice soul, very precious indeed in God's sight, and on that account abundantly rewarded. It is, it may be submitted, undoubted that certain men called mystics believe themselves to have attained union with God, and that such men frequently bring forth abundantly in their lives the fruits of the Spirit; but nevertheless strictly speaking such abundant bringing forth is not proof of the accuracy of their belief.

Something may now be said about the actual teaching of the Christian mystics, and two names, Eckhart and Scheffler, are here chosen as representative of their class.

MEISTER ECKHART (*c.* 1260–*c.* 1327) was a Dominican,

---

[1] Professor William James (*The Varieties of Religious Experience*) tells us: Nitrous oxide and ether, especially nitrous oxide, when sufficiently diluted with air, stimulates the mystical consciousness in an extraordinary degree. Depth beyond depth of truth seems revealed to the inhaler. The truth fades out however, or escapes, at the moment of coming to; and if any words remain over in which it seemed to clothe itself they prove to be the veriest nonsense. Nevertheless the sense of a profound meaning having been there persists; and I know more than one person who is persuaded that in the nitrous oxide trance we have a genuine metaphysical revelation.

CHRISTIANITY AS AN INSTITUTION

and like so many other members of his order an earnest student of Thomas Aquinas. But the methods of the two men were widely different. St. Thomas taught that for the human soul to attain to the highest truth it must be assisted by something which we call "revelation," coming from without. Eckhart on the other hand seems to attach but little value to revelation. In his opinion Divine truth is something which carries out its work within us independently of any external aid. Eckhart calls attention to the words of Jesus: *It is expedient for you that I go away; for if I go not away the Paraclete will not come unto you;* and he interprets these words to mean: *Ye have set too much joy upon my present appearance, therefore the perfect joy of the Paraclete cannot come unto you.*

Eckhart shows us the nature of his conception of God when he says:

> Some people want to see God with the same eyes with which they see a cow, and want to love God as they would love a cow. So they love God for the sake of outer riches and inner comfort, but such people do not rightly love God. . . . Simple folk fancy that they should behold God as though he stood there and they here. But this is not so. God and I are one when my soul knoweth him.

It is noticeable that in the above passage Eckhart deprecates the love of God for the sake of inner comfort. This opinion may be well contrasted with such a commonplace sentiment as that contained in Faber's well-known hymn ending:

> Father of Jesus, love's reward,
> What rapture will it be
> Prostrate before thy throne to lie
> And gaze and gaze on thee.

As the mystic believes that he is essentially one with the Deity, it follows that for him any feeling of separation from God is a mere delusion of the senses, which tends to disappear as the inner sight becomes more and more developed. The non-mystic on the other hand looks forward to a time when his knowledge of God will be fuller, and his relationship more intimate; but nevertheless according to his theological system the creature and the Creator will for ever remain essentially separate, it being through all eternity the duty and privilege of the former to worship the latter.

The foregoing prepares us for other sayings of Eckhart:

> A Master said: *God became man, whereby the whole human race is uplifted and made worthy. Thereby we may be glad that Christ, our brother, of his own strength rose above all the choirs of angels and sitteth at the right hand of the Father.* That Master spake well, but in truth I would little heed it. What would it profit me had I a brother who was a rich man, and I were poor? What would it profit me had I a brother who was a wise man and I were a fool? . . . The Heavenly Father begetteth his Only Begotten Son in himself and in me. Wherefore in himself and in me? I am one with him and he hath no power to shut me out. In the selfsame work the Holy Spirit receiveth its being and proceedeth from me as from God. Why? I am in God, and if the Holy Spirit take not its being from me, neither doth it take it from God. I am in no wise shut out.
>
> I speak in good truth and in eternal truth and in everlasting truth that God must needs ever pour himself forth to the utmost of possibility in every man who has reached down to the foundation of his being—so wholly and completely that in his life and in his being, in his nature and in his Godhead, he keeps nothing back, he must ever pour all forth in fruitful wise.
>
> It is a sure and certain truth that God is of necessity bound to seek us as though indeed his very Godhead depended upon it. God can as little dispense with us as we with him. Even though we turn away from God, yet God can never turn away from us.
>
> I thank God not that he loveth me, for he may not do otherwise; whether he will or no yet his nature compelleth him . . . therefore will I not pray to God to give me anything nor will I praise him for that he hath given me.

And the following passages illustrate Eckhart's attitude to the great problem of freewill:

> God compelleth not the will; rather he setteth the will free, so that it wills not otherwise than what God willeth. And the spirit desires not to will other than what God willeth, and that is not lack of freedom, it is true and real freedom.
>
> The righteous man serveth neither God nor the creature, for he is free, and the nearer he is to righteousness the nearer he is to freedom's very self.
>
> The man who standeth in God's will and in God's love, he but craveth to do all good things that God willeth and to leave undone all evil things that are contrary to God. And it is impossible for him to leave undone anything that God ordains. Even as a man whose legs are bound cannot walk, so it is

impossible that a man who standeth in God's will should do aught unvirtuous.

Certain men say: I have God and God's freedom; I may do whatever I please. Such understand wrongly this saying. So long as thou canst do aught that is contrary to God and his commandments, so long hast thou not God's love, even though thou mayst deceive the world that thou hast.

In fine, for Eckhart the Christian's philosophy is summed up in the phrase: "God became man that I might become God."

JOHANN SCHEFFLER (1624–1677) is perhaps better known by his pseudonym of Angelus Silesius. Originally a physician and of the Lutheran persuasion, he joined the Roman Church, became a priest and rose to be coadjutor to the Prince Bishop of Breslau. He is widely known as the author of a collection of over two hundred hymns. Of these the most familiar to English worshippers is the *Liebe, die du mich zum Bilde*, a well-known translation of which begins:

> O Love, who formedst me to wear
> The image of thy Godhead here;
> Who soughtest me with tender care
> Through all my wanderings wild and drear:
> O Love, I give myself to thee,
> Thine ever, only thine to be.

But a work, less popular than the hymns but more valuable to the student, is the *Cherubinischer Wandersmann*. In this book Scheffler puts into the form of rhymed couplets various thoughts apparently drawn, principally at all events, from earlier Christian mystics. Some examples are subjoined:

> God is in me the fire and I in him the light: do we not each partake of the other most intimately?

> I am as rich as God: believe me, man, there can be no grain of dust that I have not in common with him.

> God loves me above himself if I love him above myself: so much I give him as he giveth me from himself.

> The bird flieth in the air, the stone rests upon the earth, the fish lives in the water and my spirit in God's hand.

> Halt! whither runnest thou? Heaven is in thee; seekest thou God elsewhere, thou missest him for ever.

Man is all things; if aught is lacking in him then in truth he knoweth not his riches.

The world it holds thee not; thou art thyself the world that holds thee, with thee, in thee, so strongly captive bound.

I myself am eternity when I abandon time and self in God, and grasp God in myself.

The rose here seen by thine outer eye, has so bloomed in God from all eternity.

So long as for thee, my friend, time and place exist, so long thou failest to grasp what is God and what eternity.

In as far as my own "I" languishes and decreases, so cometh to power the Lord's own "I."

God may not make without me a single little worm: if I with him uphold it not, straightway must it burst asunder.

I know that without me God can no moment live; if I come to nought he needs must give up the Ghost.

Is my will dead? God must do as I will; I myself prescribe to him the pattern and the goal.

For the wicked is the law; were there no command written, still would the righteous love God and their neighbours.

All must be slain. If thou slayest not thyself for God, then at last eternal death will slay thee for the enemy.

A few representative passages have now been given from two representative Christian mystics. Without here submitting any opinion on the vital question whether these writers were or were not justified in their assumptions as to the essential unity of their Higher Ego with God, there are three observations which may conveniently be made:

Firstly: the ideas of Eckhart and of Scheffler may shed some light on such very difficult sayings of Jesus as those in which he tells us *My Father is greater than I*, and immediately afterwards *All things that the Father hath are mine*, and *That they all may be one; as thou Father art in me and I in thee, that they also may be one in us* (John xiv. 28, xvi. 15, xvii. 21).

Secondly: a mystic who believes that his Higher Ego is

CHRISTIANITY AS AN INSTITUTION

essentially one with God can scarcely be expected to attach great importance to theological dogmas. If a man like Eckhart be so convinced of his unity with the Deity that he neither prays for any benefit hoped for, nor thanks God for any benefit received, he cannot surely believe, with the author of the Athanasian Creed, that it is necessary to everlasting salvation that he believe rightly the Incarnation of our Lord Jesus Christ; neither is he likely to hold with Boniface VIII that it is necessary for the salvation of every human creature that he submit himself to the Roman Pontiff.

Thirdly: the Christian mystic, having an intense conviction of the indwelling of God within the human soul, and also of man's participation in the Divine nature, is likely to form an opinion of Jesus as a being in whom God specially dwelt, and who specially participated in the Divine nature. Hence the mystic is more likely to be attracted by what seems to have been the older Christian theology—i.e. that Jesus was endued with the Spirit at his baptism—than with the later—i.e. that Jesus was God Incarnate from the moment of his miraculous conception.

When attention was specially called above to the works of two mystics, Eckhart and Scheffler, it was not intended to be implied that all those theologians who are commonly called "mystics" take such a definite view of the essential identity of God and man as did the two writers named. Thus few people would deny the title of "mystic" to St. Bernard of Clairvaux, who wrote a sequence in which the following passage, addressed to Jesus, occurs:

> Celestial sweetness unalloyed!
> Who eat thee hunger still,
> Who drink of thee still feel a void
> Which nought but thou can fill.

In the above lines St. Bernard clearly desired to indicate an extremely close communion with God, without however going quite the length of Eckhart, in whose opinion the union was so complete that he felt justified in declaring that "I am in God and if the Holy Spirit take not its being from me, neither doth it take it from God."

It will now be seen why the medieval Church tended to look on mysticism always with suspicion and sometimes with active hostility. Little by little dogmatic theology had caused men to look on the Almighty Father as more and more remote; he was to be approached through Jesus, and Jesus having in his turn become remote was to be approached through his Blessed Mother and through the Saints. And the Church simultaneously came to be looked on as the divinely instituted organisation by and through which the prayers of the faithful were offered in an acceptable manner. But this elaborate system had but little interest for the true mystic: if he realised the presence of God within him he felt but small need to travel to Compostella to seek the protection of St. James, or to Canterbury to ask for the intercession of St. Thomas à Becket. Reference has already been made to Protestantism as tending to eliminate what in commercial parlance is called the "middleman," and this consideration applies with even greater force to mysticism. In consequence it would appear that in Spain the activities of the Inquisition were directed far more against mystics (*alumbrados* or enlightened ones) than against Protestants, the explanation of course being that the principles of the Reformation failed to arouse any great sympathy in the Peninsula. St. Theresa of Avila was several times denounced to the Inquisition, and one of her books, *Conceptos del amor divino*, was actually prohibited. She herself was under arrest for two years, and the immense success which eventually crowned her efforts seems to have been largely due to the fact that the attacks on her had been directed from Italy, and consequently aroused a reaction in the mind of Philip II, who disliked Italian interference in Spanish affairs.

It is especially instructive to examine the attitude of the authorities towards what is called "Quietism," that is to say the passive meditation on God, in the belief that such meditation is the highest spiritual exercise, and the chief means whereby the Creator and the individual soul can be brought into intimate communion. The best-known apostle of this school was Miguel de Molinos (*c.* 1640–1697), a Spanish priest who settled in Rome and was for a long time an intimate friend of Pope Innocent XI. Molinos collected round him a considerable following of pious and intelligent disciples, largely belonging to the best Roman society, for whose benefit he published a *Guida spirituale*, a book which was examined by the Inquisition and considered orthodox. But as Molinos became more popular the authorities perceived more clearly —what apparently Molinos himself did not perceive—that in

CHRISTIANITY AS AN INSTITUTION

his system there was really no logical necessity for a formally organised Church, nor indeed for the death of Jesus on the Cross. So Molinos was arrested: two years subsequently he made a formal retraction of his doctrines and was sentenced to imprisonment for life. He died after about ten years' incarceration. In Spain several devotees alleged to be "Molinists" were burnt in the eighteenth century.

Other examples of mystics forcibly repressed by the Church are the Cathari. These formed a very widely spread body, and are perhaps best known on account of the fact that the inner circle of the Albigenses were Cathari. The exact tenets of the body form a matter of doubt; the information that has reached us has filtered through their opponents, and much of it appears to be *pri mafacie* unreliable. (*Vide* Appendix C, p. 299, dealing with this subject.) But there seems no doubt that the Cathari *perfecti* were celibates; that their austerities rivalled those of the Christian hermits; that they ate neither meat, cheese nor eggs, nor did they drink milk; that they taught that salvation comes about by the gift of the Spirit and by man becoming the vehicle of the Paraclete; that until a man receives the Divine gift he is destined to be born again and again, but that finally all men will be redeemed. The Cathari are specially interesting on account of the influence they exercised on Catholicism. It was principally to counteract the teaching of the Cathari that the Dominican order was formed; the Catholic sacrament of Extreme Unction is believed to have been suggested by the Catharist *consolamentum*, and it was the adverse criticism pronounced by the Cathari on the character of the Old Testament Deity which led the Church to discourage the circulation of the Old Testament among laymen.

CHAPTER VIII

CHRISTIANITY OF TO-DAY

PREPARATORY to making a few general observations concerning the Christian religion as it exists at the present time, it seems desirable to recall the nature of its growth. We have seen a society, apparently quite small in number at its founder's death, increase slowly and with difficulty during two centuries, after which it took a sudden impulse and rapidly attained great popularity, eventually becoming indeed the chief religion of the Roman Empire. It seems reasonable to conclude that the Christian had during a certain period every ground for hoping that his faith would shortly become dominant throughout the habitable world. In the seventh century however such hopes received a rude shock by the rapid and spectacular success of a rival creed. There subsequently followed many years of warfare between Christian and Moslem nations; and it happened that after a kind of stalemate had been reached in the seventeenth century, the former group progressed in material civilisation incomparably faster than did its opponents. Indeed by the nineteenth century it seemed that it would have been relatively easy for the Christian powers, had they so wished, to have combined and to have completely dominated the Mahometans. But by that time the Christian nations had almost entirely lost that sense of solidarity which had caused the sovereigns of England, France and Germany to take joint action against the infidel in Asia Minor towards the close of the twelfth century. Christian powers have indeed during the last few hundred years been guilty of most sanguinary wars among themselves, and mere jealousy has proved itself sufficient to prevent them from joining in arms against the Moslem. And it must further be said, in this case to the credit of the modern Christian, that the fact is now widely recognised that religion is not rightly propagated by wholesale slaughter—by "devastating the vicious lands" of the expected proselyte—but by missionary efforts approximating somewhat more closely to the methods of Jesus and of his immediate followers.

From quite early days there existed an occasional tendency for larger or smaller numbers of Christians to sever themselves from the main body; and in the eleventh century an extremely important schism took place, the Eastern and Western groups definitely separating. Again in the sixteenth century a very large number of Western Christians severed themselves from the traditionally organised Church, and, taking the name of Protestants, formed a number of independent bodies. Between Catholics and Protestants there then ensued a very active period of violent hostility. While this hostility is by no means entirely at an end, its violence has been abated by the growth of the modern conception of the lay state, either maintaining itself neutral in all purely religious matters, or at least extending frank toleration to well-behaved partisans of creeds other than that officially adopted.

Now if the excellent Pangloss, who, as we all know, taught his pupils that in this best of possible worlds everything is necessarily disposed in the best possible manner, had lived towards the end of the nineteenth century, he would very probably have been led to conclude that Protestantism was especially the object of divine favour. We can indeed imagine that he would have spoken somewhat as follows:

> I see much that is admirable in the Mahometan religion and in the daily lives of many of its adherents. I cannot doubt therefore that this religion receives Divine approval to a very considerable degree. But on the other hand a careful comparison between Mahometanism and Christianity convinces me that the former occupies only a secondary place. And if I pursue my investigation further, and attempt to distinguish between the different branches of Christianity, the conclusion to which I come is on the whole favourable to Protestantism. It is true that as regards mere numbers, Catholicism is far ahead of its rival. But if we judge of the value of a religion by its effect on culture, enlightenment, education and moral rectitude, the result appears to be frankly favourable to Protestantism. Divide for example the American continent into two parts, north and south of the boundary between Mexico and the United States, and judge accordingly. It is true that certain Catholic countries, notably France and Italy, have attained a very high level of civilisation. But in both these countries anti-clerical influence is very strong, and in neither are the precepts of Catholicism respected with regard to the relationships between Church and State. In point of fact in Italy a condition of open hostility exists between the Vatican and the Quirinal. I

270 INTRODUCTION TO THE STUDY OF CHRISTIANITY

have no hesitation therefore in concluding that the future of Christianity and indeed of civilisation lies with Protestantism.

But the opinions of Pangloss might possibly have been considerably modified had he lived say three decades subsequently. The situation by that time had become profoundly altered. Catholicism had become far stronger in various parts of the world, and Protestantism had in the meantime come to exhibit certain very disquieting symptoms, concerning which a few comments are now offered.

It has already been seen that while Catholicism is fundamentally a religion of a Church and of a Book, in actual practice the authority of the Book has tended to be obscured in popular theology. But orthodox Protestantism for centuries avowedly based its teaching on the assumption of the literal accuracy of the Bible narrative. And in consequence grave difficulties began to arise when in the second half of the nineteenth century the scientific theories of the schools of Darwin and Lyell began to be popular. For some time Protestantism was able to maintain an attitude of simple negation in the face of such teaching as tended to cast doubts on the scientific accuracy of the book of Genesis. But as time went on Protestant ministers found it increasingly difficult to make their flocks believe that the visible universe came into being by means of six distinct acts of creation, occurring on six successive days. And when congregations came to reject this proposition, it was explicable enough that they should begin to ask: If we cannot rely on the statements of the Bible with respect to such matters as are to some extent open to verification, why should we rely on its remaining statements? Hence a great falling off in the influence of the Protestant teachers. These men are at least as earnest, intelligent and conscientious as were their predecessors, and their reading usually covers a far wider field. But they claim less authority over their hearers, and one of the most human of human weaknesses is the respect that man instinctively feels for definite affirmations, true or false, delivered in an authoritative manner. It is probably fair to say that people who call themselves Protestants at the present time are at least as truly religious as were their predecessors two generations ago. But they attend public worship far less, and they attach relatively little importance to dogmatic teaching.

On the other hand the influence of the Church of Rome on its followers has been affected to a much smaller extent by modern scientific discoveries and speculations. The Holy See has found itself in a position to some extent analogous to that which it occupied when, on the disruption of the Roman Empire, it proved to be the one existing organisation able to speak in an authoritative manner. And it has not been slow to avail itself of the opportunity so afforded. So Pangloss, had he been living at the present time, would presumably show himself as great an admirer of Catholicism as he would have been of Protestantism had he lived half a century ago. It may therefore be of interest if something be said about the position of the Roman Church with respect to the modern state, modern thought and modern society.

Three-quarters of a century ago Pope Pius IX conceived the idea of compiling a kind of code, technically called a "syllabus," which would indicate authoritatively the Church's attitude towards such matters as those above indicated. It was decided that this code should take a negative form, i.e. instead of positive dogmas being enunciated, errors were to be condemned (or rather re-condemned); and, as a result of the labours of a commission specially appointed, eighty propositions were selected as having been already stigmatised as erroneous by His Holiness. On December 8, 1864, the Cardinal Secretary of State, acting on the Pope's instructions, addressed to all the Roman Catholic Bishops a formal letter enclosing a copy of the condemned propositions.

Now these eighty "erroneous propositions" are of by no means equal interest. For example No. 31 advocates the abolition of the special courts of justice for the trying of secular causes, civil or criminal, to which a cleric is a party. But in condemning this proposition the Pope does not appear to adopt a wholly uncompromising attitude, nor does he affirm that no cleric should ever be judged by a layman. On the contrary the language used seems to imply that the matter is one on which negotiations may conveniently take place between the civil and the ecclesiastical authorities.

But the condemnation of certain other propositions shows a far more uncompromising spirit, and is indeed of a nature to give rise to considerable criticism. For example:

> 5. Divine revelation is imperfect, and is consequently subject to a continual and indefinite progress which corresponds to the development of human reason.

15. Every man is free to adopt and to profess the religion which he reputes to be true according to the light of reason.
42. In case of legal conflict between the two powers, civil jurisprudence prevails.
55. The Church should be separated from the State, and the State from the Church.
63. It is permissible to refuse obedience to lawful princes, and even to revolt against them.
78. It is justifiable that in some Catholic countries the law has provided that foreigners may enjoy the public exercise of their special forms of worship.
80. The Roman Pontiff can and should reconcile himself with, and adapt himself to progress, liberalism, and modern civilisation.

Now one cannot condemn numbers 42 and 55 without appearing to claim that there should exist a close relationship between Church and State, on the understanding that in case of conflict between the two powers the ecclesiastical law, or in other words the will of the Pope, should prevail. And one cannot condemn number 63 without appearing to condemn *in toto* all those checks on absolutism which the experience of centuries has proved to be so necessary for the progress and welfare of civilised countries. And moreover the condemnation of Nos. 5 and 15 is of a nature to cause considerable embarrassment to the faithful. If revelation is not progressive, how can one justify the fact that prior to 1854 it was permissible for a good Catholic to teach, as did for example St. Thomas Aquinas, that the doctrine of the Immaculate Conception is false? And how can one justify the further fact that prior to 1870 it was permissible for a good Catholic to believe, as did for example the bishops assembled at the Council of Constance, that the Pope is not infallible? And if a man may not accept a religion because his reason tells him that it is true, on what grounds can a Protestant be asked to accept the Roman Catholic faith?

Concerning the reception of the Syllabus by the Church, Professor Boudinhon, already referred to in these pages as a moderately-minded Catholic theologian, tells us:

> Its publication aroused the most violent polemics; what was then called the Ultramontane party was loud in its praise; while the liberals treated it as a declaration of war made by the Church on modern society and civilisation. Napoleon III's government forbade its publication, and suspended the newspaper *L'Univers* for having published it. Controversies were equally numerous as to the theological value of the Syllabus.

Most Catholics saw in it as many infallible definitions as condemned propositions; others observed that the Pope had neither personally signed nor promulgated the collection, but had intentionally separated it from the Encyclical by sending it merely under cover of a letter from his Secretary of State; they said it was hastily and sometimes unfortunately drawn up; they saw in it an act of the pontifical authority, but without any of the marks required in the case of dogmatic definitions; they concluded therefore that each proposition was to be appreciated separately, and in consequence that each was open to theological comment. That such is the true view is proved by the fact that Rome never censured the theologians who, like Newman, took up this position (*Encycl. Brit.*).

The above reasoning seems strained. The reader naturally enquires: "What are the marks required in the case of dogmatic definitions?" The reply is that it is claimed that the Pope is infallible when he, acting in his capacity of Universal Bishop, declares that a certain pronouncement on any question of faith or morals is binding on the whole Church (*vide* p. 172). It seems a little disingenuous to deny that these conditions are fulfilled in the present case. The fact that the propagation of the Syllabus was entrusted to the Cardinal Secretary of State is an indication that the Pope acted officially, and the fact that the Cardinal was instructed to send a copy to every Roman Catholic Bishop indicates the intention of imparting authoritative teaching to the whole Church. The concluding remark made by Professor Boudinhon about the position of Newman and his fellow-liberals is difficult to follow. One party in the Church affirmed that certain doctrines laid down by the Pope were infallible; the other party denied this. His Holiness himself formally condemned neither. Surely it is unfair to infer, as Professor Boudinhon appears to do, that the Pope thereby supported the position of those who denied infallibility to his own pronouncement.

It has been frequently suggested that the liberal policy of Leo XIII, the successor of Pius IX, did much to counteract the traditional conservatism of the latter. This however is only a partial truth. Leo XIII had an extraordinary faculty for making himself respected, and indeed beloved, by many of those who differed from him. But on questions of principle Leo entirely confirmed the utterances of Gregory XVI and Pius IX, concerning which he wrote (Encyclical *Immortale Dei*, 1885):

> From these decisions of the Sovereign Pontiffs it must absolutely be admitted that the origin of public power must be attributed to God and not to the multitude; that the right of rebellion is repugnant to reason; that it is not permissible either to individuals or to societies either to omit to take into account religious duties or to treat different religions in the same way; that the unrestrained liberty of thinking and of publicly manifesting one's thoughts ought in no way to be placed among the rights of citizens, nor among matters worthy of favour and protection.

And on the question of absolutism Leo XIII wrote in the Encyclical *Quod apostolici*, 1878:

> If it happens however that princes heedlessly go too far in the exercise of their power, Catholic teaching does not permit the individual to rebel on his own account against them, for fear that the tranquility of order may be more and more disturbed, and that society may receive still greater injury. And when the excess has got to the point when no further hope of safety appears to remain, Christian patience teaches that the remedy should be sought in merit and in urgent prayers to God.

The successor of Leo XIII, Pius X, in his Encyclical *Vehementer nos* (1906) wrote concerning the nature of the Church:

> Scripture tells us, and the tradition of the Fathers confirms to us that the Church is the mystical body of Christ, a body governed by Pastors and Doctors, a society of men in the bosom of which chiefs are to be found who have full and perfect powers to govern, to teach and to judge. It results that this Church is in its essence an unequal society, that is to say a society embracing two categories of members, the Pastors and the flock; those who occupy a rank in the different degrees of the hierarchy, and the multitude of the faithful. And these categories are so distinct one from another that in the pastoral body alone reside the right and authority necessary to urge and to direct all the members towards the aim of the society; as for the multitude it has no other duties than those of allowing itself to be led, and like a docile flock of following its Pastors.

It can hardly be questioned therefore that the general principles of the Roman Church harmonise far better with those of an absolute civil government than with a liberal one. Our own generation has seen for example that after the Italian Government had become absolutist it was able to enter into a close working arrangement with the Vatican (February 11,

1929), and thereby to put an end to a quarrel which had lasted for half a century. Two days after the signature of the respective treaty, the Pope was reported to have said with reference to his negotiations with Signor Mussolini:

> We must say that we were most generously helped by the other side. It may be that there was also needed a man such as Providence has caused us to meet, a man unaffected by the prejudices of the "Liberal School" (*Address to a delegation from Milan University*, February 13, 1929).

Subsequent events in Abyssinia and elsewhere have proved how wholly accurate was His Holiness in describing Signor Mussolini as "a man unaffected by the prejudices of the Liberal School."

The foregoing quotations from papal utterances, illustrating as they do the attitude of the Roman Church towards civil governments, may assist the reader to understand the somewhat paradoxical fact that those monarchs whose general principles would presumably cause them to be the most faithful followers of the papal policy, have occasionally experienced great friction in their relationships with the Holy See. For example Louis XIV in 1685, following the counsel of his clerical advisers, revoked the measures of toleration granted to Protestants by the Edict of Nantes (1598), and he afterwards subjected his Protestant subjects to exceedingly harsh treatment, prohibiting for example medical men to attend them in sickness. But simultaneously the King consistently nominated to vacant bishoprics ecclesiastics specially chosen for their disavowal of the extreme papal claims, and to these ecclesiastics the Pope with equal consistency refused to grant letters of institution. Hence it came about that at the time when the Pope was illuminating the Vatican in honour of the revocation of the edict (which revocation he described as "the finest act the King had ever performed") many dioceses of France were one by one being left unoccupied. In 1688 there were thirty-five sees awaiting bishops, and it was only in 1693 that the King finally decided to come to terms with the Papacy. The explanation is of course that Louis XIV was by nature a despot, and as a despot he could not on the one hand accept the principles of papal authority as laid down by Gregory VII and Innocent III, neither could he on the other hand tolerate the obvious desire of his Protestant subjects to conduct their religious affairs without interference on the part of the Crown.

Another matter which strikes the notice of the student is the fact that, while the Roman Church itself is international, its government is Italian. As is of course well known, the College of Cardinals when electing a Sovereign Pontiff has full liberty of choice, and indeed in past centuries there have been many Popes of nationality other than Italian. But it is generally believed that public opinion in Italy would not in our day tolerate the idea of a non-Italian Pope, and in modern times we are compelled to think of the Pope as an Italian, having his seat of government in Italy, and surrounded by an immediate *entourage* of Italians. It is indeed noteworthy that the Syllabus of Pius IX contained the following "condemned proposition":

> 35. There is nothing to prevent a decree of a General Council, or the consensus of all nations, from transferring the Sovereign Pontificate from the Roman Bishop and from the town of Rome to another Bishop and another town.

It appears therefore to be definitely implied that the papal office is absolutely identified with that of Bishop of Rome, and that not even the decree of a General Council nor the universal consensus of Christians would justify the conferring of the papal tiara on the Bishop of some other city.

And when relationships between the kingdom of Italy and the Vatican are considered, attention is naturally drawn to the fact that the latter, by the Lateran Treaty of 1929, became the holder of Italian Government 5 per cent Bonds to the value of a thousand millions of lire and thereby acquired, apart from any other consideration, a very strong interest in the stability and prosperity of the Italian State.

The foregoing observations naturally raise two questions which the reader may put to himself: (*a*) is it consistent with the gospel of Christ that one nation should be given, with respect to matters of religion, that special pre-eminence which Italy would acquire if the papal claims were generally acknowledged? and (*b*) if the former question be answered in the affirmative, has Italy any special claim to merit that pre-eminence?

Concerning question (*a*) it may be suggested that it is usually believed by Christians that until the birth of Jesus the Jews occupied a very special position among the nations of the world, and were in a very particular sense the object of divine favour. At first glance therefore there would appear to be nothing illogical in the suggestion that under the new dispensation some other nation might acquire that special favour which the Jews are stated to have lost. On the other hand Paul would probably have demurred at accepting this doctrine, because he taught that in Christ there is neither Greek nor Jew, circumcision nor uncircumcision, Barbarian, Scythian, bond nor free (Col. iii. 11).

Question (*b*) is obviously one which cannot be answered in a few words, but one observation can be placed before the reader. It is generally admitted that there are important points of divergence between the respective mental outlooks of the Italian and the Anglo-Saxon. Such divergence has for example been brought quite recently into prominence owing to Italian action in North Africa and in Spain. But it is easier to judge impartially of matters which are less recent, and which affect us less directly. Let us take, therefore, as another example the works of St. Alfonso Liguori, a writer, formerly at any rate, regarded by many English and French Catholics with marked distaste. Now notwithstanding the opposition to his teaching, St. Alfonso was consecrated bishop in 1762, was declared "Venerable" in 1796, was canonised in 1839 and obtained the supreme rank of "Doctor of the Church" in 1871.

That the works of St. Alfonso are an expression of Italian mentality, and impress the average Englishman unfavourably, seems to be recognised to some extent by Cardinal Newman when he says (*Apologia*):

> S. Alfonso Liguori, it cannot be denied, lays down that an equivocation, that is a play upon words, in which one sense is taken by the speaker, and another sense intended by him for the hearer, is allowable if there is a just cause, that is in a special case, and may even be confirmed by oath. I shall give my opinion on this point as plainly as any Protestant can wish; and therefore I avow at once that in this department of morality, much as I admire the high points of the Italian character, I like the English character better; but in saying so I am not, as will be seen, saying anything disrespectful to S. Alfonso, who was a lover of truth and whose intercession I trust I shall not lose, though on the matter under consideration, I follow other guidance in preference to his.

And concerning the teaching of St. Alfonso and other Italian writers with reference to the Blessed Virgin Mary, Cardinal Newman tells us in the same work:

278 INTRODUCTION TO THE STUDY OF CHRISTIANITY

> Such passages . . . were not acceptable to every part of the Catholic world. . . . Such devotional manifestations in honour of Our Lady . . . are suitable for Italy but they are not suitable for England.

Should the reader care to follow this matter up and to study for himself the writings of St. Alfonso, he is likely to come to the conclusion that the writings have in actual practice done considerable harm; that they are emphatically a product of the Italian mind; and that the extraordinary honour extended to the author by successive Popes can be explained at least in part by the fact that the Popes themselves were Italians, and therefore more able than an Englishman would be to appreciate and to sympathise with the subtleties of the Saint's reasoning.

If we were to say: "The English mental outlook is superior to the Italian," the statement would be certainly discourteous and quite possibly untrue. But it can hardly be doubted that a healthy English mind tends to emphasise an aspect of truth which the Italian mind tends to overlook, and consequently the world would be morally far poorer if it were generally admitted that there existed one supreme and irresponsible human arbiter on all questions of morality, and that this arbiter was an Italian.

It now seems desirable to say something about the general manner in which Catholics and Protestants respectively find themselves compelled to deal with the various questions in dispute between them. An impartial observer who had never given the matter any very serious consideration, might be inclined to say that as each side had an interest in putting forward its own case in the most attractive manner possible, a certain perversion of the facts was just as likely to be made by the one as by the other. But it will nevertheless be seen that a distinction does in point of fact exist; and this distinction will be exhibited more clearly by means of one or two illustrations.

Let us suppose that our impartial enquirer studies the public utterances of successive Popes during for example the last century, and compares them with the utterances of some prominent non-Roman ecclesiastics: say for example successive Archbishops of Canterbury throughout the same period. Now if the result of such comparison were wholly favourable to the papal cause, or in other words if the successive Popes were clearly seen to excel the Archbishops in bringing forth in their pronouncements the fruits of the Spirit—love, joy, peace, long-suffering, gentleness, goodness, faith, meekness, temperance—the Protestant controversialist would not necessarily be disconcerted at the discovery. We can indeed imagine him replying somewhat as follows:

> The Popes are chosen, under circumstances of extraordinary solemnity, by mechanism carefully designed to ensure that the successful candidate is a man of quite outstanding aptitude for his exalted office. On the other hand the election of the Archbishops of Canterbury is known to be a mere fiction; they are really appointed by the Crown, and in actual practice the general public never knows exactly why or how they are chosen. So if it can be proved that they are men of no great suitability for their posts, one can only reply that it is indeed surprising that they are not worse than they are. But all this does not bear directly on the Protestant case against the Papacy, which case is not necessarily that modern Popes are not spiritually minded and able men, but rather that they both preach false doctrine and improperly claim to be Vice-Regents of God on earth.

But if the impartial enquirer, as the result of his study, had formed a wholly contrary view, and had decided that the Archbishops of Canterbury appeared to bring forth the fruits of the Spirit to a greater degree than did the Popes, the conclusion would be exceedingly damaging to the papal claims. According to the Roman view any post-Reformation Archbishop of Canterbury is an arch-enemy of the Holy and Immaculate Bride of Christ, outside of which there is no salvation, and such Archbishop is cut off from any sacramental means of grace, and consequently prevented from receiving into his corporal and spiritual being that body, blood, soul and divinity of Jesus which the humblest members of the true Church may receive at the hands of any ordained priest. In consequence, while Roman theories by no means exclude the possibility of certain Popes being incapable and indeed wicked men, and of certain Protestant divines being both capable and spiritually minded, the papal apologist could hardly contemplate the possibility of a series of heretical Archbishops of Canterbury, throughout a long term of years, bringing forth the fruits of the Spirit in greater abundance than the contemporary occupants of the throne of St. Peter brought forth such fruits.

It will be seen therefore that it happens that the Roman controversialist is at a disadvantage with respect to his Protestant opponent in that the former, in order fully to make out his case, has to prove so much more than has the latter. The Protestant has no hesitation in admitting that God has left man without any visible guide with respect to a vast number of important matters; the Catholic on the other hand has formed a general theory, of which the most striking feature is that this world is subjected to the Pope as the Vice-Regent of God (*qui Dei et Domini nostri Jesu Christi vices gerit in terris*) and that the Pope is an infallible source of divine truth. In consequence all historical facts have to be examined by the Catholic in the light of this theory, and hence there is necessarily a great temptation for him, when he finds that the theory does not readily harmonise with the facts, to adjust the latter to the former.

Some Roman Catholic writers seem to have appreciated this difficulty, and have attempted to meet it by what seems to be practically discouraging the free study of Church History. Thus Cardinal Manning in his *Temporal Mission* calls the appeal to Scripture and antiquity "essentially rationalistic," and further on in the same work he says:

> "The appeal to antiquity" (i.e. the appeal behind the present teaching of the Church) "is both a treason and a heresy. . . . I may say in strict truth that the Church has no antiquity. It rests upon its own supernatural and perpetual consciousness. . . . The only divine evidence to us of what was primitive is the witness and voice of the Church at this hour."

Clearly however it would be quite impossible for Cardinal Manning or anyone else to hope that the public generally would refrain from studying history for fear of discovering facts which fail to harmonise with preconceived theories. Hence it has come about that a certain adjustment of the facts by controversialists has indeed been made. A few examples will be given of incidents concerning which controversy has taken place.

At the beginning of the seventeenth century a story was put into circulation to the effect that Matthew Parker, who became Anglican Archbishop of Canterbury under Queen Elizabeth in 1559, was never consecrated, or rather that his only consecration took place at a tavern called the "Nag's Head," where one "Scory, an apostate monk" touched his head with a Bible and bade him receive power to preach the word of God. Now it so happens that the contemporary records of the consecration of Parker are exceptionally ample and convincing, and there is no reasonable doubt that the ceremony really took place in the manner prescribed by English ecclesiastical law. The only vestige of truth that can be found in the legend is the fact that one of the consecrating bishops was in fact named Scory. But let us suppose that the contrary had been the case, and that the so-called "Nag's Head fable" had been true. The result would of course have been unfavourable to Protestantism, but nevertheless the position of the great bulk of Protestant thinkers would have been but little affected thereby. They would reply somewhat as follows:

> We take our stand on the belief that in the first century of our era certain supernormal events took place, and that these events had the effect (*a*) of modifying profoundly the relationships between God and man, and (*b*) of setting up a certain code of morality. It is therefore the duty of the modern Christian (*a*) to take advantage of the Way laid open nineteen centuries ago, by which Way he can approach the Father, and (*b*) to act in accordance with the code propagated by Jesus. This is our religion, and nothing that could possibly have happened in the time of Queen Elizabeth can conceivably modify it.

Let us now take an allegation made against the Roman position. The Council of Constantinople of 680 anathematised Pope Honorius I for heresy; the then reigning Pope (Agathus) was represented at the Council, and his successor (Leo II) explicitly approved of its sentence. Now it is clear that by the very nature of the standpoints of the contending parties, it is impossible that any fact could be adduced as damaging to the Protestant position as is the condemnation of Honorius I to the Papal claims to infallibility. We are not surprised therefore to find that after the sixteenth century the Roman Breviaries cease to mention this condemnation. A Breviary dated 1520 contains the entry (under the date of June 28th): *In which synod were condemned Sergius, Cyrus, Honorius, Pyrrhus, Paul and Peter . . . who asserted and proclaimed one will and operation in our Lord Jesus Christ.* In modern Roman Breviaries (under the heading June 28th) one reads the following: *In this Council were condemned Cyrus, Sergius and Pyrrhus, who preached only one will and operation in Christ.* It is clear therefore that in this respect the record of the facts is adjusted to fit the theory.

To the foregoing it may quite conceivably be replied that the Protestant controversialists also have every interest in presenting their case in the most favourable light possible, and hence it would be very unfair to assume that one of the two sides has a monopoly of misrepresentation. But the fundamental difference between the two sides is, as has already been pointed out, very considerable. And this difference will perhaps be made clearer if we remember that such men as Philip II of Spain, Louis XIV and Napoleon I of France and William II of Germany have all in turn been intensely unpopular among the English public, but nevertheless any reputable modern historian may be trusted to write concerning any one of the four with at least something approaching to impartiality. But if a historian accepts as a basic assumption the allegation that the successive Popes are Vice-Regents of God on earth, and are in a very special sense the chosen vehicles and mouthpieces of the Holy Spirit, then *ex hypothesi* there cannot be any question of impartiality. Indeed, if we accept the Roman position, impartiality instead of being a virtue seems to be—to use the language already quoted of Cardinal Manning anent appeals to antiquity—"at once a treason and a heresy."

A further matter concerning which there is a marked contrast between the teaching of modern Protestantism and that of Roman Catholicism is the doctrine of eternal punishment. From the earliest times Christians have uniformly adopted the starting-point that all men are sinners (Rom. iii. 9 and 23). The life and death of Jesus, however, were held to afford the sinner a means of escape from the punishment of his sins; but it was simultaneously taught that the Church possessed the Keys of Heaven, and consequently the individual benefited or otherwise from the death of Christ according as to whether or no he died reconciled to the Church. In the latter event he was doomed to an endless future of never-ceasing torment. From a strictly legal point of view it is easy to argue that such torment is a punishment for sin, but nevertheless, seeing that all men, good and bad, are held to have incurred the Divine wrath, it seems inevitable that the faithful should have come to regard suffering in the next world as a punishment for having failed to become reconciled to the Church. And as it is taught that the first essential in order to effect such reconciliation is the acceptance of the Church's dogmatic teaching, it has often been said that the result of the system was to substitute the creed for the ten commandments. That is to say that while no one could truthfully allege that the Church actually ceased to preach Christian morality, nevertheless such morality came in practice to be regarded as of vastly less importance than the acceptance of Catholic dogma and the maintenance of an attitude favourable to the claims of Rome. It will be seen therefore that while there is much difference of opinion as to whether or no the doctrine of the eternal torture of the damned is true, there can be no doubt whatever that it is a doctrine highly advantageous to the position of the Roman Church. At the time of the Reformation, Protestant divines still continued to hold strenuously to the same doctrine: they did not of course teach that sinners would be eternally damned for not being reconciled to Rome, but they consistently taught that damnation would result from rejection of the dogmas of Christianity as accepted by Protestant bodies. So they continued to take their stand on the Athanasian Creed, and to insist that *it is necessary to everlasting salvation that he that would be saved believe rightly the Incarnation of our Lord Jesus Christ*. But as and when Protestantism came to find itself faced with rationalism, and had to submit its teachings to the light of human reason, it found itself gradually compelled to preach two propositions: (*a*) God is a just and righteous Judge, and (*b*) in so far as is consistent with the former proposition, God is merciful. And it was felt that these propositions were incompatible with the doctrine of eternal punishment, because, even supposing that the effect of sin is really much more terrible than we human beings can conceive, it is hardly reasonable to think that any one man can in a single lifetime commit sins sufficiently atrocious to merit eternal torture as an expiation. It has consequently come about that probably the majority of modern Protestant divines either repudiate altogether the doctrine of everlasting damnation, or at least let it drop into the background. Those theologians who continue to teach this doctrine are sometimes actuated by wholly laudable motives, i.e. they conscientiously believe the teaching to be true, and they think that its rejection on the part of Christians generally would entail an enormous increase of wickedness in this world and of consequent damnation in the world to come. Sometimes however such theologians appear to outsiders to be actuated by less worthy motives—an overwhelming desire for authority and control over the minds of men, coupled with a certain satisfaction at the thought of the terrible fate about to befall those of whose conduct they disapprove, or, more especially, from whose doctrinal views they differ. In particular the Church of Rome, which consistently maintains its policy of exacting obedience rather than of appealing to reason, lays special emphasis on the doctrine of the everlasting duration of punishment. An interesting example of such emphasis is quoted by Miss Betham-Edwards in her study of that great liberal Catholic theologian Jean Reynaud (1806–1863). She tells us:

> With regard to Jean Reynaud's condemnation of the theory of eternal punishment, the conclave of bishops at Perigueux decreed as follows:—
>
>> As regards the doctrine which the author puts especially forward with respect to the punishment of the wicked after death, we condemn it likewise, we repel it, and we have it particularly in horror, because it is infinitely pernicious. In truth the divine love is only too often stifled in the heart of man under the weight of passions; what would happen if a hypocritically flattering doctrine were to come to destroy fear, and to offer to the generation of the perverted a God under whose government vice having attained liberty would be allowed full scope (*les vices affranchis se mettraient à l'aise*)?
>
> But the closing sentence shows best the temper of the bishops:—
>
>> Finally we declare that even if, not merely a man or the whole world but, to imagine the impossible, an angel from heaven were to teach a contrary doctrine, our own should remain for all Christians the object of a wholly firm and entirely immutable faith. If anyone act otherwise, let him know that he cuts himself off from the Catholic faith, and that he has incurred those same eternal penalties the existence of which he denies.

The obvious difficulty of presenting to the faithful this truly awful doctrine, while at the same time teaching the justice and the love of the Almighty Father, has occasioned a curious air of unreality in such popular devotions as deal with the fate of the wicked. Thus for example that great saint, Francisco Xavier (1506–1552), wrote a hymn *O Deus, ego amo te*, of which two verses are here given:—

CHRISTIANITY OF TO-DAY

> My God, I love thee; not because
> I hope for heaven thereby,
> Nor yet because who love thee not
> Are lost eternally.
>
> .   .   .   .   .
>
> Then why, O blessed Jesus Christ,
> Should I not love thee well,
> Not for the sake of winning heaven,
> Or of escaping hell?

This hymn finds a place in more than one well-known collection intended for the use of non-Catholics, and frequently forms a part of evangelical missionary services. But if anyone takes the trouble to paraphrase the first verse he can hardly fail to be struck by the extraordinary incongruity of addressing the Deity with an expression of disinterested affection, reminding the Almighty at the same time that a cessation of such affection would entail everlasting punishment.

We have quoted above the words of the Athanasian Creed: "It is necessary to everlasting salvation that he that would be saved believe rightly the Incarnation of our Lord Jesus Christ." As this statement may be said to mark the point where traditional Christianity definitely breaks away from other religions, it may be desirable further to examine the words in question. It will be seen that they assume the truth of three propositions:

(a) In the first century of the Christian era certain very remarkable occurrences took place in Palestine, the chief actor therein being a public preacher named Jesus of Nazareth.

(b) Jesus was not merely perfect man, but was also perfect God, being in fact the second Person of the Blessed Trinity. In him the divine and human natures were united in one Person. The result of this union, or Incarnation of God in man, is of the very highest importance for us members of the human race, because Jesus by his death "hath destroyed death and by his rising again hath restored to us everlasting life."

(c) In order however that the individual may attain everlasting life and may otherwise benefit by the incarnation, death and resurrection of Jesus, it is necessary that he believe the accuracy of proposition (b), it being of course clear that proposition (a) presents no great difficulty.

It is as regards proposition (c) that traditional Christian teaching clashes so notably with twentieth-century thought. Thinking men and women increasingly find it hard to believe that their eternal salvation can depend on their right interpretation of facts alleged to have occurred in Asia Minor nearly two thousand years ago. If we find it intensely difficult to form a correct judgment as to the causes and responsibilities of the Great War, an event still fresh in the memories of most of us, how can we possibly be sure of appreciating rightly the existing evidence relative to events which took place in Palestine in the third decade of our era? We are taught that the life and death of Jesus brought about a new relationship between God and man, and as it were created a new remedy for the spiritual illnesses of mankind. Is it reasonable to suppose that a right comprehension of the nature of this remedy is necessary for its efficacy? Analogy with the material world would prompt us to reply in the negative. For example, scientists have discovered that certain substances found in different foodstuffs are necessary for maintaining our bodily health. But no one could possibly think that an accurate scientific knowledge as to the nature and effect of vitamins is necessary to keep a man in reasonably good physical condition. And it is at least possible that there is some analogy between our spiritual health and our bodily health. If it be true that the human race became estranged from God, and if reunion with God be our aim and goal, and if such reunion has been facilitated in some manner transcending human intelligence by the earthly mission of Jesus, then it is *prima facie* reasonable to hope that the benefits thereby accruing can be enjoyed by those who earnestly desire reunion with God, but who for one reason or other have erroneous ideas, or even no ideas at all, about such mission.

We remark that Peter, shortly after the Ascension, is reported to have said of Jesus: "Neither is there salvation in any other; for there is none other name under heaven given among men, whereby we must be saved" (Acts iv. 12). But the vision subsequently granted to him at Joppa profoundly modified his exclusiveness, and led him to realise that God is indeed the Father of all men. We find that he immediately afterwards told Cornelius: "Of a truth I perceive that God is no respecter of persons, but in every nation he that feareth him and worketh righteousness is accepted with him" (Acts x. 34, 35). And again we observe that Paul, writing to Timothy (i. iv. 10), says that God is the Saviour of all men, especially of those that believe. This seems to show unequivocally that Paul did not consider the acceptance of dogma as essential to salvation. It is of course true that there are certain passages (e.g. Gal. iii. 22) which have been adduced to prove the contrary. This question has already been touched on (*vide* p. 121) but at the risk of appearing to go over the same ground a second time, it may be well to observe that in those passages of the Epistles and Gospels in which "belief" seems to be stressed as an essential for salvation, it seems not unlikely that the authors' meaning may have been something like what a physician has in mind when he says to a patient: "I can assure you that if you will only have confidence in me, you will get well." Here the physician obviously means that if the patient's confidence be sufficient to induce him to carry out faithfully the treatment indicated, he is almost certain to get well. It is not suggested that the patient will be cured by merely saying to himself: "Dr. Blank is a very able practitioner." And in the same way, the phrase "to have faith in Jesus" may be reasonably interpreted to mean "to adopt the method of Jesus, as set forth in the Gospels and as further explained and elaborated in the Pauline Epistles."

It has already been remarked that the Epistle to the Hebrews contains passages which have been interpreted, especially by Protestants, in a manner out of harmony with the teaching of other Christian writers. For example the text *Without faith it is impossible to please (God)* (Heb. xi. 6) is a very favourite one with a certain type of preacher. But if the quotation be continued, we read: *For he that cometh to God must believe that he is, and that he is a rewarder of them that diligently seek him.* It appears that what is here meant by faith is, as already suggested, a conscious effort on the part of the individual to raise his being towards God, and the author assures us that God rewards those who so seek him. It will be observed that such faith presupposes a belief in the existence of the Deity, but does not necessarily presuppose any specific dogmatical tenets as to the Divine Nature. And the writer of the Epistles to the Hebrews does not, in the passage in question, tell us that in order to obtain the desired reward any conditions are necessary other than that man should firstly believe in God's existence and secondly diligently seek him.

As a contrast to the foregoing it may be well to call attention to Faber's well-known hymn, of which the last verse is as follows:

> Jesus is God: let sorrow come
> And pain and every ill,
> All are worth while, for all are means
> His glory to fulfil;
> Worth while a thousand years of woe
> To speak one little word,
> If by that "I believe" we own
> The Godhead of our Lord.

The above lines may be compared with the words of Jesus himself: *Not every one that saith unto me, "Lord, Lord," shall enter into the Kingdom of Heaven, but he that doeth the will of my Father which is in heaven* (Matt. vii. 21).

We now approach the conclusion to which the considerations set forth in the foregoing pages appear to lead. In the first few centuries of our era Christianity was propagated among men, for the most part very uneducated, of widely different races, languages and religions. It was therefore humanly speaking impossible that it could have performed its function of disciplining men's souls unless it had presented its teaching in definite dogmatic form, the preacher saying in effect: *What you have hitherto believed is wrong: I affirm this to be right: Your duty is to accept as true what I tell you.* Or, as St. Remi expressed it when baptising Clovis: *Bow thy head: adore what thou hast burnt, and burn what thou hast adored.* But in the twentieth century the standard of culture among the more civilised nations is wholly different from what it was in the early centuries of Christianity. There are to-day thousands of people who are unable to believe that the New Testament ought to be interpreted and accepted in a certain traditional manner, and that if they fail so to interpret and to accept it, God is no longer their Father and they are definitely cut off from the spiritually living. It is to such that the present treatise is primarily addressed. To them it is suggested that the Gospels and Pauline Epistles do not profess to give us in clear and unequivocal language exact information as to the nature of the personality of Jesus. And it is indeed difficult to believe that such exact information can be necessary to men's happiness in the world to come. But the New Testament does give its readers a vast amount of instruction as to the method of Jesus, and it is this method that the disciple is called upon to follow. And moreover, if and when the disciple takes up his cross and follows Jesus, he may reasonably be encouraged to do so in the conviction that God is his Father, and that his sonship is not necessarily lost on account of any erroneous ideas which he may hold either as to the nature of the founder of Christianity, or as to the status of any living ecclesiastic resident in Rome or elsewhere.

It may be of interest to study the words of a very popular hymn commencing *O little town of Bethlehem*, by Bishop Phillips Brooks. Two extracts are subjoined:

> So God imparts to human hearts
>   The blessings of his heaven.
> No ear may hear his coming;
>   But in this world of sin,
> Where meek souls will receive him, still
>   The dear Christ enters in.
>
> O holy Child of Bethlehem,
>   Descend to us, we pray;
> Cast out our sin, and enter in,
>   Be born in us to-day.
> We hear the Christmas Angels
>   The great glad tidings tell:
> O come to us, abide with us,
>   Our Lord Emmanuel.

Examining the above lines in the light of traditional Christianity, we naturally conclude that the author accepted two basic propositions: (*a*) Christ was born as a human being in Bethlehem in or about B.C. 4; and (*b*) the spiritual progress of each individual soul depends upon its capacity for enabling Christ to be born and to develop within itself. These two propositions are of very different natures; the former is a part of exoteric Christianity, and is taught freely to all comers; the latter may in a sense be called semi-esoteric Christianity, because, although no secret is made about the doctrine, nevertheless it is in actual practice not considered suitable for explaining to children and to prospective converts.

It is noteworthy that the two propositions are wholly independent in the sense that theoretically it is possible that either might be true and the other false. It may possibly assist us to appreciate the relationship between the two propositions if we recall to mind the "alabaster box of ointment of spikenard very precious" of which we read in Mark's Gospel. Such doctrine as directly affects the life of the human soul and its communion with the Deity may be compared to the "very precious spikenard." On the other hand such doctrine as that set forth in what we have called proposition (*a*) may be compared to the alabaster box containing the ointment. The box without its contents would be a useless ornament: the ointment without a suitable receptacle could not be conveniently transmitted from one person to another, and would quickly deteriorate. There is here an analogy, albeit incomplete, with the Christian faith. If the early apostles and missionaries had taught the birth of the Christ Spirit within their hearers, and had made such teaching the principal point of their message to mankind, then their doctrine would have been too similar to Neo-Platonism and other popular philosophies to permit of its being considered as a unique revelation. (We have already seen, on p. 187, that Augustine abandoned Neo-Platonism for Christianity partly because the latter offered him a "religious founder" while the former did not.) But on the other hand it would seem that the weakness of traditional Christianity has been the excessive drawing of attention to the alabaster box rather than to the ointment contained therein. It is easy to teach children to repeat the statement that Jesus Christ was conceived of the Holy Ghost and born of the Virgin Mary, but intensely difficult to explain to them how the indwelling of the Christ Spirit may possibly affect their individual souls. So from generation to generation the difficulty has been shelved, and while time and care have been lavished on the study of the less important words and acts of Jesus, the fundamental truths as to union with God through Christ have been too often allowed to drop into the background. In this way traditional Christianity has unhappily fallen short of its divine mission, with the effect that is only too familiar to us.

The above observations raise a very pertinent enquiry: if it be admitted that a Deity exists, and that this Deity yearns for complete union with each individual human soul, and if such union may be brought about by man availing himself of the aid of the Divine Christ Spirit, then what need was there for the Passion of Jesus, or indeed what essential difference is there between the system taught by Paul and that taught by Plotinus? The preceding pages of this treatise will possibly have prepared the reader for the difficulty of answering these questions. The accounts we possess of the life and work of Jesus were compiled, as we have already seen, long after the event by writers who did not as a rule possess the theological temperament, and who did not give us their own deductions from the facts they related. We also notice the disinclination of Paul to comment on the teaching, parables and miracles of Jesus, just as we similarly notice the disinclination of early Christians to make pictorial representations of any of the scenes of the Passion of Jesus, notwithstanding the fact that they freely depicted him both as a thaumaturge and also in an ideal manner: e.g. as the Good Shepherd.

But while the difficulties of the subject are great, it seems to be something more than a mere tenable hypothesis that in the fullness of time the Almighty Father specially chose one human being, who on account of his superlative merits became the vehicle of the Christ Spirit, and to borrow the language of Paul of Samosata,

> coalesced with God so as to admit of no divorce from him, but for all ages to retain one and the same will and activity with him, an activity perpetually at work in the manifestation of God.

And there seems nothing unreasonable in the belief that as a result of the complete union between God and man, effected in the person of Jesus, the union (albeit less complete) between other human beings and God became in some transcendental manner greatly facilitated. It must of course be admitted that we can hardly suppose that an inhabitant of Athens living in B.C. 200 was necessarily precluded from becoming a Son of God, but that as a result of the mission of Jesus an Athenian living four centuries later did in fact possess that potential privilege. But what we know about even the best of the ancient religions leads us to infer that the doctrine as to union with God was jealously kept secret from the mass of humanity, and initiation was an arduous and painful process which only a very small proportion of even "the wise and prudent" could hope to pass through. And it is surely not unreasonable to believe that after one specially chosen human being had by divine ordinance and by his own superlative merits attained perfect union with the Godhead, the way for the rest of humanity was laid more open; the time came when whosoever had ears to hear was enabled to hear, when it might be said figuratively that the veil of the Temple was rent in twain, and when all who desired to worship the Father were freed from the necessity of undergoing the training of the Mystery Schools and became encouraged to worship in spirit and in truth.

Rudolf Steiner, in one of his essays (*Human Conscience*) puts forward a proposition harmonising with the foregoing. He says:

> In order that man should find God-nature in his inner soul it was necessary that Christ should enter into the development of humanity as an external historical event. If Christ, the Deity, had not been present in the human body of Jesus of Nazareth; if he had not appeared as the conqueror of death in the Mystery of Golgotha—man would never have been able to understand the indwelling of the Deity in the inner soul.
>
> To assert that man could understand the Divine inner penetration without the external historical Christ Jesus, is equivalent to claiming that we could have eyes though there were no sun in the world. As against the one-sided view of philosophers that the origin of light must be sought in the eyes, since light cannot be perceived without eyes, we must ever put forward Goethe's statement that the eye is "created through light for light." If no sun were to enlighten space, no eyes could have been formed out of the human organism. The eyes are created by light and, without the sun, there would be no eyes to perceive. No eye is capable of perceiving the sun without having first received from the sun the power of perception. In the same way there can be no inner understanding and knowledge of Christ-nature without an external Christ-impulse. As the sun in the Cosmos is to sight, so is the historical Christ Jesus to that which we call the permeation with God-nature in ourselves.

Steiner arrived at the above conclusions through what he called "spiritual science," that is to say he believed that he acquired his knowledge when his consciousness was on a higher plane, and he was thus enabled to perceive truths actually hidden from the average human being. Obviously the appeal of such statements can hardly be to strict logic. But nevertheless many earnest enquirers have been led to feel that the view of the mission of Christ as above set forth harmonises as no other theory harmonises with scientific knowledge and with the history of mankind, as well as appealing to all that is most sacred and profound in human consciousness.

In studying the Christianity of our own day, we ought not to forget that, like everything else, it is the net result of all the forces to which it has been subjected since its inception. In so far as these forces have been favourable to its right development, we reap the advantage; in so far as they have been unfavourable, we inevitably suffer the consequences. And it so happens that the methods now adopted in Russia to propagate Bolshevism as a militant creed enable us to appreciate, far better than the last generation could have done, the general lines on which medieval Christianity was imposed on the bulk of the people. Lenin and his colleagues have practically laid down a code of dogmas based on certain affirmations with respect to mankind and to the universe in general; and current Russian writers on history, sociology and philosophy are compelled to adapt their theories to the official creed. A distinguished Russian professor, exiled from his own country, tells us that:

> Creative philosophical thought cannot flourish in such an environment, and it amply accounts for the shuffling, the endless repetition, the monotony, the limitedness of Soviet philosophy, its petty sophistries, the reciprocal accusations and denunciations, the fundamental necessity of lying; neither talent nor genius can make any headway (Nicolas Berdyaev: from an essay contributed to *Questions Disputées*, 1933).

The foregoing language may, at least in part, be applied to medieval Western Christianity, to the Church of Innocent III and of Torquemada; and it would seem that the initial error, both in Russia and in Western Europe, has been the demand that all individuals shall think alike, and it is from the results of this initial error that we to-day are suffering. It has not always been remembered that the Christian Church is a community of believers striving to attain atonement with God through his Christ Spirit: unquestionably members of this community should tend to think on the same general lines concerning religious matters, they should hold the faith in unity of spirit, in the bond of peace and of righteousness of life, but enforced unity of thought, so destructive of personality and of intellectual advancement, is in no way a desirable characteristic of the Church of Christ.

In conclusion permission may be asked to remind the reader that the present treatise is a mere *Introduction to the Study of Christianity*, and the author in no way claims to have written

294 INTRODUCTION TO THE STUDY OF CHRISTIANITY

a History. Many of the subjects herein dealt with are in the highest degree controversial, and the utmost that the author can hope is that a train of thought may be initiated in the reader's mind, assisting him in some measure to arrive at his own conclusions thereon.

APPENDIX A

EXTRACTS FROM BHAGAVAD GHITA,
GIVEN FOR SAKE OF COMPARISON WITH
THE TEACHING OF THE JOHANNINE DISCOURSES

ALL these sacrifices of so many kinds are displayed in the sight of God; know that they all spring from action, and, comprehending this, thou shalt obtain an eternal release. O harasser of thy foes, the sacrifice through spiritual knowledge is superior to sacrifice made with material things; every action without exception is comprehended in spiritual knowledge, O son of Pritha. Seek this wisdom by doing service, by strong search, by questions, and by humility; the wise who see the truth will communicate it unto thee, and knowing which thou shalt never again fall into error, O son of Bharata. By this knowledge thou shalt see all things and creatures whatsoever in thyself and then in me. Even if thou wert the greatest of all sinners, thou shalt be able to cross over all sins in the bark of spiritual knowledge.

Chapter IV.

I am the cause, I am the production and the dissolution of the whole universe. There is none superior to me, O conqueror of wealth, and all things hang on me as precious gems upon a string. I am the taste in water, O son of Kunti, the light in the sun and moon, the mystic syllable OM in all the *Vedas*, sound in space, the masculine essence in men, the sweet smell in the earth, and the brightness in the fire. In all creatures I am the life, and the power of concentration in those whose minds are on the spirit. Know me, O son of Pritha, as the eternal seed of all creatures. I am the wisdom of the wise and the strength of the strong.

Chapter VII.

I am the goal, the Comforter, the Lord, the Witness, the resting-place, the asylum and the Friend; I am the origin and the dissolution, the receptacle, the storehouse, and the eternal seed. I cause light and heat and rain; I now draw in and now let forth; I am death and immortality; I am the cause unseen and the visible effect.

Chapter IX.

I am the same to all creatures; I know not hatred nor favour; but those who serve me with love dwell in me and I in them. Even if the man of most evil ways worship me with exclusive devotion, he is to be considered as righteous, for he hath judged aright. Such a man soon becometh of a righteous soul and obtaineth perpetual happiness.

Chapter IX.

Having obtained this finite, joyless world, worship me. Serve me, fix heart and mind on me, be my servant, my adorer, prostrate thyself before me, and thus, united unto me, at rest, thou shalt go unto me.

Chapter IX.

For those who worship me, renouncing in me all their actions, regarding me as the supreme goal and meditating on me alone, if their thoughts are turned to me, O son of Pritha, I presently become the saviour from this ocean of incarnations and death. Place, then, thy heart on me, penetrate me with thy understanding, and thou shalt without doubt hereafter dwell in me. But if thou shouldst be unable at once steadfastly to fix thy heart and mind on me, strive then, O Dhananjaya, to find me by constant practice in devotion. If after constant practice, thou art still unable, follow me by actions performed for me; for by doing works for me thou shalt attain perfection. But if thou art unequal even to this, then, being self-restrained, place all thy works, failures and successes alike, on me, abandoning in me the fruit of every action.

Chapter XII.

APPENDIX B

SUFFERING AND SHAME AS FACTORS IN SPIRITUAL DEVELOPMENT
(P. 92)

MANY Christian authors have emphasised the shame and humiliation experienced by Jesus on the occasion of his Passion, but have not always remembered that shame and humiliation formed part of at least some of the ancient mysteries wherein the neophyte was perfected in spiritual knowledge. The following illuminating quotation is from an article by Mr. Cecil Harwood in *Anthroposophy* for Easter 1930:

> At certain Dionysian Mysteries it was the custom for the procession of those who were to become the Initiates ($\tau\epsilon\lambda\epsilon\tau\alpha\iota$) of the gods to be subjected on the way to a ceremonial cursing and reviling by the lookers-on. The meaning of such a custom is not clear, except perhaps to those who try to experience in imagination the effect of such a reviling on the neophyte as he advanced to the temple. It was surely to strengthen in him the feeling that every man's hand was against him, that he must be strong in the lonely mysteries of his own ego which he was now seeking to fulfil. Such a feeling of the effect of this reviling can only be strengthened and deepened by the contemplation of the life of the Christ. He too was reviled, and forsaken even of God, and, at the last, he uttered the word which the Gospel writer took from the old Mystery language ($\tau\epsilon\tau\epsilon\lambda\epsilon\sigma\tau\alpha\iota$)—the Mystery is fulfilled.

APPENDIX C

THE RELIGION OF THE ALBIGENSES

It is stated in the text (p. 214) that such knowledge as we possess of the tenets of the Albigenses is almost exclusively derived from their adversaries. The reader may be interested in examining a typical example of the statements made by orthodox writers concerning this body.

An article attributed to the Benedictine Abbot Dom Butler, and contributed to the *Encyclopædia Britannica*, contains the following:

> The Albigenses have received much sympathy, as being a kind of pre-Reformation Protestants; but it is now recognised that their tenets were an extreme form of Manichaeism. They believed in the existence of two gods, a good (whose son was Christ) and an evil (whose son was Satan); matter is the creation of the evil principle, and therefore essentially evil; and the greatest of all sins is sexual intercourse, even in marriage; sinful also is the possession of material goods, and the eating of flesh meat, and many other things. So great was the abhorrence of matter that some even thought it an act of religion to commit suicide by voluntary starvation, or to starve children to death. . . . Such tenets were destructive not only of Catholicism but of Christianity of any kind, and of civil society itself. . . .
>
> In 1208, after the murder of a papal legate, Innocent III called on the Christian princes to suppress the Albigensian heresy by force of arms, and for seven years the south of France was devastated by one of the most bloodthirsty wars in history, the Albigenses being slaughtered by thousands and their property confiscated wholesale.

Two points especially strike the reader, the first of these being the inherent improbability of several of the above statements. Why should it be necessary to engage for seven years in "one of the most bloodthirsty wars in history" in order to confiscate the property of people who hold the possession of material goods to be sinful? And how could people who hold sexual intercourse, even in marriage, to be the greatest of all sins, survive in the struggle for life, and continue to be for several centuries the object of an extremely violent, if possibly ntermittent persecution, on the part of the orthodox Christians?[1] The obvious inference is that Dom Butler has represented the Albigenses in general as inculcating a degree of asceticism which could hardly have been attempted by more than a very few exceptional members of the inner circle of the body (*Cathari* or *perfecti*).

The second point which strikes us is that what Dom Butler says about the Albigenses sounds so very much like what a hostile and not wholly well-informed critic might be expected to say about the Catholic regular clergy. The great religious orders, male and female (excluding however the tertiary orders), owing obedience to Rome, prohibit their individual members from owning personal property, in which indeed they follow the example of the early Christian Church. They also prohibit marriage, and this prohibition applies to the Roman Catholic secular clergy. All of them forbid the use of flesh meat throughout certain seasons of the year, and some indeed (e.g. the Minims) permanently exclude from their diet such articles as meat, eggs, milk, butter and cheese. It is true that we do not hear of Catholic ascetics deliberately starving themselves to death, but we can hardly doubt that the early death of many of them (e.g. St. Francis of Assisi) has been directly brought about by malnutrition.

The remaining point raised by Dom Butler is that of the dualism alleged to be taught by the Albigenses. Here again it would seem that the case is not quite fairly presented. The most outstanding point of the teaching of the Albigenses, as against their Catholic opponents, appears to have been the rejection by the former of the doctrine of eternal punishment. The Albigenses believed in the ultimate extinction (at all events as far as the human race is concerned) of evil. The Catholics appear to preach that that great mass of humanity which does not "submit itself to the authority of the Roman Pontiff" will throughout all eternity form part of the kingdom of Satan and remain permanently separated from God. While therefore it seems untrue to say that either the Catholics or the Albigenses acknowledged the existence of two opposing deities, the accusation is more comprehensible if brought against the former than against the latter.

[1] We find that Albigenses were put to death for their faith as early as 1022. The great persecution preached by Innocent III commenced about 1209. In 1245 at Montségur two hundred of the heretics were burned in one day. The Inquisition continued to take active steps to crush the heresy throughout the thirteenth century, and it was not until about 1330 that the persecution of the body came to an end owing to the practical extinction of its partisans.

APPENDIX D

With reference to Page 216

PORTUGUESE EXPEDITIONS

GONDIN DA FONSECA (*Portugal na Historia*, 1932) devotes a chapter to the reproduction of interesting passages from Portuguese sources, specially selected as shedding light on the mentality which formerly stimulated expeditions to the East. For example, we have the following quotation from João de Lucena's *Life of Father Francisco de Xavier*, in which we are given details concerning a battle against Moslem seamen:

> When the soldiers of Jesus saw that it was clear that their Lord was fighting on their side, all of them called with one voice on his most unconquered name (*por seu invitissimo nome*) and flung themselves on the enemy as if they had wished to conquer with the work and energy of their bare hands, seeing that they ran no risk, the artillery having already acted so efficiently. Four of our boats rammed six of the Moors', killing with musket-fire, with lance and with sword, some two thousand in half an hour. Those who remained, after some had fought with courage, fearing rather the fury of our men than a jump into the river, flung themselves therein, so that in a short time all the boats were surrounded with struggling soldiers. Of these, however, as they were getting tired of fighting, and half dead with fear, some burnt with powder and others badly wounded, none got out of the water alive. ... The number of dead in the enemy's fleet was four thousand, for the greater part people of position (*gente limpa*), attendants of King Achem, according to the confession of fifteen of them who, after all was over, were captured in a *proa* and tortured. On our side four men were lost—one for every thousand—and indeed the mere work of killing so many people might have caused more (*on our side*) to die if the most holy name of Jesus had not constituted both strength and weapons for his warriors. (*Só do trabalho de matar tanta gente puderam morrer mais, se o santissimo nome de Jesus não fôra aos seus guerrerios forças e armas.*)

APPENDIX E

With reference to P. 257

TOLERATION TOWARDS NON-CATHOLIC BODIES

It is a remarkable fact that respect for its general principles has sometimes caused the Holy See to demand the non-toleration of Protestantism even in circumstances in which it would appear to outsiders that such demand was not merely useless but positively prejudicial to Catholic interests. We know for example that the French Catholic clergy suffered severely from the great outburst of anti-clericalism at the time of the Revolution of 1789. In 1809 Napoleon imprisoned Pius VII, who during his long captivity might have been expected to have been led to the conclusion that the Catholic clergy should attempt to carry out their sacred mission without too great friction with the (then dominant) anti-clerical party in France. But on the contrary we find that within two months of his release from Savona the Pope addressed (April 29, 1814) to the Bishop of Tours the Apostolic Letter *Post tam diuturnas*, giving various instructions to the French Episcopate, and specially enjoining the bishops to make certain representations to Louis XVIII with reference to the proposed Constitution. The Pope, on the subject of liberty of conscience, wrote:

> A fresh subject of regret, with which our heart is still more bitterly afflicted, and which, we confess, causes us an extreme torment, grief and anguish, is the twenty-second article of the Constitution. Not only does it permit the *liberty of cults and of conscience*, to employ the actual terms of the article, but it promises support and protection to this liberty, and moreover to the ministers of what are called *cults*. There is indeed no need for a long dissertation, in addressing such a bishop as yourself, to make you see clearly how mortal is the wound with which the Catholic faith in France is smitten by this article. By the fact that the liberty of all cults is established without distinction, truth is confounded with error, and the Holy and Immaculate Bride of Christ, the Church outside which there can be no safety, is placed in the same rank as the heretical sects and even as Jewish perfidy. In promising favour and support to the heretical sects and to their ministers, not only their persons but also their errors are tolerated and favoured. . . .

His Holiness instructs the French bishops to seek audience of the King and to point out:

> what a fatal blow to the Catholic religion, what a peril for souls, what ruin for the faith, would be the result of his consent to the articles of the said Constitution. . . . Inform him on our behalf that we cannot persuade ourselves that he will wish to inaugurate his reign in causing to the Catholic faith a wound so deep as to be nigh incurable.

INDEX

Abdul Walid of Cordoba (Averroes), 224
Abélard, P., 224
Acre, fall of, 139, 194, 233
Acts of Apostles, 26, 33
Adhemar, Bp., 232
Agathus, Pope, 281
Agrippa, King, 91
Albigenses, 211, 214, 215, 267, 298–299
Alcacer Kebir, 230, 234
Alcibiades, 60
Alexander, Bishop, 126, 133
Alexander II, 98, 231
Alfonso Liguori, S., 277, 278
Alva, Duke of, 245
Ambrose, St., 143, 225
Ammonius Saccas, 187
Anastasius, Creed of, 131
Andrew, St., 57
Angelus Silesius, *see* Scheffler, J.
Antioch, Synod of, 132
Apelles, 119
Apocrypha, 149–150, 152, 254
Apolinare Nuova, S., at Ravenna, 144
Apollinaris, 129
Apollo, 108
Apostles, choice of, 39
Apostles' Creed, 117, 118, 125, 127, 132
Aquinas, Thomas, 220, 261, 272
Archelaus, 37
Areopagus, Paul's speech on, 96
Ariston, 108
Aristotle, commentaries on, 224
Arius and Arianism, 126, 127, 133, 134, 184
Arjuna, 74
Arnold, Matthew, 23, 90, 92, 155
Arnold, Thomas, 229
Assumption of S. Mary, 138
Athanasian Creed, 283, 285
Athanasius, 124, 126, 127, 133, 177
Attila, 191, 192
Augustine of Canterbury, St., 193
Augustine of Hippo, St., 176, 178, 179, 185, 186, 190, 202, 224, 225, 290
Aurelian, Emperor, 125
Averroes, 224

Babylon, 169
Bacon, F., 15, 240
Bacon, Roger, 222–223
Bahia, 250
Barnabas, St., 86, 126, 156
Basilidians, 111
Basle, Council of, 257
Beauvais Cathedral, 217
"Benefit of Clergy," 216
Berdyaev, Nicolas, 293
Berengarius, 247
Bernard, St., 232, 265
Betham-Edwards, Miss, 284
Bethlehem, 18
Bhagavad Ghita, 24, 73, 295–296
Bible, the, 148 *et seq.*
Birth-Stories, 102–111
Bishops, 156, 200
Boanerges, 39
Boleyn, Anne, 241
Bolsena, Miracle of, 220
Boniface VIII, Pope, 173, 248
Book of the Dead, 22
Boudinhon, Dr. Auguste, 172, 203, 272, 273
Brandt, Gerard, 228
Breath (Spirit), 38, 114, 116
Brooks, Bishop P., 289
Buddha, Gautama, 104, 135
Butler, Abbot, 298, 299
Byron, Lord, 18

Callixtus I, 128, 144
Calvin, J., 249, 259
Camões, Luiz de, 215, 216, 232
Campion, Edmund, 246
Cana of Galilee, 57, 58, 110
Candelaria Brotherhood, 223
Canon of New Testament, 150 *et seq.*
Canon of Old Testament, 148 *et seq.*
Canterbury, See of, 212, 241
Cardinals, College of, 206, 276
Caroline of Brunswick, 238
Carpaccio, 180
Carpus, 153
Catacombs, 142, 143, 144, 145, 180
Catalina, Queen, 240, 241
Catarina dei Medici, 241

304 INTRODUCTION TO THE STUDY OF CHRISTIANITY

Cathari, 214, 267, 299
Cather, Miss Willa, 17
Celibacy of Clergy, 79, 210, 222, 250, 267
Celsus, 176, 181, 182
Cerdo, 118
Chalcedon, Council of, 136, 159
Charlemagne, 201, 230
Charles V, 201, 240, 241, 257
Charles X, 230
Charles the Hammer (Martel), 194, 201
Chillingworth, 254
Chrishna, 74, 104
Christians as a Jewish sect, 76-95
Christmas Day, 110
Chrysostom, St. John, 111, 162
Church of Rome, *see* Roman Catholic Church
Cathari, 214, 267, 299
Clement I (Clemens Romanus), 117
Clement III (Guibert of Ravenna), 208
Clement IV, 222
Clement VII, 240, 242
Clement of Alexandria, 111, 241
Clovis, 288
Codex Sinaiticus, 16
Codex Vaticanus, 16
Coke, Chief Justice, 252
Commodus, Emperor, 183
Communal system, 78
Communion, Institution of, 45-46, 218, 219, 258
Conrad III, 232
Constance, Council of, 257, 272
Constantine, 133, 184, 185, 201; donation of, 185
Constantinople, Council of, 177, 281; stormed, 211
Cordoba (Cordova), 235
Cornelio, 259
Cornelius, 85, 286
Cosmas Indicopleustes, 179
Coué, School of, 40
Cowper, W., 256
Cranmer, Abp., 210
Creed, Apostles, 117; Athanasian, 130 *et seq.*, 285: Nicene, 127 *et seq.*
Crookes, Sir W., 19
Crusades, 194, 196, 211, 232, 233; Children's, 233

Cumont, F., 183
Cyprian, St., 163, 164
Cyril, St., 138, 165, 190
Cyrus, 25
Damasus, 203
Dante, 185
Darius, 16
Darwin, C., 270
David, 45
Deacons, 155, 156
Desmoulins, Camille, 122
Diogenes Laertius, 108, 109
Dionysian Mysteries, 297
Disciples, Commission to the, 65-66
Divine Pymander, 23-24
Dollinger, Prof., 203
Drugs, 260
Duns Scotus, 223, 225

Ebionites, 95
Eckhart, Meister, 260-263
Eddington, Sir A., 102
Edessa, 232
Egyptian Trinity, 114, 115
Eleusinian mysteries, 60
Elijah, 255
Elizabeth, Queen, 200, 244, 245, 246, 247
Eons, 122, 131
Epiphany, 38, 111-112
Essence, 127
Essenes, 79
Eugenius III, 232
Eugenius IV, 257
Eusebius, 35, 127, 143, 177
Eutyches, 129, 132
Eutychus, 50

Faber, F. W., 261, 288
Faustus, 123
Fawkes, G., 243
Felton, 244
Filioque, 204
Fish symbol, 143, 144
Fitzherbert, Maria, 238
Fonseca, G. da, 300
Fourth Gospel, 13, 46; authorship, 53, 68 *et seq.*; prologue, 53-55, 170
France, Anatole, 97, 98, 140-141, 229
Francis, St., 139, 299
Francis II, Emperor, 209, 242
Frederick I, 232
Frederick II, 233

INDEX

Gadarene swine, story of the, 40
Gallicanism, 191
Gallio, 97, 98, 99
Gama, *see* Vasco da Gama
Gautama Buddha, 104, 135
Genghis Khan, 98
Genseric, 191, 192
Gentiles, conversion of, 85
George IV, 14, 238; V, 185
Gibbon, E., 180, 190
Gilbert, Canon, 219
Gnostics, 39, 111, 119, 120, 121, 122, 123, 124, 125, 126, 135
Gore, Bp., 192
Gospels, commencement of the, 36–37
Gregory I, 193
Gregory IV, 207
Gregory V, 185
Gregory VII (Hildebrand), 206, 207, 208, 209, 210, 211, 216, 225, 231, 243, 247, 275
Gregory XVI, 254, 273
Gregory of Tours, 138
Guibert of Ravenna, *see* Clement III

Hagiographa, 149
Harnack, A., 175, 179, 187
Haroun al Raschid, 230
Harwood, Cecil, 297
Hebrews, Epistle to the, 15, 87 *et seq.*, 287; Gospel of, 35
Henri II, 241
Henri III, 243
Henri IV, 243, 253
Henry III, 94, 214
Henry IV, 208, 213, 238, 240
Henry VI, Emperor, 202
Henry VIII, 239, 241, 242, 244, 249, 252
Hermes, 143
Herod, 51, 103, 107, 108
Herodotus, 16
Hilary of Arles, S., 111, 132, 191
Hilary of Poitiers, 133
Hilda, St., 200
Hildebrand, *see* Gregory VII
Holy Roman Empire, 208
Home, D. D., 19, 20
Honorius I, 281
Horus, 114
Hypatia, 190

Ignatius, 109, 156
Immaculate Conception, 79, 100, 108, 109, 132, 173, 225, 272
Inge, Dean, 19, 42
Innocent I, 171
Innocent III, 211, 213, 214, 215, 216, 233, 275, 293, 299
Innocent XI, 266
Irenaeus, 36, 156, 170
Isidore of Seville, 202
Isis, 138

James, I, 243
James, Prof. W., 260
James, St., 39, 56, 86; Epistle of, 87 *et seq.*
Januarius, St., 122
Jerome, St., 35, 133, 168, 185–186, 225, 254
Jerusalem, siege of, 43; temple authorities at, 46; Jesus at, 58, 59; Council of, 115
Jesus, baptism of, 37, 55; life and mission of, 39–42; teaching of, 42–44, 48; family connections of, 44–45; passion of, 46 *et seq.*, 63–65; preaching, 39, 99, genealogy of, 44–45; resurrection of, 48, 50–52
Jews, 24, 25, 182; Christians as a Jewish sect, 76–95
Joad, C. E. M., 102
Johannine discourses, 72–74, 295–296
John, King, 211, 212, 213
John, Apostle, 56
John the Baptist, 37, 38, 39, 55, 89
John XII, Pope, 201
John XXIII, 257
Jonah, 145
Joseph of Copertino, St., 20
Josephine, 253
Joshua, 25
Julius II, 191, 221
Justin, 71, 100, 114, 190

Kamsa, 105
Keenan's *Controversial Catechism*, 171
Kephas, 39
Khalil, Sultan, 139, 233

Langton, Stephen, 212
Lasserre, Henri, 153
Lateran Treaty, 276
Lazarus, raising of, 60–62, 146

Lenin, 293
Leo I, 112. 190–191, 192, 193, 211
Leo II, 281
Leo III, 201
Leo IV, 230
Leo IX, 205, 206, 210
Leo X, 139, 240
Leo XIII, Pope, 151, 152, 225, 273, 274
Leopold of Austria, 202
Liberius, Pope, 133
Liesse, 140
Lisbon, 170, 247
Livy, 117
Locke, John, 127
Logos, doctrine of, 177
Loisy, M. Alfred, 14
Lord's Supper, Institution of the, 45–46
Loreto, Holy House, 139, 140
Loreto, Our Lady of, 139, 140, 141, 217
Louis VII, 232
Louis XI, 213
Louis XII, 253
Louis XIV, 213, 275, 282
Louis XVIII, 301
Lourdes, 18
Lourdes, Our Lady of, 140
Lucena, J. de, 300
Luke, St., 33, 36. 37, 38, 40, 42, 45, 48, 49, 50, 56
Luther, Martin, 249
Lyell, 270
Lystra, 126

McCabe, J., 235
Maeterlinck, Maurice, 17, 18
Magi, 110, 112
Magna Charta, 213, 249
Mahomet and Mahometanism, 95, 187, 193–201, 215, 223, 226, 229–236, 248, 268, 269
Maia, 135, 138
Malachi, 157
Malchus, 40, 64
Malory, Sir Thomas, 15
Manes, 123
Manichaeism, 186, 191, 298
Manning, Cardinal, 153, 207, 219, 280, 282
Manuscripts, 15–16

Marcion and Marcionites, 119
Maria Maggiore, S., 141
Mark, St., Gospel of, 33 *et seq.*
Marriage, 57, 110, 252, 253
Martel, C., 229
Martet, Jean, 122
Martha, 71
Martin, St., 133
Mary, St., cult of, 134–141
Mary, Queen of England, 240, 245
Mary, Queen of Scots, 244, 245
Mary of the Snow, 141
Mass, 252
Matthew, Gospel of, 15, 20, 21, 34 *et seq.*
Maxentius, 184
Maya, 104, 135, 138
Mazarin, 213
Messiah, 25, 55, 56, 57, 77, 80, 103, 162
Milman, Dean, 236
Milton, J., 205
Ministry, Christian, 155–158
Miracles, 17–21, 58, 59, 60–62
Miriam, 135
Mitchell, J. M., 187
Mithraism, 183, 186
Moffatt, Dr. J., 27, 38
Molinos, Miguel de, 266, 267
Monothelites, 129
Montségur, 227, 299
More, St. Thomas, 210
Mosaic Code, 77, 79
Mother of God, 137
Motley, J. R., 228
Muratorian fragment, 150
Murillo, 221, 222
Museo Kircheriano, 142
Musset, A. de, 92
Mussolini, 275
Mysticism, 259–260, 267

"Nag's Head" fable, 280, 281
Nantes, Edict of, 275
Napoleon, 253, 283, 301
Neo-Platonism, 186, 187, 290
Nestorius, 129, 132
Newman, Cardinal, 17, 21, 122, 255, 273, 277
New Testament, 150 *et seq.*
Nicea: Council of, 127, 132, 174, 184; Creed of, 130, 178

Nicholas I, 203
Nicholas II, 206
Nightingale, Florence, 200
Norfolk, Duke of, 245, 246
Noah, 144-145

Olinda, 250
Origen, 95, 123, 135, 163, 175-179, 187, 255
Orpheus, 143
Orvieto, Cathedral of, 221
Osiris, 114
Otto I, 201

Padua, Cathedral at, 223
Paganism, influence of, 96 et seq.
Pallavicini, Cardinal, 258
Pangloss, 184, 269, 270
Papal power, growth of, 201-215
Papias, 34
Paraclete, 83, 84, 267
Parker, Archbishop, 280, 281
Pascal, Blaise, 106
Patrizi, Cardinal, 172
Paul III, 241
Paul IV, 236
Paul of Samosata, 124, 125, 126, 132, 291
Paul of Tarsus, apostleship, 22,28-29; career, 26 et seq.; possible auditor of Jesus, 27; serpent incident, 52
Pauline Epistles, 13, 14, 15, 22-32, 45, 287, 288
Pelagianism, 189
Pentateuch, 148, 199
Pepys, S., 234
Père Lachaise Cemetery, 224
Periclitione, 108
Perigueux, 284
Peter, St., 83; imprisoned by Herod, 51; at Joppa, 286
Peter, St., Basilica of, 160
Peter the Hermit, 194, 232
Petrine Claims, 160 et seq., 249
Philip II, 95, 242, 245, 247, 266, 282
Philip Augustus, 211, 212, 232
Piers Plowman, 251
Pilate, Pontius, 27, 37, 127
Pippin the Short, 201, 230
Pius II, 257
Pius V, 244

Pius VII, 301
Pius IX, 14, 216, 225, 271, 273, 274, 276
Pius X, 14, 274
Pius XI, 275
Plato, 73, 100, 108, 109, 224
Plotinus, 186, 187, 290
Polycarp, 71
Polygamy, 199
Portuguese expeditions, 216, 230, 300
Proclus, 190
Prophets, Book of, 149
Pseudo-Matthew, 38, 103, 104, 105, 109
Pseudo-Mark, 148
Pseudo-Luke, 38, 103, 104, 105, 109
Protestantism, 247-258

Quakers, 77, 90
Quicunque Vult, see Athanasian Creed
Quietism, 266

Racine, 242
Rahab, 94
Ramadan, 197
Raphael Sanzio, 191, 221
Remi, St., 288
Renan, E., 21, 73, 80
Revelation, Book of, 61
Reynaud, Jean, 284
Richard I, 202, 232, 233
Richelieu, 213
Rio de Janeiro, Cathedral at, 223
Robertson, J. M., 13, 105, 135
Roman Catholic Church, 13, 14, 17, 20, 111, 138, 151, 153, 154, 158-160, 173, 201-215, 236 et seq., 250 et seq., 269 et seq.
Rome, See of, 158-160, 173, 185, 231
Romulus, 120
Rosicrucians, 39
Rouen, See of, 210
Rubens, P. P., 139
Rudolph II, 237

Sabbath Day, 255
Sabellius, Sabellianism, 128, 129, 224
Saladin, 233
Sarpi, Paolo, 238

Scheffler, Johann (Angelus Silesius), 263–267
Schlegel, A. W., 229
Schuré, E., 145
Schweitzer, Albrecht, 42
Scory, Bishop, 280
Sebastian, St., Church of, 142
Sebastião, King, 230, 234
Ségur, Mgr., 172
Seignobos, C., 258
Sens, Council of, 224
Sepher Yetzira, 113
Serveto, Miguel, 258
Seville Cathedral, 217
Sexual problems, 30–31
Shelley, P. B., 259
Sicilian expedition of, 415, 60
Siena Cathedral, 217
Sigismund, Emperor, 202
Silas, 51, 52
Simon, 39
Siricius, 209
Sixtus V, Pope, 247
Sobeski, King John, 234
Socinians, 259
Socrates, 73
Soissons, Council of, 224
Son of God (title), 28, 79: of Man, 79, 81
Sosthenes, 99
Sozini family, 259
Spensippus, 109
Speyer, Diet of, 248
Stanley, Dean, 140
Steiner, R., 292
Stephen, 76
Substance defined, 127
Sunday, 95
Sun God, 135, 143
Swithun, St., 209
Syllabus, 272, 276
Sylvester, Pope, 185
Synoptic Gospels, 13, 34–74, 118

Tabitha, 51, 220
Tertullian, 123, 124, 131, 135, 175
Tharaud, J. and J., 195
Theophilus of Antioch, 37, 71
Theophylact, 162

Theresa, S., 187, 200, 266
Thomas, St., 224, 225
Thurii, 61
Toledo Cathedral, 99, 217
Toledo, Council of, 130
Torquemada, 293
Trallis, Church at, 109
Transubstantiation, 220, 221
Tre Fontane, 32
Trent, Council of, 13, 14, 15, 258
Trinity, Doctrine of the, 112 *et seq.*, 119, 131, 132, 135, 141
Trismegistus, 23, 24
Trullo, Council in, 151
Tyrannus, 99
Tyrrell, Father, 14

Urban II, 231
Urban IV, 220
Ursula, St., 180, 181
Usury, 226

Valentinian III, Emperor, 191
Vasco da Gama, 215
Vatican Council, 171, 172
Venice, 180, 237
Verbal accuracy, 16–17
Victor I, St., 174
Victricius, Bishop, 131
Vienna, 209
Vincent, St., 133, 171, 173
Voltaire, 134, 169, 239

Wesley, C., 42, 105, 249
Westminster Abbey, 217
Whitman, W., 80
William, Duke, 231
William II, 282
William of Orange, 243

Xavier, F., 284, 300
Xenophon, 73

Yathrib, 193, 194

Zebedee, 39, 56, 57, 68, 94
Zenobia, 125
Zephaniah, 157

For Product Safety Concerns and Information please contact our EU
representative GPSR@taylorandfrancis.com
Taylor & Francis Verlag GmbH, Kaufingerstraße 24, 80331 München, Germany

www.ingramcontent.com/pod-product-compliance
Lightning Source LLC
Chambersburg PA
CBHW071346290426
44108CB00014B/1450